TRANSFORMING
MUSIC EDUCATION

COUNTERPOINTS: MUSIC AND EDUCATION
Estelle R. Jorgensen, General Editor

Transforming
Music Education

Estelle R. Jorgensen

INDIANA
University Press

Bloomington & Indianapolis

This book is a publication of

Indiana University Press
601 North Morton Street
Bloomington, Indiana 47404-3797 USA

http://iupress.indiana.edu

Telephone orders   800-842-6796
Fax orders   812-855-7931
Orders by e-mail   iuporder@indiana.edu

The paper used in this publication meets the minimum
requirements of American National Standard for Information
Sciences—Permanence of Paper for Printed Library
Materials, ANSI Z39.48-1984.

Manufactured in the United States of America

Library of Congress Cataloging-in-Publication Data

Jorgensen, Estelle Ruth.
    Transforming music education / Estelle R. Jorgensen.
        p. cm. — (Counterpoints : music and education)
Includes bibliographical references and index.
    ISBN 0-253-34172-8 (alk. paper) — ISBN 0-253-21560-9 (pbk. : alk.
paper)
    1. Music—Instruction and study.   I. Title.   II. Series : Counterpoints
(Bloomington, Ind.).
    MT1 .J678 2003
        780'.71—dc21

                                            2002004913

1   2   3   4   5   08   07   06   05   04   03

For my parents—my first teachers

CONTENTS

Preface

Many music teachers have passed through my classrooms, and I have talked with many more in this country and abroad about their lives and work. Making sense of my own experience, the stories I have heard other teachers tell, and the educational writers whose work I have read is a tall order. In my first days as a teacher I was eager to succeed in an educational system I took for granted. I attributed my unease about what I saw, heard, and felt to my inexperience as a teacher and musician. As evidence to the contrary mounted inexorably over the years, I began to wish to speak in my own voice, subvert the status quo, and reconstruct the system. Finding a space to be truly heard among the host of others in music education, powerful and well-connected policy makers—men and women who control the rostrums and publications where one can speak or write with freedom—has been one of the major challenges of my life.

Many of my students are happy, contented musicians and teachers, pleased with how things are in general education. They believe that they can make important contributions to education and are eager to move on to the studios, colleges, schools, and religious places in which they have chosen to teach. They see the status quo as an imperative and are reluctant to consider the notion that music education may be in need of transformation. Critical of the spate of national reports berating schools and education systems, they rise to the defense of how things are and the efforts of earnest and hardworking teachers who are doing their best in the interests of their pupils. Such students are sometimes impatient with others for whom the educational journey has been less pleasant and who are critical of the way things are. The problem with the dissatisfied ones lies, they say, with a lack of being able to adjust to the system and not with the system itself. I am pleased to learn from these students and to know that they have had such happy and fulfilling experiences as students and teachers. And I am encouraged by their hopefulness and devotion.

Others are not so happy. I meet many refugees from the classroom, disenchanted with the lack of liberty they possess as teachers, beset by the host of directives that impede their work, angered by the paternalistic attitudes of those administrators who wield power over them and fail to appreciate their efforts. There are those who are very lonely. In the words of one teacher, "I feel like an island in the midst of an ocean." Overworked and underpaid, she is very much alone with little support for her work, little time to spend with her colleagues, and still less to spend with her family. There are those who are afraid. Some express fear for their lives with armed guards patrolling their school corridors, threatened in their classes by disrespectful, angry, violent, and uncouth students or by anonymous threats via e-mail, telephone, or the Internet. Some are afraid that they do not know all they should know. Others fear that what they know and value is no longer relevant in a world that is changing dramatically. And still others fear that their influence no longer really counts in a society where mass media operatives, talk show hosts, entertainers, and Internet advertisers are the most potent purveyors of public knowledge. As one experienced teacher put it, "I feel like a pebble on the shore when the tide has gone out." Her fear of jeopardizing her teaching position, losing the livelihood upon which her family depends, and alienating the authority figures in her work life keeps her silent. Some confess, "I no longer enjoy teaching children"; "I no longer enjoy music." Gone are the hope, joy, and love of connecting with students or of the art that led them to teaching in the first place. In their place I hear the voices of weariness, discouragement, and ennui.

Over the years I have sometimes been embarrassed by the ways education is regarded, studied, and practiced. Despite the fact that teachers face some of the most urgent and important challenges in society, the field draws relatively few intellectuals, lovers of wisdom, or outstanding practitioners of their particular specialties. Instead of attracting the best and brightest students, education often interests those who cannot get into other fields. In the university at which I teach, the academic achievement of incoming future teachers is among the lowest of the incoming undergraduate population, and this is all too common. A pervasive anti-intellectualism in education manifests itself in such problems as lack of interest in scholarship, uncritical acceptance of ideas and practices, idolizing of science, and obsession with instructional and research methods. Symptomatic of this situation is the fate of educational philosophy and history, which have fallen on particularly hard times. As the prophets and seers have been displaced by the empirical researchers and social scientists, there has been a declining regard for the long and distinguished narratives of education and for the critical insights that would help guard the profession against repeating past mistakes and making ill-conceived plans. Pretentious jargon invoked by educational scientists and theorists often cloaks a paucity of strong scholarship, steady conviction, and clear application. This research is frequently unintelligible to the teachers it is supposed to benefit, and few teachers read it. Sometimes I long for the simple, clear, well-thought-through, and unequivocal statements by the educational architects of bygone days, uncluttered as they were by pretentious posturing and excessive equivocating.

Also, much contemporary popular and elite culture is coarse and crass. I recall the advertisement unveiled by the Coca-Cola Company during a prime-time Olympic telecast program depicting a female athlete in Nike shoes escaping from her male pursuer armed with a chainsaw in motion. A public outcry forced the removal of the advertisement, yet the very fact that a multinational company thought it constituted good advertising shows clearly that something is amiss in our culture. There are many other symptoms of a culture gone awry. Many churches now rely on projected words on a large screen because parishioners can no longer read music and are uninterested in singing from printed scores or in parts from their hymn-books. Too many high school graduates do not play their instruments or sing after they leave school and become, instead, passive consumers of music. Orchestras, theaters, dance studios, art galleries, bookshops, choirs, and other vehicles and places of live culture disappear because they are no longer financially viable. Popular culture in all of its forms sold by the media so silences other forms of musical expression that they are not known by young and old alike. Many can no longer sing a melody or part in tune, and it is not unusual for the wait staff in a restaurant attempting to sing "Happy Birthday" to a patron to embarrass themselves, and those of us who know the tune and can sing it, by chanting the song in a monotone. Many do not know the names of prominent musicians and cultural figures in the past, let alone recognize their compositions and performances. Too few know how to select a broad range of music for their sound recording collections at home, which movies to attend, what plays to see, how to visit an art gallery, which musical groups to go and hear, without relying on popular opinion or the views of self-styled pundits. Some adults are afraid to audition for a play, a choir, or an instrumental ensemble because they do not know how to sing or play at sight, or they are afraid to go out dancing because they do not know the traditional and social dances. Too many spend most of their leisure time seeking light entertainment, playing video games, and watching television. They rarely read a serious book, read to their children, listen to their children read to them, watch a documentary film, or use the library or Internet for research purposes. And meals are often taken in such haste that families spend little time about the dining table discussing and debating ideas, playing games, sharing their ideas and feelings with one another, or making music together, and thereby building bridges between the generations.

Publicly supported schools are under continued assault. In the United States, especially, one sees a flight from the public schools to private, parochial, charter, and home schools. Public schools, especially those in large urban centers, are the only options for some of the country's most impoverished students, and grave inequities persist. Against the stories of teachers who have transformed their schools, new buildings constructed, computers placed in every classroom, and more teachers hired, there are the images of broken-down school buildings, absentee students, and disheartened teach-ers working in Third World conditions. Along with the decline of the American public school is a growing fragmentation of education and an ongoing seepage from the common school. The common school was a nine-teenth-century democratic experiment in which American children irre-spective of their wealth, social status, ethnicity, and linguistic group might be educated together in the cause of the republic. More than a century after the founding of publicly supported schools in the United States, these schools were belatedly desegregated in the hope that this move would create a more inclusive society and transcend the barriers of race, ethnicity, class, and gender. Now, mounting resegregation in education threatens to undo society's common bonds, ghettoize its inhabitants, and tear its fabric apart. Advocates of school choice abound, but the numbers of those who cannot choose grow larger as they also become poorer and more disadvantaged.

Much has been made in American education of the need for teachers to focus on the "basics" of reading, writing, and computing in the school curriculum. Where this narrow approach to education persists, society fails to contest those things that are amiss in culture. Reading, writing, and computing constitute a very small part of culture. Crudity, crassness, banality, and incivility result when a society fails to take care of its culture. And the narrow education advocated by those interested only in basal skills and the pursuit of purely instrumental ends shortchanges students by denying them a liberal education—a rich, holistic, balanced, intellectual, physical, emotional, spiritual, and cultural development that ought to be their birthright.

A society that espouses democratic ideals relies for its continued existence on the education of its citizens. Without their continued engagement in the political process as informed participants, a democratic republic is easily undermined. Throughout history, democratic arrangements have been the exception rather than the rule. One reason may lie in the fragility of democracies. They are readily overtaken by powerful individuals or interest groups, who seize power for their own ends if the citizens do not remain vigilant. Apathy on the part of citizens within the republic is just as much a danger as threats from outside its borders. And to its credit, the United States has been at the forefront internationally in educating its population. Still, the persistence of such problems as adult illiteracy, drug addiction, a culture of violence, and widespread lack of interest in political and cultural matters is symptomatic of the fact that all is not well in the republic or its cultural life.

For those of my students who think that nothing is amiss in education, I reply that even if this were the case, education is always in need of transformation. The passing of one generation and the coming of another is evidence of this ongoing renewal. The perspectives of teachers and their students, situations in which they teach and learn, and the broader societal contexts are changing, for better or worse. My point in this book is to suggest that music teachers need to help shape culture and the directions in which society moves. Teachers and educational policy makers cannot afford to remain passive or reactive. Nor should they leave the work of transformation to others. Rather, they need to commit to transforming education toward a humane and civil society. And given the nature of their subject matter, musicians and artists are especially positioned to create a powerful model of a humane and holistic music education that can help to transform education generally and those who undertake or undergo it.

So you ask: What should music education be about and for? What can musicians and educators do to model and engender educational transformation? What principles should guide this transformation? This is a book about why music education should be transformed, what is meant by transformation, how educational and musical transformation function, and some directions in which music education might be transformed. I suggest in these pages that reforming music and education is not enough; tinkering on the edges of these fields will not suffice. Contra those who believe that systemic educational changes are not called for, I propose a radical and fundamental change in the nature and objectives of music education and, through this transformation, a transformation of general education and culture.

I view music educational transformation as a dynamic process involving many voices. Music and education are dynamic, living things, in the process of changing and adapting to the wider society and culture of which they are a part. Any systemic intervention or action affects not only the system and its environment but also those who seek to change it. There are tensions between the status quo, which is itself a dynamic and gradually changing entity, and those ideas and practices that would radically, systemically, or fundamentally alter the system and even its environment, between those who set out to make changes and the system that affects them and shapes their thinking and acting. Nor is this transformation ever complete. It is always ongoing. Its effects are both intended and unintended, because its architects lack complete knowledge and perfect foresight. There is always the element of surprise or the unexpected, the dialectic between anticipated and resultant realities.

Musicians and educators are engaged in a fundamentally social, political, and cultural enterprise. The challenges are inherently complex, difficult to grasp conceptually and meet practically. These challenges have an important bearing on what can be accomplished in classrooms, studios, and all the other places teachers teach. They frame instructional activities in compelling ways and need to be addressed directly. This may be an uncomfortable undertaking for those with vested interests in the present system or for those who for many reasons would prefer things the way they are now. However, this cannot be helped, because the search for truth is often uncomfortable and disconcerting, especially when those things one has held dear are challenged.

As a microcosm of general education, music education provides a window into what happens in educational generally. It also can be an agent for change not only in education but also in the wider society. The arts are important ingredients of cultural life, and education fundamentally involves the transmission and transformation of culture. This link has been recognized since ancient times, and the idea has persisted to our day. As a means of enculturation, education is fundamentally about the arts. They, along with other instrumental school subjects, are among its basic elements and have been so throughout recorded history.

When the arts go awry, where they are ignored or marginalized, the broader society of which they are a part is likewise at risk. As lenses on cultural life, the arts demonstrate what is taking place in cultural and social life more generally. In Mary Renault's tale, *The King Must Die,* her hero, Theseus, the heir to the King of Athens, comes to the Labyrinth of Crete as a bull dancer. He finds that the Cretans have lost interest in their traditional fine pottery and sculpture and have become preoccupied with novelty. Incredulous that his own rough clay figure should be taken seriously as a work of art, Theseus exclaims that the Cretans no longer value their artistic and cultural traditions, their civilization has decayed, and the island is ripe for the taking. So it can be in our time.

What follows is a quintet of essays. In chapter 1 I set the stage for what follows by identifying some contemporary challenges for music education and my dialectical approach to them. In chapter 2 I show why systemic transformation is needed in music education. In chapter 3 I describe the educational transformation I have in mind. I distinguish images of educational transformation, demonstrate how each contributes to our understanding yet is flawed in some way, and map some of the ways in which educational transformation can function as a humanizing, civilizing, and ennobling agency. In chapter 4 I examine several musical images whereby music is conceived and analyze specific ways in which musical transformation takes place. In chapter 5 I sketch some specific features of music education that when taken together reveal a dialectic and holistic approach to musical and educational transformation, and I tackle important practical questions of how this analysis can be helpful to music educational policy makers and its potential impact on education and culture.

This book constitutes a thoroughgoing criticism and reconstruction of traditional music educational theory and practice in the sense of unmasking problems that are hidden from view and confronting those that are more clearly evident. My international experience as a teacher has taught me that it is far easier to deconstruct a set of ideas and practices than to reconstruct them. Beyond the important task of analysis and criticism is that of synthesis and reassembly of a whole that is being renewed and made transformative in its impact. And to this end, I offer a list of symptoms of transforming music education—that is, what a transforming music education would look like.

Some may argue that the vision I portray is idealistic—that it cannot be realized fully in practice. To some extent, they may be right. However, for me, music education is a profoundly hopeful and optimistic endeavor. Hope, faith, joy, and love undergird it. Given human nature, these qualities are never realized fully, but without them music education falters. It lacks direction because hope and faith constitute imperatives that support attempts to improve a situation. It also lacks humanity, because joy and love underlie individual happiness and corporate well-being. Forces of systemic selfishness, arrogance, bigotry, exclusiveness, marginalization, repression, oppression, violence, and patriarchy still work against the noblest intentions of human beings. And the only reason I can see for engaging in artistic and educational activity is the hope, even the belief, that somehow one can make a difference, improve the situation, enrich human experience, and foster and celebrate the good, the true, and the beautiful, wherever they may be found.

Estelle R. Jorgensen
Bloomington, Indiana
March 2002

Acknowledgments

This book has been a long time in the making. I am especially indebted to my students at Indiana University School of Music, to my colleagues here and abroad, and to my teachers who bequeathed a rich legacy in their printed words and the memory of their being. Much of what follows in these pages has been mulled over in my classes, lectured about, discussed, and criticized. I am thankful for the opportunities I have had to teach students and musicians who by dint of their verve, intellect, imagination, thoughtfulness, and courage have been my teachers, and for the rich musical environment in which I have been privileged to work and study. While these gifts can never be repaid, I hope that those colleagues and students who provoked this offering will at least consider it a down payment.

Transforming
Music Education

1

Setting the Stage

We live at a time of profound change. This reality fundamentally affects our understanding of the world and human relationships, the way we live, our beliefs and values, and our relationships with others. Now, more than ever before, we see ourselves as inhabitants of planet Earth, living in a fragile world that we can sustain or destroy. We have more information about the world and the people and things in it than before. Still, tribalism, warfare, and fear and mistrust of different others are as strong as ever. The technology at our disposal has revolutionized human life, yet along with devices that potentially improve the quality of life, there remain the modern-day electronic "sweatshops," continuing divisions between rich and poor, and other symptoms of dehumanization and greed. Even though the mass media make human want and suffering patently clear to us, poverty and violence continue to afflict city and countryside alike. Unprecedented and massive population movements have contributed to cultural diversity and richness on the one hand and racism, cultural imperialism, fear, and anger on the other. A global economy fostered by international trade, investment, and monetary policy offers many possibilities to relieve human suffering and enhance living standards, and yet colliding with nationalistic, ethnic, and hedonistic aspirations creates political problems, racial hatred, political unrest, and economic exploitation. As a result, we face enormous challenges and differing realities than in the past.

Music provides a window on some of these important cultural and societal changes. Technological developments in computing, sound recording, and synthesis have changed the face of musical composition, performance, and listening.[1] Sight has become as important as sound in music making, particularly in such genres as film, video, and rock music. The keyboard and computer provide important means of synthesizing sound, composing music, and preparing scores. Technological advances have permitted diverse live and recorded music listening experiences ranging from the solitary

listener to mass audiences of thousands or even millions of people. Popular
mediated musics, or those propagated for and by the media, have become
truly international, as have Eastern and Western classical musics. Even traditional or vernacular musics that historically were practiced within relatively small geographical areas are performed and heard internationally,
especially through their links with popular culture. At the same time,
groups fear that their traditional cultures are in danger of disappearing
under the influence of popular music. Inventions provide the means to
democratize music and to compose, perform, record, and distribute it
widely, yet they ghettoize musical publics and fragment musical tastes. Live
music is threatened where musicians cannot make a livelihood or the public does not attend and support live performances. And materialism fostered through concerted advertising by multinational corporations creates
an environment in which spiritual and artistic values are downplayed in
favor of a widespread desire for economic security and material well-being.
International marketing of music and artists makes some music widely
available. At the same time, it silences others who cannot obtain venture
capital and afford to distribute their music extensively. And it undermines
and devalues amateur participation in music making by subjecting it to
comparison with exacting professional and commercial standards.[2]

Such a world could not have been envisioned in the early nineteenth century, when publicly supported schools were established and when music was
among the first subjects introduced into general education throughout the
Western world. True, mounting industrialization, urbanization, and international trade—forces that were to mushroom in the twentieth and into the
twenty-first century—were already evident. Immigrants were swelling the
populations of larger cities and towns throughout the world, and scientific
and technological discoveries were changing the face of industry and daily
life. Still, in the West, Western culture was considered the cornerstone of
education, and educational ends were more or less agreed upon. Cultural
uniformity was accepted without question, and the dissenting voices of
women and minorities were more or less silent. Notions of the good, the true,
and the beautiful could be described with relative surety, and the philosophical ideas of such writers as August Comte and Herbert Spencer reinforced a
widespread belief that Western civilization represented the epitome of societal development thus far and that human progress would continue.[3]

It is not surprising that in the United States the uncertainty, ambivalence,
and fear engendered by mounting "multiplicities and pluralities" should
have resulted in a drift to conservatism over the past decades, to the safety
of well-worn paths and ideas, and appeals to a mythic and idealized past.[4]
Notions of liberalism, especially as was expressed by educators, although
once espoused by American educational thinkers, came to be blamed for society's ills. Conservative agendas dominated education in the late twentieth and
early twenty-first centuries and contributed and sustained a "monochromatic" culture driven by capitalist ideas and democratic political ideologies.[5] To

criticize this agenda could earn one the label of Marxist, political subversive, throwback to the sixties, or even anti-American.[6]

In the face of these major shifts and movements, Western classical music and the "high" arts remain normative.[7] Performing ensembles and music classes that foster music listening and audience development are a mainstay of school music programs.[8] Music teachers are among the staunchest advocates of national standards and examinations.[9] Too often, criticisms of the assumptions, purposes, and methods of musical instruction are bypassed, and differences of opinion are personalized rather than attributed to underlying systemic problems.[10] Like education generally, the specialty of school music is largely bureaucratic, leaders have a self-interest in preserving the status quo, and teachers are trained as technicians to follow directives issued by educational authorities.[11] Teaching methods remain generally didactic, emphasize prescribed subject matter and procedures, and utilize assessment approaches to validate this instruction.[12]

There have also been important changes. Much more attention is now given to teacher preparation; multicultural awareness has increased; new approaches to assessment have been developed; systematic philosophical examination of commonplaces has begun to emerge; school restructuring efforts have forced music teachers to take a more active role in advocacy for the arts and curricular development; and creative ways have been devised to relate music to its social context, other arts, and school subjects and to take advantage of recent technological advances. Still, in other fundamental respects and like other school subjects, music instruction remains very traditional, and its rationale has changed little since the early part of the nineteenth century, when publicly supported schools were established.

Present Challenges

In music education there is a "widespread loss of faith in our educational present." Teachers disagree about their objectives, especially since they serve an increasingly diverse constituency, and society expects more of its schools than ever before. This crisis is expressed in cultural life, especially music among the other arts. In his book *The House of Music,* Samuel Lipman suggests that music teachers face a crisis in music and education that is "nothing less than a calling into question, by the spirit of the age, of their justification for existence as artists and teachers." As Lipman sees the problem, in music, a new phenomenon in music history has emerged, namely, the widespread lack of interest in the contemporary compositions of professional classical musicians. Also, musicians are conflicted about what counts as music and preoccupied with music of the past. Serious music, Lipman states, has been "swamped by demotic musics to the extent that it has taken on the character of a *recherché* amusement for the few."[13]

Lipman's view reflects a sense of crisis evident at the turn of the twenty-first century in musical education worldwide. Among a host of examples that might be cited, in the United States, the National Commission on Music Education's report entitled *Growing Up Complete: The Imperative for Music Education* proclaimed, in the words of Wynton Marsalis, that "our culture is dying from the inside" and urged a national campaign to revitalize musical instruction in the public schools.[14] The Consortium of National Arts Education Associations was also motivated to put teeth into arts programs and meet widespread skepticism about the serious purpose of musical and artistic instruction in schools by adopting *National Standards for Arts Education*. Likewise, in the United Kingdom, although a broad curriculum for national examinations in music was in place to include performance, composition, popular and world musics, and traditional historical and theoretical subjects, many teachers and students were unwilling to treat popular music with the same regard as classical music, and a gap remained between musical ideology and educational practice.[15] Elsewhere, despite the fact that efforts to democratize music and include popular and vernacular musics in the musical canon challenged notions of cultural imperialism, traditional ideas of the dominance of classical music (especially that emanating from the West), the narrowness of musical curricula, and the validity of Western notions of music itself were difficult to dislodge.[16] These instances of a disquiet among music teachers signaled by an array of campaigns, committees, commissions, and consortiums illustrate the degree to which musical education, like education generally, has become institutionalized and professionalized and in need of transformation. Today's world seems a far cry from the nineteenth century, when such teachers as Émile Chevé, Sarah Glover, Julia Crane, John Curwen, John Hullah, Elam Ives Jr., Joseph Mainzer, Lowell Mason, Nanine Paris, and William Woodbridge could respond individually to the lack of musical education they perceived in their time and devise and implement methods of mass musical instruction in public and private schools.[17] Now, educational change is difficult to achieve without institutional leadership, support, or control of one sort or another.[18] Colleges and universities, school boards, accrediting agencies, certification requirements, state curriculum guidelines or mandates, professional associations, national standardized tests, and unions are among the forces to be taken into account in negotiating any significant changes in music and music education. In the United States, for example, MENC—The National Association for Music Education speaks on behalf of its members, forges alliances with professional and business interests, publishes scholarly and professional journals and other materials, constitutes task forces, organizes conferences and symposia, regulates the conduct of special research interest groups, endorses curricular materials, and through a variety of other means exerts considerable power on music education theory and practice in this country. Widespread change in American music education seems almost impossible without its support or acquiescence, and transformation needs to be conceived in institutional as well as individual terms.

Institutional Control of Education and the Difficulty of Achieving Change

Institutions serve several important purposes. They provide ways of tackling tasks in the public domain. John Dewey noted that the presence of the poor, indigent, young, mentally ill, and old, among others who are dependent on society, necessitates corporate action that transcends individual hedonistic concerns.[19] In his view, some projects such as education, public works, and law and order surpass individual interest and require the attention of the public or the state. It is in the public's interest to designate individuals to act on its behalf in carrying out these tasks and to sustain their work by such means as taxation, fees for services rendered, and charitable gifts. This argument underlies the concept of publicly supported schools throughout the world and, in particular, vocal music in general education, making it possible for all children to be musically and generally educated irrespective of their particular ethnic, social, cultural, or economic backgrounds.

Institutions organize corporate activities. They control significant aspects of collective life by standardizing or normalizing systems of goal-seeking, recruitment, communication, conflict resolution, responsibility allocation, role coordination, information exchange, loyalty maintenance, cooperation, competition, evaluation, and socialization, or by disciplining and excluding those who do not meet or accede to the group's expectations.[20] Policies governing such things as lines of communication, departmental organization, grievance procedures, courses of study, practical teaching experience, and teacher qualifications provide some measure of coherence in the institution's operation, help to delineate it from others, and ensure its survival. For example, colleges, universities, and their accrediting agencies; state teacher licensing boards; and professional associations provide mechanisms whereby their members work together to establish and maintain certain expectations of teacher education, ensure that unqualified persons do not teach, and guarantee that instruction at least meets certain minimal standards.

Institutions provide stability in social life. By invoking norms, governing conduct, imposing sanctions, socializing the young, and preserving traditions and wisdom from the past, they foster peaceful interaction between the individuals in a society. By clarifying general expectations, they promote civility and contribute to the happiness of citizens. This stability provides an environment in which the arts can flourish.[21] For example, musical institutions such as the National Association of Schools of Music can stabilize curricula of member schools and help to create conditions that foster musical education in the academy over the long term.[22]

At a time when the mass media dominate communication, when many differing voices clamor to be heard, institutions provide a way for those who share common interests to break through the general din and make themselves heard in the public spaces.[23] Without such concerted action, individuals may not be noticed, especially where large institutions such as commerce play a dominant role in controlling access to the media. By virtue of its size, for example, the MENC along with various national artistic and commercial organizations can command the attention of government, business, religious, media, and other institutions with which it deals on matters of music and artistic educational policy, and the National Association of Schools of Music can constitute a powerful entity in accrediting and regulating its member schools within academe.

Still, various systemic flaws within institutions resist change. The dehumanizing forces of exclusivity, oppression, violence, patriarchy, selfishness, and disdain of different others pervade all societal institutions.[24] There is a dark side of the family, church, state, business, orchestra, choir, opera house, concert hall, conservatory, music studio, and school, among the various agencies of music making and musical education.[25] Notwithstanding the desire of some teachers to embrace an ethic of caring for students as well as subject matter, ever-present institutional realities of sexism, racism, classism, ethnocentrism, sectarianism, and homophobia make this difficult to achieve in practice.[26] Notions of freedom, equality, inclusiveness, and humanity invariably collide with systemic pressures toward conformity, injustice, exclusivity, and inhumanity; as a result, they are only ever achieved partially, if at all.[27]

These dehumanizing and oppressive forces are systemic; they permeate every societal institution and are embedded in institutional beliefs, values, norms, structures, and practices. They exist in every musical, artistic, and educational group and are almost impossible to eradicate because they are so widespread and taken for granted that they form a part of common sense. Why is this? The answers are complex. Theologians look to human nature, to innate and cultivated dispositions to evil; philosophers and cognitive scientists, to the nature of mind and meaning-making; physiologists and psychologists, to physiological mechanisms, needs, and drives; anthropologists and sociologists, to the collective unconscious, cultural contexts, and social influences.[28] All of these perspectives provide valuable insights into humanity.

Paulo Freire directly engages the question of how to confront these oppressive forces and create emancipatory or liberating education. In his view, oppression is difficult to eradicate because those who are oppressed carry within them the "image" of the oppressor.[29] So deeply are human beings affected by their experience of oppression (they absorb the attitudes, values, and practices of the oppressor) that they associate liberation with the beliefs and actions of the oppressor. In spite of themselves and without even realizing it, when they achieve a measure of power, they tend to act like their oppressors. Thus, disenfranchised groups of poor, female, ethnic, racial, religious, or other minorities exhibit the selfsame qualities of patriarchy, exclusivity, oppression, even hostility to their fellows or different others that they abhor in their oppressors. For Freire, the only way out of this dilemma is through the process of emancipatory education, or what he called *conscientização* (or conscientization)—that is, becoming conscious of evil within society and acting to transform the situation and liberate the oppressed.[30] This transformation cannot be accomplished by individuals acting alone. Only through acting in solidarity with others within a community can people come to recognize their oppression; imaginatively envisage what might be otherwise possible; gain courage to transform their community and society toward achieving freedom, justice, and civility; and realize their creative powers to the fullest extent possible.[31]

Cultural and Educational Problems

Beyond the institutional character of all education and the difficulties of achieving systemic change are problems both cultural and educational. The latter part of the twentieth century witnessed what are sometimes described as "culture wars," a contest between the so-called high and esoteric Western culture of the past and contemporary mediated popular culture, and between European and other cultural traditions. These contests were expressed musically in clashes between beliefs, values, and practices of Western "art" music, so-called classical music, and popular musical expressions of jazz, country, rock, rap, and others, each in turn achieving some measure of respectability the longer it lasted. As well, the increasingly multicultural and diverse societies of the West included musical traditions from Africa, Asia, Oceania, and South America that lay outside the mainstream of western European tradition. Some of these traditions were classical in their own right, while others were popular or practiced traditionally. The confluence of these many musics raised questions about which musical traditions should predominate, which should be included in the curriculum, and how to reconcile the claims of many varied musics on teachers and their students.[32] Was musical multiculturalism a desirable or achievable goal? If so, how should it be achieved? How could musics with such disparate values and aesthetics be included in the music program? How could or should these disparate, sometimes conflicting, musical voices be heard with integrity? In the face of these and many other questions, music teachers were naturally conflicted about their musical purposes, plans, and procedures.[33]

Regarding education, the nineteenth-century experiment with publicly supported and comprehensive schools seemed to run out of steam toward the end of the twentieth century and was berated on all sides for its perceived failures. In the United States the common school was established with a view to strengthening and sustaining a democratic political system. At its nineteenth-century beginning it served as a means of educating the poor and underprivileged. Gradually, it increased its reach to include the middle class and most of the population. The last few decades of the twentieth century, however, witnessed a spate of reports critical of the schools, strident calls for higher standards and increased accountability, published accounts of the failure of public schools, the rise of alternative charter schools and private schools, and an increased commitment to home schooling to which the well-to-do or disenchanted could escape. The flight from public schools following on the enforced desegregation of public schools (borne largely by blacks, who felt the brunt of busing to the suburbs) exacerbated the difficulties faced by teachers in urban schools, widened the gaps between rich and poor, black and white, and reinforced the racism and classism in American society.[34] Many young people entered the teaching profession with high hopes and found, instead, that they could not do what they wanted to do—meet the needs and interests of students as they wished—so straitjacketed were they by administrative directives, testing and evaluative procedures, and professionally, politically, or self-imposed curricular standards, requirements, and expectations. Lacking appreciation and financial and other rewards for their work, and feeling very much alone in their schools, they became disenchanted with public education. In the face of the mounting problems in their classrooms, insufficient resources, and inadequate organizational and scheduling arrangements and support, many teachers became so discouraged that they left the profession altogether or left the public schools to more congenial teaching environments. Despite an enormous investment in music teacher preparation, the revolving door to public school music teaching necessitated a constant supply of new recruits to replace those who had left. Teachers who remained were able to adapt to the educational system, often working in spite of it yet reluctant or powerless to change it, and unable to provide the sorts of quality experiences to which they felt their students were entitled.[35] Education was clearly in need of systemic change. But how, and in what direction, to change it? And how to achieve that change in practice?

At a time of dramatic and pervasive societal change, potent and effective mass mediated culture, and compelling and seductive materialism, educational and cultural transformation seem to be required. The drama of this change may seem to overshadow all other periods of change historically. Yet, looking back over musical and educational history, others before our time have had to deal with crises of their own that impelled them to think and act for change. As with other areas of culture, some periods of musical history demonstrate more dramatic change than others do. The inexorable transformation from Gregorian chant to the electronified music of today seems more the rule than the exception.[36] Each generation needs to renew education and culture for its particular time and place—its Janus faces to the past and future—and this renewal constitutes the seeds of musical, cultural, or societal transformation. In times of great uncertainty and change such as ours, this challenge to transform music, education, and society seems especially daunting.

It is important, here, to highlight the persistent connection between education and culture—a connection that provides the grounds for a transforming model for education.[37] In his magisterial study of *paideia*, Werner Jaeger demonstrates the role of education in ancient Greek thought as an agency of enculturation, of becoming a cultured person.[38] The values underlying *paideia* are spelled out by Socrates, Plato, and others in their train to include music (construed more broadly in that time as the arts) as a foundational element.[39] Notions of education as enculturation and the centrality of the arts as educational agencies resurface later in the writings of Friedrich Schiller, John Dewey, Herbert Read, Harry Broudy, Mortimer Adler, Elliot Eisner, Maxine Greene, and Charles Fowler.[40] To conceive of education as enculturation, as these writers do, requires placing culture at the heart of education.[41] Regarding music along with other arts as important manifestations of human expression suggests that they should be central and essential to a complete education. Downplaying or excluding musical and artistic instruction degrades education and culture because instruction constitutes a necessary part of sustaining any culture or society and because what happens in music or the arts plays out in culture and in education conceived as the process of enculturation. Including and supporting musical and artistic instruction enhances education and culture. These twin notions—the conception of education as enculturation, and the interconnectedness of music, culture, and education—seem sufficiently established to provide reasonable grounds for my move to view musical education as a microcosm and agent of transforming general education.

To call for educational transformation is not to denigrate the well-meant efforts of educators past and present. It is not to disparage what is just for the sake of change. Nor is it to claim that the work of transformation has yet to begin. Others have recognized the need for change, and there have always been educators who have sought to renew themselves and their work toward transformative ends. Within music one thinks of a galaxy of teachers throughout the ages and ongoing efforts within educational institutions, such as the MENC, to renew the work of teaching, learning, and instruction for our time.[42] My call for musical and educational transformation should be read as a mark of respect for these many efforts. Standing on the shoulders of those who have gone before, my purpose is to propose a vision of what a transformed music education might look like and to suggest that as the work of musician-teachers among other artists is transformed, so the wider work of education can also be transformed.

The complexity and intractability of these practical and theoretical challenges cannot be met with facile or simplistic approaches and solutions. Music teachers and other educational policy makers need an approach to thinking about multiplicities and complexities that avoids the pitfall of what Charlene Morton describes as "add and stir" approaches in which the old is merely assimilated or accommodated into the new, or vice versa.[43] Notions of assimilation and accommodation invoke cultural imperialism or ethnocentrism in which, for example, a particular cultural or musical practice is taken to be normative. Nor does one wish to throw out the old simply because it is old; what is old may be exceedingly precious, to be kept at all costs.[44] There is the ever-present danger of failing to recognize the value of traditional things, especially in a society preoccupied with change. And not only is the educational enterprise already under way, but each participant and observer has a partial understanding of it, and one's ideas and actions have unintended consequences. The spaceship is in flight, and repairs must be undertaken in mid-voyage.

Thinking Dialectically

One way of viewing these complex issues is through a dialectical approach.[45] The word *dialectic* carries its own baggage, and it is important to clarify what I mean by the term and explore some of its advantages and limitations. Prefacing this discussion, I recognize that reflection occurs not in a vacuum but against the backdrop of particular times, places, cultures, literatures, and individual perspectives. Certain beliefs and practices gain currency, and it is sometimes difficult to swim against the tide of their popular acceptance. Yet swim the change agent must. Skepticism—the conviction that there must be something wrong with the most cherished or plausible idea, even if it be of one's own making—provides the impetus toward criticizing and clarifying ideas and practices. Its exercise is an act of respect for the effort expended and achievements of one's fellows, and a corrective to the tendency for unexamined assumptions to become dogma, or what Freire calls "sectarianism"—the refusal to skeptically or critically examine one's ideas.[46] As Israel Scheffler reminds us, dogmatism, absence of surprise, or doubt may be more comfortable intellectual positions, but they signal "epistemic weakness" and closed-mindedness.[47] Educational policy makers seeking greater truth face the prospect of belief on the one hand and doubt on the other. Definitive solutions forged for all time seem out of reach. Recognizing this reality does not invalidate the effort to build a philosophy, as some educational thinkers have and are attempting to do. It simply underscores the tentativeness of these formulations.

My interest in dialectical analysis began early in my teaching experience. I found myself caught between two worlds: the world of the desirable and the world of the possible. I was forever analyzing, comparing, and contrasting things, seeing the instructional process ripe with alternatives that might be meritorious or desirable yet practically impossible to achieve simultaneously. I was forced to choose among possibilities, whether it be the tenor of the music program, repertoire, or methodological approach, and these choices affected my program in important and inescapable ways. If I chose too much of one thing, something else suffered, and as I analyzed my experiences, I saw how difficult were some of these decisions about how to reconcile disparate, sometimes conflicting aims and methods and how crucial my decisions were to the success of my teaching.

During the 1970s I was introduced to the notion of ideal types by the Canadian sociologist Henry Zentner. In company with other sociological theorists, Zentner conceives of theoretical or ideal types as logical or polar opposites that may be systematically compared by means of a profile of characteristics, where certain aspects of each extreme may be melded to form empirical types.[48] For Zentner there are two orders of types: ideal or logical types that constitute purely theoretical entities or polarities, and empirical types exemplifying the various clusters or profiles of characteristics in the phenomenal world. Following Zentner, I sought to identify polar opposites (or theoretical types) in music education by which I could more clearly distinguish the ground between them. As a teacher, I had earlier recognized that this "ground between" constituted the principal stuff of education.[49] In this ground between lay important problems and potentials that seemed to make the difference between poor, competent, or brilliant teaching and learning. Yet it fell through the cracks of my learned paraphernalia of musical and educational taxonomies, frameworks, concepts, skills, objectives, and methods. I thought to spotlight this ground between by focusing in turn on one logical extreme and then another, and through systematically comparing these opposites, to understand more clearly how they commingled in the empirical world. This analysis would then constitute a springboard to reflecting about how they ought to commingle.

I came to see that the notion of synthesis to which I had earlier been attracted was problematic, simplistic, and reductionistic. It was problematic in that it did not address the question of how to meld things that were logically contradictory and mutually exclusive. It was simplistic in that it failed to address the variety of combinations inherent in the polarities identified, the various ends to which they may be put, and the possibility that only certain aspects of these polar opposites could be melded to varying degrees, and even then, the outcomes might be very fragile. It was reductionistic in assuming that the analysis should be construed at a high level of generality concerned mainly with social issues. Nor were things as neat and tidy as my theoretical world seemed to be. I learned that empirical experience in the psychological and social world invariably differs from theoretical postulates about it. Conceptions and categories of empirical experience are often murky and fuzzy, weak syndromes in which one thing invariably blurs into another. And there are inevitably tensions, conflicts, and paradoxes.[50]

I also came to recognize a tension between identifying theoretical positions and making choices between alternatives based on them. Choice is a problematical process, and it is difficult for choosers to assess comparatively alternatives in advance of their implementation.[51] The unintended consequences that flow from all human actions are exacerbated by the difficulty of *a priori* hypotheses, estimation, and prediction, of assessing which alternatives are better than others in advance of the fact. In attempting to forecast the likely impact of implementing alternatives X and Y, I observed that teachers generally focus on the imagined future and practical consequences that flow from X and Y rather than on the refutation of past evidence about them. In this respect, their choices may differ from those of researchers in the scientific tradition. Given a choice between X and Y, the exclusion of one or other alternative eliminates a string of desirable and undesirable consequences following from that option and forecloses an alternative that might have turned out to be the better one had it been selected. Not to make the choice, however, necessitates finding a practical way to combine X and Y and minimizing the undesirable consequences of combining them.

I noticed that music teachers, many of whom are women, make choices based mainly on the practical demands of their classrooms. They are remarkably unwilling to exclude alternatives and foreclose their options. For example, each of the music instructional methodologies (construed broadly to refer to what and how the music teacher teaches) such as those by Émile Jaques-Dalcroze, Percy Scholes, Zoltán Kodály, Carl Orff and Gunild Keetman, Shinichi Suzuki, Murray Schafer, Patricia Shehan Campbell, and Doreen Rao has desirable and undesirable features.[52] Historically, when music teachers have been free to do so, they have often opted for an eclectic methodological position even though the assumptions underlying these methods conflict and contradict each other.[53] This tendency suggests that teachers make situated judgments on the basis of practical experience rather than rational theories and instructional methodologies, a hypothesis consistent with the findings of Carol Gilligan, Lyn Mikel Brown, and their colleagues concerning the different ways women and girls view the world.[54] I suggest, more broadly, that music teachers, as do their colleagues in other teaching fields, make decisions on other bases than logical judgment and externally mandated or more or less universally accepted rules or standards.

Also, I saw that prescriptive instructional methods do not last very long. They are superseded because teachers invariably find them shortsighted or lacking in one respect or another, and they go in search of an antidote. For example, within a year of the publication of the latest editions of school music textbook series published by the Macmillan and Silver Burdett companies, some teachers were already complaining that the curriculum was off-putting to children.[55] If history repeats itself, it will just be a matter of time before present editions of basal series will have run their course only to be supplanted by others, as textbooks are redesigned to better fit perceived classroom realities and those of electronic or Internet-based publishing. This ongoing and repetitive process contributes to the observed faddishness of music education practice.[56] I am inclined to believe, however, that given the tendency of teachers toward eclecticism, such faddishness should be laid principally at the door of the architects of educational ideas and methods rather than the teachers themselves.[57]

A Critique

In characterizing my dialectical approach, Iris Yob writes that it is not to be read as an *"either/or* conclusion or a simple *both/and* synthesis" but rather a *"this-with-that* solution," whereby "the view not center stage in our attention would potentially be exerting its influence and offering course corrections even from the wings." It "does not weigh the strengths and weaknesses" of the two alternatives "to determine which one has more strengths and fewer weaknesses" so as to "plump for the more compelling net result," nor does it "blend [both alternatives] together in some kind of bland, undifferentiated

mix where the weakness of one [is] canceled out by the strengths of another, and vice versa." Instead, there is a sense in which both perspectives
coexist, "held in dialectical tension with each other."[58] In this view, teachers analyze the theoretical possibilities flowing from the implementation of
alternatives X and Y, determine if it is possible to combine them and in
what ways, create the appropriate "mix," and adjust or correct the balance
between them so as to maximize the advantages and minimize the disadvantages of the theoretical possibilities either taken alone or resulting from
their combination.

I agree that the either/or conclusion may limit the options too much,
and the simple both/and synthesis may neglect the difficulties inherent in
synthesizing things in tension with each other.[59] The this-with-that solution, drawing as it does on a dramatic metaphor in which alternatives
teachers face are actors on a stage, seems to come closest to the process I
am trying to articulate. It seems to work rather like Vernon Howard's distinction between the artist's peripheral and focal awareness.[60] Howard
explains that the artist (read teacher) is grappling with various skills, some
of which are in the foreground while others are in the background.
Sometimes it may be necessary to translate peripheral awareness into focal
awareness, attend to a particular aspect, and then, when it is learned or
mastered, relegate it to peripheral awareness. Even when the skill is in
peripheral awareness, it is still operating as part of the means whereby the
artist (teacher) makes course corrections along the way toward the making
of a work of art. It is an integral part of the artistic process.

Although the analogy between the teacher and Howard's artist is not
fully congruent, it can be helpful in explaining the dialectical process. Let
us say that teachers are considering two contrasting objectives, both of
which they wish to pursue. They are likely to follow one and then the
other, the one constituting a correction for the other and thereby influenc-
ing the other even when it is not the focus of attention. For example, Keith
Swanwick and June Boyce-Tillman represent this process in the tension
between the two sides of their music curricular spiral in which the learner
progresses through several levels of musical knowledge, moving alternatively between rational and intuitive approaches to music.[61] I cannot agree
with them that the process is as mechanistic as they suggest, with the
particular ordering of elements in their curricular spiral, or with the specific
configuration of their conception of musical knowledge. Still, the idea that
music curriculum is dialectical and it is not always possible to pursue all
aspects at once is consistent with my own thinking. We agree that the practical exigencies of exposition require that teachers and students sometimes
focus on one thing to the exclusion of others, later shifting their attention
elsewhere as other interests and needs emerge.

Among the advantages of this dialectical approach are its open-endedness,
interconnectedness, and situatedness, allowing for multiple solutions to educational problems. It is analogous to a hypertext, or an interconnecting system

of branching networks from various nodes that make it possible for a person to choose where to enter the system, which texts to select, and in what order. Nicholas Burbules and Thomas Callister Jr. cite the metaphor of rhizomes—certain grasses and plants that have a decentralized root system—to illustrate how hypertexts work.[62] They see hypertext as "a hybrid term, meaning both the particular technological developments that have made textual fragmentation and complex cross-referencing possible and convenient, and a theoretical view of the text (any text) as decentered and open-ended, which has been with us for a long time."[63] Hypertext emphasizes the connectedness of information and provides freedom for people to read the text from their individual perspectives and in their own ways. It presumably allows for multiple solutions to theoretical and practical problems, seeing that people enter the system from different points, have incomplete knowledge of it, make their own connections and interlinked pathways, and ultimately come to see it from various perspectives.

These qualities correspond to the nature of social or open systems. Those within a social group have a partial view of it based on their particular roles within the system, and they make decisions based on incomplete information. They enter at different times and go in different directions, toward different ends. They make their moves bodily, emotionally, intuitively, imaginatively, and logically. Construed as social systems, then, music and education are appropriately viewed from a dialectical perspective.

Also, my dialectical approach is consistent with dialogical education in which various points of view are analyzed, discussed, and debated in an ongoing conversation between members of an educational community.[64] For Freire and Greene, the multiple perspectives and pluralities in dialogical education constitute strengths as well as challenges for education.[65] Such education potentially enriches personal and corporate understanding of different others, empowers individuals within communities to struggle for freedom, and humanizes societies by valuing the ideas and personhood of those who might otherwise be marginalized or ostracized because of their differences. It goes beneath the superficial differences between people to enable them to see the deeper similarities that connect them with others. Notwithstanding that music is made in a myriad of different ways around the globe, all those who make it share a common humanity and invoke music to celebrate, to mourn, to encourage, to pray, and to remember their lived experience. In many cultures they do not even think of what they do as music viewed through Western eyes as separate from other aspects of their lives.[66] This shared humanity is a powerful connection between the music makers and takers of the world. A dialectical approach to music seems an appropriate way of revealing commonalities as well as differences in music making and taking between and among people.[67] Musical dialectics become apparent through musical dialogue as people talk about and enact their differing musical ideas, just as the dialogues are necessitated because of the musical dialectics. Both are inextricably interconnected and worked through experientially.

Despite these advantages, one of the principal achievements of feminist thinking over the past three decades has been to show the problematical character of dialectical resolution—how deeply embedded are male-dominated structures of meaning in self and society, and how profoundly difficult it is to change them. In counterpoint to the idealistic desire to give voice to those who have been silenced; to overcome boundaries of gender, age, color, language, ethnicity, social class, and religion that separate people; and to work toward such ideals as inclusiveness, equality, freedom, and human dignity are the forces of institutionalized subversion of these ideals: patriarchy, marginalization, repression, and dehumanization.[68] Against the bright picture of community is its dark side fraught with hypocrisy, tension, betrayal, and destruction, as efforts to enhance and enrich human experience through community are subverted.[69] Nel Noddings describes this dark side as "the tendencies toward parochialism, conformity, exclusion, assimilation, distrust (or hatred) of outsiders, and coercion."[70] Despite educators' best efforts to create and sustain dialogue, an open-ended system in which multiple solutions can be implemented and tolerated, and in which all can participate fully, other forces invariably contradict, countermand, or crush these efforts. While acknowledging these difficulties, I think a dialectical approach is worth pursuing even if only as an ideal. The alternative of foreclosing this possibility on the grounds that it might be thwarted is depressing, demoralizing, and ultimately dehumanizing.

Yob regards my this-with-that solution of holding things in tension as problematical because the flaws of each alternative still remain and the weaknesses as well as the strengths of each are multiplied.[71] I concur but plead that, practically speaking, I cannot see how this can be avoided. Noddings seeks to find a way between establishing "some of the desirable features associated with community: a sense of belonging, of collective concern for each individual, of individual responsibility for the collective good, and of appreciation for the rituals and celebrations of the good" while at the same time avoiding the oppressive aspects of community.[72] And I agree that in an imperfect and sometimes evil world in which the good often seems fragile, virtues can be turned into vices if indeed they can ever be realized. In his essay, "Vice into Virtue, or Seven Deadly Sins of Education Redeemed," Scheffler identifies vices that may be turned into virtues, and his argument can just as easily be turned on its head to show exactly the opposite—that virtues may be turned into vices.[73] This reality necessitates constant vigilance on the part of educators in order to minimize the dark side of things that might otherwise be virtuous.

Some may see this dialectic approach as masking an underlying bifurcated and dualistic world. They may say that it does not go far enough. One of the insights of feminist among other postmodern thought is the recognition that people are wholes, unities, not conglomerations of separate qualities of mind and body, intellection and emotion, or physical and spiritual entities. Rather than pairs of actors or dancers, Yob sees a whole actor or dancer, representing the whole person.[74] I reply that dialectics are *not* dualities in disguise. As polarities or weak syndromes, they intersect; it is difficult, practically speaking, to separate them. But polarities should not be confused with dualities, which by definition cannot intersect or meld one with the other. Notwithstanding their interrelatedness, and here I am sure Yob would agree, there are advantages to making conceptual distinctions between one thing and another if only to see the "ground between" more clearly. And I do not deny that people act as whole persons. Yob may be focusing on the ontological character of the actors (or dancers) themselves, whereas my dialectical approach is directed toward the epistemological dilemmas these persons confront and how they go about solving them practically speaking. Yob's view and mine may, in fact, be in tension. Rather than undermining the argument, her view evidences the possibility of even more dialectics than those I have observed. And this possibility reinforces the value of multiple and differing perspectives—a notion about which we both agree.[75]

Another potential flaw in this dialectical approach is its failure to provide a rational structure for curriculum. Returning to my analogy of the hypertext, learners may get lost in the system because they may be shortsighted or do not have the advantage of knowing the logical structure upon which a field of study is built before they enter it. The onus is presumably on them to invent a structure, forcing them to reinvent the wheel or otherwise idiosyncratically grasp the field. Nevertheless, the logical claims of a particular subject demand an orderly progression of events. Educators cannot escape the need to sequence material because of the finite capacities of learners to grasp new material at a given time. Such sequencing demands privileging of some information over other information, so that the learner comes to systematically understand a structure of the field of study (even if this is one of many possibilities). Because the learner enters the hypertext at any point and goes to any other in the system, the immediate interests of the student are placed over and above the requirements of the subject and its underlying rational structure, and the claims of rationality are downplayed in favor of intuition and imagination as the learner explores the various parts of the hypertext. Failing to provide a logically sequenced series of assumptions and focusing on problems that are individually and collectively grasped rather than on concepts that are structurally and rationally articulated, the hypertext is limited in the extent to which it can provide a structural knowledge of the subject matter.

I reply that the analogy between hypertext and my dialectic approach can only be pressed so far. It ultimately fails because a hypertext is a closed system, whereas my dialectical approach is a genuinely open-ended one. The freedom suggested in the hypertext is illusory because the author has supplied the material in the first place.[76] Also, unforeseen events surprise teachers and students alike, because they fail to fully grasp the wider, changing reality. Further, while subject matter has inherent structure, it is unlikely that it has only one structure, yet music education policy makers have historically treated music as if there is only one view of musical structure—that associated with Western classical music. In this emphasis on musical structure over students' attitudes and preferences, particularly in our time, the dialectic between the student and the subject matter may be forgotten.[77] The student's mind-set should also figure into the teacher's decision about how to structure the educational process and bring the student and subject matter together.[78]

This leads me to the related observation that my dialectical approach does not provide a single, simple or clear direction for practitioners. In *In Search of Music Education,* I suggested that there is really no such thing as the one high road to music education, notwithstanding that throughout history, music teachers along with their colleagues in other fields have sought one.[79] Joseph Schwab and Scheffler have shown that even though theory and practice overlap (and Schwab is inclined to separate them more than Scheffler), they constitute two conceptually distinct if practically interrelated realms.[80] Just as a theoretical proposition is capable of several hypothetical solutions in practice, so it is difficult to connect any singular theoretical position to a particular practice, such is the interrelatedness and ambiguity between an idea and its practical realization. I see this ambiguity as a strength in that it provides space for teachers to devise their own solutions to the particular challenges they face. Instead of being technicians who unthinkingly employ the ideas and approaches of others, teachers have the opportunity to act as professionals in creating instructional situations that meet the particular needs of their students.[81]

Another problematical aspect of the this-with-that solution, and one that I can only presage in this chapter, is the case in which alternatives are irreconcilable and mutually contradictory, in which this cannot be combined with that. I am inclined to the view that many apparently dichotomous cases turn out to be fuzzier than on first glance. For example, it might seem difficult to combine the elitist ethic underlying the Church of England choir school, in which only a few musically talented boys are selected for intensive musical and liturgical training, with the universalistic ethic underlying an English primary school, in which it is presumed that all children irrespective of talent shall have some limited musical and religious training. Values underlying the one seem inconsistent with the other. Yet some Church of England choir schools exemplify universalistic qualities by offering school membership to girls and boys beyond the cathedral or chapel choir (as well as offering choir membership to girls), and some primary schools illustrate elitist qualities by incorporating select choirs of auditioned members within their school curricula. In those cases where one or another alternative must be selected, however, it is important to recognize that this dialectical approach constitutes a process whereby teachers and their students explore their alternatives and the possibility of the ground between them before prematurely foreclosing either option. It provides a systematic way of analyzing alternatives and focuses as much on the process of philosophical reflection as on its practical outcomes. Given the freedom to act in this manner, teachers and their students likely will arrive at differing solutions that fit their particular perceptions of their times and places.

A more pressing question arises: What are the principles by which teachers and their students adjudicate the dialectics they face? I concur with Scheffler, Paul Hirst, R. S. Peters, and Robin Barrow that logical and moral tests constitute two principal means whereby alternatives may be examined and choices made among or between them.[82] In other words, reason, intuition, and imagination play important roles in teachers' and students' decision making. Educational decisions cannot be scientifically refuted. They are only ever justified because ultimately they are based on values that ultimately are defended philosophically.[83]

Freed from the claims of perfection and comprehensiveness, this dialectical approach can facilitate discussion of the many challenges that face the field today, particularly those relating to transforming music and education. It is not a philosophy among philosophies, but a tool for negotiating among different philosophies, theories, and methods. As such, it provides a lens through which teachers can view their work and a way of articulating the conceptual and practical framework for music and education.

Summary

To sum up, I have suggested that the work of music teachers provides a window on the work of education generally. Teachers face complex systemic problems that are at once societal, artistic, and educational. These problems can best be addressed by individuals in solidarity with others in communities where the multiplicities and pluralities of contemporary societies are represented and voiced. One practical way of working through complex educational issues and arriving at multiple perspectives on them is by taking a dialectical, this-with-that approach that constitutes a way of thinking through options before prematurely foreclosing them. As dialectics are voiced and negotiated in the process of dialogue between teachers, students, and those interested in their work, these dialogues, in turn, engender further dialectics. Despite the fact that this approach is a potentially flawed and fragile endeavor, it offers a way to envisage transforming music education that respects and listens to the other and draws on reason, intuition, imagination, and feeling. In so doing, it creates a space where many voices heretofore silenced can be heard. And as transformation occurs in music education, its effects potentially ripple out into education and society.

2

Justifying Transformation

In this chapter I suggest that music education needs to be transformed for two reasons. First, the mortality of human beings and the fact that education is carried on by one generation after another necessitates transformation if it is to succeed in the long term. Second, because it is undertaken by human beings, music education is beset by systemic problems that afflict the wider society. Always, education seems to have important and far-reaching dehumanizing and oppressive aspects. Individual and collective efforts toward transforming music education and achieving greater humanity, civility, justice, and freedom are difficult if not impossible to undertake and achieve in practice. The ongoing challenge for music educators is to resist pervasive tendencies toward banality, crudity, and violence in contemporary culture and renew society toward refinement, physical restraint, personal dignity, love of wisdom, and care for others. And although music education is an inherently flawed social system itself in need of transformation, it can constitute an agent of change toward civilizing and enculturating society at large.

The first argument for transformation is a relatively simple one. Viewing music education as the means whereby a particular group, institution, or society is able to survive from one generation to the next suggests that teachers seek to transmit to the young the personal and social attitudes, beliefs, practices, skills, expectations, and dispositions to enable them to survive and flourish in the particular group of which they are a part. As one generation gives way to the next, each also needs to decide which beliefs and practices to preserve and which to change. Especially at a time in which change is pervasive worldwide, this reexamination of traditions constitutes a part of the ongoing process of transformation whereby people make beliefs and practices their own, and a group adapts to changing circumstances yet still preserves certain traditional perspectives and practices. Without schooling, socialization, and enculturation, a group would be without the means to transform itself across the generations.

The second argument for transformation is more complex because it concerns normative objectives of music education—that is, those to which groups, institutions, and societies ought to aspire. Instead of ploughing over ground that has been well worked elsewhere, my argument is grounded on principles that predicate educational transformation. I am in the company of those who believe that education ought to be humane. It ought to be directed toward such ideals as civility, justice, freedom, and inclusion of diverse peoples and perspectives.[1] It ought to take a broad view of the world's cultures and human knowledge and prepare the young to be informed and compassionate citizens of the world.[2] It ought to address not only material things but the aspirations and longings of the human spirit.[3] And it ought to provide learners with the skills and dispositions to participate in their governance actively and intelligently, and prompt and empower them to act toward the betterment of their world.[4] This is a radical and critical pedagogy—one that is not satisfied with the status quo and seeks to realize ideals, even if imperfectly, in the phenomenal world.[5]

In taking a normative stance in respect of educational practice, I see systemic problems that militate against the ends of freedom, civility, justice, humanity, and inclusivity. In the field of music education, there are problems of gender, worldview, music, education, tradition, and mind-set—issues that apply to education more broadly. Having identified these systemic problems opens the door to seeing how music education can be transformed toward this humane and inclusive vision. And it is to this task that I turn.

Gender

It is a commonplace that music and education are gendered in their historical tendency to exclude women and girls or marginalize them from the mainstream of musical life; to prescribe and proscribe certain musical activities for each gender; and to perpetuate white, male, heterosexual perspectives on music theory and practice in what counts for musical knowledge.[6] Historical and ethnological examples of sexism abound. Sexist attitudes and practices are evident in music education; traditional music making; the school music textbook industry; the music recording industry; the music education research establishment; the professional performance and management business; music education associations; universities, conservatories, and private studios; the print and electronic media; and national or state examination systems.[7] All of the societal institutions I have studied—family, religion, politics, music profession, and commerce—reveal, sometimes starkly, that women are often relegated to informal music making, restricted to the performance of certain music or musical instruments or to amateur rather than professional music, and excluded from positions of leadership and authority or from particular musical events.[8] Notwithstanding the best intentions on the part of many musicians and teachers, music education has been riddled with sexism for a long time.

I am concerned with what music education might be missing by excluding or marginalizing the voices of women, and what it could gain by discovering the territory of the might-have-been or might-be, of possibility rather than actuality. Greene points to the need to become "demystified" or "wide-awake" to the situation and recover things that have been buried by human ignorance, neglect, opposition, or destruction.[9] In another vein, Scholes invokes a different metaphor in describing the music teacher's task as one of removing obstacles to understanding, much as one might repair an impassable road cluttered with debris.[10]

Recovering buried treasure or removing debris are helpful metaphors for discovering women's contributions to musical meaning making and practice. Female perspectives and practices have been ignored, devalued, and deliberately obscured, buried under the weight of male institutions, structures, and rules. This loss can be remedied by mining women's perspectives and practices or by removing the clutter of male perspectives and prerogatives that have otherwise obscured them from view. Seeing that male viewpoints are inherently narrow, inaccurate, and misleading if taken to represent the whole of human experience, finding or recovering women's ways of knowing and doing can broaden the realms of knowing and being. The feminine voice is different, and the female perspective brings a richness to human experience that is ignored or silenced to the detriment of the entire human race. Recovering and articulating that perspective is a necessary first step in the process of accepting it into the mainstream of human thought and practice. In accomplishing this, it is important to recognize how invisible this perspective often is. Even Freire laments that his vision of liberating education within *Pedagogy of the Oppressed* failed to include women and girls. His use of exclusive language betrayed his shortsightedness; in spite of the fact that he worked tirelessly to develop a truly inclusive and liberating educational system, he did not recognize how deeply patriarchy was ingrained in his own thinking and how oppressive it was to the very people he sought to liberate.[11] It was only later, after women wrote to him, that he realized his error. And I suspect that Freire's experience is shared by many others.

Gender has come to include the entire range of sexuality and with that, the prospect of increasing complexity in the ways in which music and education are conceived. For example, Elizabeth Gould's autobiographical account of music education from the perspective of a "white, middle class, middle-aged lesbian who works as an arts administrator and first-year university lecturer in the midst of completing a doctoral dissertation" leads her to question music education practices, to a sense of marginality, alienation, and powerlessness, and prompts her to work toward transforming the individual and corporate lives of music educators.[12] Were her account to be dismissed because it is unscientific, critical of the status quo and all who stand to gain from it, or representative of a minority of women, much would be lost. More than half of the music teachers and their students are women and girls, with varying sexual identities, and their perspectives along with those of other minorities need to be included in music educational thought and practice if one is to envisage all that might be possible.

Further, it is simplistic to associate "masculine" qualities exclusively with males and "feminine" qualities only with females. Social-psychological research suggests, rather, that a mix of these qualities is desirable for well-adjusted men and women. Empirical studies of musicians show, for example, that most are somewhat androgynous, possessing traits that might be labeled masculine and feminine.[13] The feminine voice, like the masculine, is to be discovered in both males and females and is not the exclusive prerogative of women and girls. It may have been suppressed, repudiated, or never grasped, acknowledged, or articulated by men and women, boys and girls alike.

How would music, music making, and music education be different if the feminine perspectives were to prevail? In answering this question, feminist writers have suggested some important differences. The feminine tends to emphasize art as centered in the present, joyful, playful, and erotic, in contrast to the masculine view of art as directed toward the future, purposeful, work-oriented, and cerebral. In the feminine view, art is a part of life, whereas in the masculine view, art is a discrete entity apart from life. The feminine approach to art is holistic, contextual, and thereby unified, whereas the masculine approach is logocentric, decontextualized, and therefore alienating. Feminine epistemology is drawn in terms of "soft boundaries" between categories or "weak syndromes" in which one category melds into another, thereby focusing on the "ground between" categories, whereas masculine epistemology is drawn rigidly and dichotomously, in terms of rule-sets and "hard boundaries" in which distinctions are clear-cut.[14] The feminine perspective of art is feelingful (including emotion and corporeality) in contrast to the masculine perspective, which is intellectual. Feminine organization of art is universalistic, informal, communal, cooperative, and egalitarian, whereas masculine artistic organizations are elitist, formal, individual, competitive, and hierarchical; feminine art is corporately shared, whereas masculine art is hoarded as a source of power. Feminine art is subjectively evaluated, whereas masculine art is objectively evaluated.[15]

Would that things were this simple or clear-cut. But they are not. Notions that men intellectualize music whereas women feel it, or that men make music competitively and hierarchically whereas women make music in cooperative and egalitarian ways, seem unsupported by the empirical evidence I have seen and go counter to the tendency toward androgyny among musicians that Anthony Kemp has observed. The alternative is to rest such mutually exclusive, antithetical, dichotomous, or ideal-typical constructs (depending on how they are read) on taken-for-granted or stereotypical ideas of femininity or masculinity—notions that in the West have their modern roots in Renaissance ideals.[16] Either way, Lucy Green faults the theoretical claims that women and men make music differently and that these differences can be found *in* the music. Such a view fails to take account of the crucial distinction between what she describes as music's "inherent" meaning—that is, its significance discernible in regard to its syntactic structures as understood by the initiates in a particular musical tradition—and its "delineated" meaning, or music's reference to and association with other things through aspects of the musician's display, performance, marketing of the musical event, and so forth. At best, she argues, male and female differences should be attributed more to music's delineated rather than its inherent aspects.[17]

I am less persuaded than Green is that her distinction between inherent and musical meaning is as clear-cut as she seems to believe it to be. Rather, for me it constitutes an instance of a soft boundary or weak syndrome in which the one seeps or melds into the other. Rules that ground musical practice are themselves formulated within a societal context, a phenomenon that Leonard Meyer recognized several decades ago.[18] If these rules are taken to be social constructs and form the basis for musical theory and practice, then it seems inescapable that the syntactic aspects of music would, to some extent, be read appropriately as "social text,"[19] thereby blurring the boundary between Green's inherent and delineated musical meaning. On the other hand, irrespective of how they play out in practice, stereotypes of femininity and masculinity are regularly used, taken for granted so that they become a part of common sense and are used as a basis for shaping social conduct. It is not surprising, then, that feminists would have appealed to them as a means of showing important potential differences in the musical perspectives and practices of men and women, even if these differences may be less clear-cut than they imagined, especially when applied in the arena of formal music making. Seeing that formal music making is so dominated by male beliefs and practices, and empirical evidence of women's musical beliefs and practices is comparatively limited, projecting what might be if women's perspectives were to be included equally alongside men's is necessarily speculative. However, viewed ideal-typically, in terms of logically contrasting theoretical positions or matters of emphasis, and allowing the caveat of inevitable murkiness, theoretically and practically, the notion that men and women make music differently, as feminist writers have proposed, can be recuperated.

In the phenomenal world, instances probably fall along a continuum between theoretically feminine and masculine extremes.[20] At first glance, the masculine profile seems more or less consistent with characteristics shared by the great musical traditions (such as the classical traditions of the world) because these musics are often viewed as cerebral; purposeful; requiring delayed gratification in the sense of practicing for a future performance; separated from everyday life; logocentric; exemplifying rigid rule-sets; exhibiting hard boundaries; organized in elitist, formal, and hierarchical ways; and objectively evaluated. The feminine view, by contrast, looks like those small musical traditions (those vernacular traditions limited mainly to relatively small geographic areas) where the playful and erotic elements are emphasized; the arts serve everyday life purposes; music is viewed informally and holistically; boundaries are soft in the sense that actors in musical events move easily from one role to another, or ideas and practices meld from one to the other; and music is a felt rather than intellectually construed experience, cooperatively and communally shared and subjectively evaluated.

On closer examination, however, the situation is much more complex than this, and counter-examples readily spring to mind. For instance, to the extent that mediated music or international popular music constitutes a great tradition, it seems feminine in significant respects—for example, in its present-centered, playful, informal, erotic, and felt qualities—while among small traditions, such vernacular musics as Balkan epic song and the traditional communal music making of the aboriginal peoples of Australia and Papua New Guinea seem masculine in important ways, especially in their exclusivity of women and those outside their tribe and the use of music as an expression of magical power over others.[21] This evidence would again support reading feminine-masculine differences ideal-typically, as logical extremes between which particular instances of music can be plotted. Rather than dichotomous entities, they can better be construed as weak syndromes in which one gradually blurs into the other, where neither probably exists in "pure" form in the phenomenal world. However, to the extent that a theoretical distinction between delineated and inherent musical meaning is defensible, they probably should be construed more in terms of delineated musical associations and references than musical syntaxes and structures.

Some writers, such as Heide Göttner-Abendroth,[22] suggest that the predominant patriarchal view of art should be "inverted" so that the matriarchal view dominates. They see artistic and musical transformation in terms of a substitution of one set of values for another—for example, the matriarchal for the prevailing patriarchal worldview. I am uncomfortable with this approach because it substitutes one potential tyranny for another. Also, each view taken by itself is too limited. Göttner-Abendroth's patriarchal view excludes the felt aspects of art—its erotic, playful, and immediate value in everyday, ordinary life. Her matriarchal view excludes the values of discipline, intellectual appeal for a relatively few initiates, hierarchical organization, and separateness from the ordinary, everyday world. A dialectical approach that holds both perspectives in view while seeking to work through aspects that remain in tension one with another, even though they are sometimes difficult to meld or reconcile, seems preferable because it allows both perspectives to be taken into account in forging solutions. This approach requires arriving at solutions experientially and particularly. The actual working out of principles takes place within circumstances that vary across individuals, times, and places. Even where the community may agree on certain values, beliefs, and practices, their precise realization will and should differ from one individual or situation to another.

In making this point, I am committed to the view that the feminine and masculine views of music, to the extent that these can be defended, each have advantages and disadvantages. I do not see one as necessarily prior to, or better than, the other. Rather, as different perspectives, they each have something to contribute to the whole of humankind. Men may be especially concerned with the importance of rules and of clear organizational and objective purposes regarding music making; women may be particularly interested in caring relationships, inclusiveness, informality, egalitarian procedures, process, and passion in music making. Women may take an objective, hierarchical, and goal-oriented approach, while men may be subjective, egalitarian, and process-oriented in regard to music making. Excluding or marginalizing feminine or masculine perspectives, however, limits music education and forces it to hop or limp on one leg. Green shows how masculine perspectives now dominate in English music education and are encoded within general education.[23] The same is true throughout the world. Transforming music education with regard to gender would mean elevating feminine perspectives and including them genuinely and equally alongside masculine ones—a process that, as I show later, would necessitate fundamental changes in music and education.

Against this possibility needs to be weighed the lack of understanding and unwillingness of some men to share power with women and others different from themselves, open their minds to divergent ideas that go counter to their preconceived beliefs, assume individual responsibility for their actions rather than excusing themselves because of societal pressures on them to act in certain ways, and change those attitudes and practices that exclude and marginalize women and their ideas. There is the concomitant problem of those women who are blind to their present marginalization in the profession, fearful of change, complicit in their oppression, and unwilling to exercise the personal responsibility required to change the status quo. These powerful, oppressive forces are shaped psychologically, socially, institutionally, culturally, and theologically. They must be met squarely if musicians and educators, individually and collectively, are to transcend the lopsided ideologies and realities of the past and present, deal honestly with gender-related issues, and forge a broader vision for the future.

Worldview

Christopher Small describes the impact of Western scientific and technological thinking on music and education.[24] Among other things, the scientific worldview relies on rationality, causal linearity (in which one thing can be said to directly cause another), inductive thought, and empirical evidence in the phenomenal world. It also employs technology to achieve the most efficient means of production, values the consumption of material goods, and relies on invention and commercial enterprise to further its ends.[25] The result of this kind of thinking, Small argues, is that the arts are devalued in society, and education is directed toward preparing children to think materialistically, restrictively, scientifically, technocratically, and commercially. In the United States such thinking gives rise to the view that the purpose of

education is to ensure that this country is the preeminent nation economically and competes effectively in the international marketplace.[26] Spiritual
and artistic things are marginalized in the school curriculum because they
are generally not seen to be useful in achieving these ends.

Against the backdrop of this industrial worldview, Small suggests that musicians and educators should espouse another paradigm—that of preparing children as artists, creators of music rather than just consumers of it.[27] For him,
music among the arts offers the possibility of escaping the tyranny of science
and industrial technology, of rationality and standardization, by embracing an
artistic worldview that emphasizes intuition and imagination, individuality and
spirituality. Drawing from cultures outside the West, Small demonstrates musical values such as cooperation and inclusiveness in counterpoint with Western
values of competition and exclusiveness. Music teachers, he believes, can play
an important role in shaping this new musical and cultural worldview.[28]

In reflecting on the changes taking place in cultural life and civilization as
a whole, Alvin and Heidi Toffler have been among the most politically
radical writers of our time.[29] The Tofflers see history in three huge waves,
each of which crashed upon the other to create massive dislocation and was
fiercely contested by the remnants of the preceding one. First came the
wave of agricultural settlement, then a wave of industrialization, and next a
wave of information explosion. This third wave now upon us forces massive
global changes even as it is strongly resisted by those who have an industrial mind-set and who fear the destruction of the status quo. The Tofflers
characterize third-wave societies as culturally heterogeneous rather than
homogeneous; "demassified" (in the sense of being able to customize production) rather than "massified" (or relying on mass production);
economically interconnected rather than disconnected systems; politically
global rather than nationalistic in outlook; information-based rather than
based on traditional raw materials of land, labor, and capital; emphasizing
intellectual rather than manual labor; and organized in "flat" rather than
"pyramidal, monolithic and bureaucratic" institutions and structures.

Against the factory—the model for the industrial age, with its values of
standardizing products, centralizing production, maximizing outputs, con-
centrating resources, and bureaucratizing organizations—is pitted the computer—the model for the information age, with its values of customizing
products, decentralizing production, minimizing inputs, dispersing resources,
and individualizing organizations. New virtual organizations replace their
industrial counterparts organized around particular tasks, predominantly
service-oriented, able to deliver specialized and customized goods and services rapidly to specific individuals and groups. Because decisions are taken
at an organization's periphery and dispersed throughout it rather than
undertaken by its top or central management, these new organizations need
to be very nimble and responsive to their clients or customers. Creative
thinking and a high level of educational skill are required at every point in
the organization and on the part of every individual within it.

Corresponding changes occur in societal institutions. During the industrial age the school and factory assumed activities previously undertaken in the home. The third-wave society "re-empowers the family and the home" and in so doing, recognizes the diversity of an institution previously standardized and restricted in concept. Alternatives from home schooling to home work enable functions that had been delegated to or usurped by other institutions to be retaken by the family and home. Likewise, in the state, rather than emphasizing majority rule, the third-wave society emphasizes "minority power," recognizes and supports cultural diversity, and invites citizens to invent and participate in new sorts of democratic political arrangements.

The seeds for this new paradigm have been with us for some time. Among the vanguard of those who recognized a paradigmatic shift, Susanne Langer's writing was seminal to subsequent psychological formulations of the nature of mind and knowing.[30] Langer understood that already, by the mid-twentieth century, positivism was giving ground to a philosophical preoccupation with meaning making through symbol systems. She saw that scientific worldviews were predicated on discursive symbol systems that constituted only a portion of the range of systems. Others characteristic of the arts and the religions she called, for want of a better term, "presentational" or "non-discursive." As Howard Gardner and Jerome Bruner acknowledge, her view of mind and the nature of human feeling opened a realm of understanding about cognitive science and human psychology, giving rise to notions of multiple intelligences or ways of knowing. These insights were subsequently captured in views of schooling as fundamentally concerned with multiplicities and pluralities rather than universals and unilateral standards.[31]

One may contrast the old scientific or technocratic worldview, dependent on logic and rationality, linear notions of causality, and the primacy of scientific understanding, with the new symbolic-centered world, relying on intuition and imagination, viewing multiple causes and perspectives, recognizing the fallibility of understanding, embracing pluralism, and regarding the arts and the religions as valid alternative perspectives to the sciences. While some educators might wish to move beyond the old to the new paradigm, explore its potential for music among the other school subjects, develop artistry, and create diverse programs relating specifically to the needs of particular students, music education like education generally is by and large stuck in the old and restrictive view. Concern with articulating national standards is just one symptom of the reluctance to let go of standardized and normative thinking, to explore the musics of the world in ways that are true to them, to tailor-make dynamic curricula to students rather than espousing a one-size-fits-all curricular approach. Truly diversifying curricula flies in the face of standardized thinking in which concepts and features that constitute the building blocks of the curriculum are formulated normatively in ways that suggest that they are agreed upon by the profession at large. That educators and politicians rely on such standards as indicators of teacher accountability is further evidence of the resilience of the old paradigm and those who endorse it.

Each of these paradigms has aspects to recommend it. The old scientific or industrial paradigm is predicated on such values as efficiency, rationality, practicality, accountability, and productivity, which can contribute to public education. The new symbolic or informational paradigm acknowledges the complexity and diversity of the present world, the importance of intuition and imagination as ways of knowing, and the role of human ingenuity in finding solutions to contemporary challenges—values consistent with a rich artistic life in schools and all the other places where learning takes place. Despite the difficulties of finding a way through these competing, sometimes conflicting worldviews, deciding which of the old to hold onto and which of the new to accept, transforming education necessitates meeting these challenges. There lurks the ever present possibility, however, that this project will be thwarted by powerful oppressive forces arising from institutional inertia to change and the limited views of those with an interest in seeing one or other paradigm prevail.

I am not sure that the new paradigm guarantees the results that Small hopes for in his vision of artistic education. Rather than constituting a counterpoint for the old industrial paradigm, the new information age may constitute a radical extension of it, further compounding its detractions. The computer may foster a new sort of factory, in which people are dehumanized and oppressed as extensions of the machines they operate, huddled into new varieties of crowded factories. Workers may use their brains and creative powers to a greater extent than in the past, but this may mask the economic pressures imposed on them by their new superiors or social circles.[32] In the increasingly centralized world of multinational corporations, in which wealth is concentrated in a minority of the population, ideals of economic efficiency and productivity may still drive corporate and social life. Artists and musicians may find themselves compelled to justify their activities in economic and political terms that can be readily understood by corporate interests rather than in artistic or musical ways.[33]

Small's view, expressed in his most recent writing, seems more consonant with the Gaia hypothesis—a radically different paradigm than the scientific, industrial, and information age paradigms I have just sketched.[34] In this view, the notion of stewardship rather than exploitation of resources—land, capital, people, and technology—prevails because all things are interconnected with, and independent on, others and must therefore be nourished and otherwise cared for and about.[35] Cooperation rather than competition constitutes the driving element of human interaction. Artistic activity, intuitive and imaginative thought, and human ingenuity and enjoyment are more highly prized than scientific and technological enterprise, narrowly rational thought, and economic efficiency. People live as dwellers in harmony with the earth and as caretakers of it. Holistic approaches to personhood and relationships take precedence over atomistic and dualistic approaches to humanity. Spiritual values are more highly prized than material things, meanings are constructed within the frameworks of particular social and cultural contexts rather than universally construed and mandated, and process is a greater preoccupation than product.

Such an artistic worldview has much to recommend it. As a complement to scientific and informational approaches, it humanizes people by promoting spiritual values, civility, cooperative enterprise, and stewardship of resources. The artist approaches the world and human products with an eye to detail, elegance, expressive purpose, technical prowess, intuitive understanding, and imaginative conception. These qualities are vital in a world in which rationality, instrumentalism, and materialism are paramount values. Artistic products enrich individual and corporate experience and provide the means whereby people may express their innermost feeling and communicate with others through their stories, myths, rituals, dances, poems, paintings, musics, and dramas. This is especially the case for music, which among the other arts is made vocally as well as instrumentally.

Still, taken alone, the scientific or technological views on the one hand and artistic views on the other each constitute a limited perspective. Art and science provide particular ways of understanding. Each has validity. While they share many commonalities, they differ in the questions they ask and the ways in which they frame their responses. In the search for a broad vision, one cannot substitute for or stifle the other. Rather, they are in dialectic in the sense that one or the other takes center stage from time to time. As they are difficult to intermix, their combination may generate discontinuities, stresses, and paradoxes. It is also unlikely that they ever exist in pure form. Instead, they are weak syndromes as one melds into the other in the phenomenal world and instances cluster or fall along the continuum from one polarity to the other.

In spite of the potential inherent in the artistic paradigm, music teachers in the past have directed relatively little philosophical attention to the conceptualization and development of artistry. Howard has been at the forefront of those who have focused on these issues.[36] Regrettably, his work has been largely overlooked by philosophers and empirical researchers in music education, although writers who have explored notions of musical practice owe much to his thinking.[37]

Howard's notion of artistry is based on the Western classical music tradition, and is limited and applicable particularly to that tradition. For example, Howard emphasizes the musician's rational deliberation as well as imaginative cognition, sequential mastery of technical and critical skills, individual effort, and development of sophisticated conceptualization and jargon associated with musical craft, among other attributes that seem to fit Western classical music. These qualities seem somewhat at odds with the ways in which artistry is developed in musical traditions outside the West or in vernacular traditions the world over. For example, traditionally, much musical learning by African and African American peoples is unsystematic, informal, imitative, and osmotic; contextualized within occasions that are not strictly speaking pedagogical; and intellectualized differently than Western classical music.[38] It is self-evident that musical artistry should be viewed within the rubric of a particular musical practice—an assumption with which Howard would likely agree—yet it remains to be seen how broadening his analysis to include a plethora of musical traditions would affect the validity of his conception of artistry. And if the development of artistry could be broadened to constitute the raison d'etre for education generally, it is unclear as to how music and education might be transformed in the process.

Artistic worldviews seem more fragile than their scientific, industrial, or informational counterparts. They bow to the pressures of hedonistic, economic, materialistic, and competitive motives. Today, spiritual values are less visible than economic values of enterprise and materialism, artistic products are generally regarded as having less instrumental value than scientific and industrial products have, and the formal aspects of art are generally seen as less compelling than their functions and purposes are. Given these realities, it is not surprising that scientific, industrial, and informational worldviews gain the ascendancy, institutionally ingrained pressures toward dehumanization triumph, and humanity is the poorer. Fostering artistic and spiritual worldviews in an environment that is uninterested in, if not hostile to, them is a challenging undertaking for musicians, educators, and those interested in their work, and is prone to problems if not defeat.[39]

Music

The particular musical beliefs and practices of a people help shape the institutions they create. It is a commonplace that music—whether conceived principally as an aural art existing for its own sake or as one of several interrelated arts in the service of corporate ritual—is a part of culture and profoundly influenced by the particular places and times in which it is created and performed. It does not exist as a separate entity apart from its social context but is intertwined with and inseparable from it. What is less often stressed is that society is as much shaped by music as music is shaped by society.[40] Through singing and playing musical instruments, people create a corporate sense of their identity. The texts their songs employ and the values their musics express reinforce their beliefs and practices and educate their young. This has been true since antiquity. The ancients understood that music is interconnected with spiritual and political life. Not only did they teach their wisdom to their young through songs and rituals, but their artists, actors, poets, storytellers, prophets, singers, instrumentalists, and dancers looked for inspiration to an imagined future as much as to an imaginatively reconstructed past, thereby helping to subvert and transform society as they also conserved and transmitted traditional wisdom.

As far back as recorded history takes us, two streams of musical tradition have been evident: the music of common people and that of an elite or few. The first, the music of common people, exists in every society I have studied. This music is popular, commonly known, simple enough to be within the capacity of most (if not all) members of the particular group for which it is taken to be music, and transmitted orally from one generation to the next. Whether it is appropriately referred to as folk, indigenous, vernacular, or popular music depends on one's point of view. It might be folk music if it is intended to represent the music of everyday life of a people, indigenous if taken to represent the music of aboriginal peoples of a particular place (although the notion of *aboriginal* is a problematical concept), vernacular if considered to refer to the music of one's native place, or popular if generally loved and widely understood and practiced in a society. It is cultivated because it is accessible to most, if not all, people within a particular group. As such, it expresses their feeling—thought, emotion, and physical sensation—about their lived realities. It articulates their hopes, desires, dreams, fears, and concerns about life. And it deals with such central questions of life as "Who am I?" "Why am I here?" "Where have I come from?" and "Where am I going?"

Against this music of the common person is that known best by a privileged elite, whether it be a Native American shaman, Hindustani ustad, Jewish cantor, Christian liturgical singer, Buddhist monk, or Western professional musician. Because music often forms a part of religious ritual, an aura of spiritual power transfers to the music connected with, and musicians who participate in, these rituals. Historically, the more complex the rituals, the more complicated the music associated with them, and the greater the distinction between common and elite music. The development of a class of professional musicians in Europe during the Middle Ages is a case in point.[41] At that time, the establishment of guilds formalized requirements of musicians, provided for systematic training, and prevented unqualified persons from entering the profession. In succeeding centuries, the technical requirements of musicians gradually increased to such a degree that by the twentieth century, professional music making lay outside the reach of the ordinary person. Now, classical musicians are trained through years of arduous practice to master a large body of repertoire, performance practice, theoretical analysis, and music history and to acquire an extensive musical vocabulary and a host of associated skills, both musical and otherwise.[42]

Knowledge of a large body of musical wisdom cannot be left to happenstance but is passed on systematically from one generation of musicians to the next. During the Christian era the ideal of the musician as artist/craftsperson emerged, in which a few talented persons were selected to follow a way of life centered on music and taught by skilled exponents of their instruments. Nor could human memory be relied on as the only or principal repository of musical repertoire. It was also necessary to notate musical scores, to ensure adherence to the composer's intention. Thus, a literate musical tradition emerged. This, in turn, required more extensive training on the part of musicians, adding further to the specialization of their roles and contributing to the growing breach between the music of the common person and that of a musical elite.

Throughout history, one also finds an intimate relationship between the musics of religious and artistic elites and the exercise of power, whether religious, political, or economic. From antiquity, political and religious leaders have employed music in their service, and they continue to do so to this day.[43] Elite music is often associated with a society's establishment, whether it be the Indian intelligentsia or the English upper class, since such music supports and reinforces values with which the establishment might wish to be associated, identifies a group having particular social or economic status, and differentiates it from others. Whereas an eighteenth-century nobleman displayed his prowess through artistic endeavors, his counterpart today—the wealthy patron—likewise demonstrates and secures economic and political power through supporting the arts.[44] Also, seeing that elite music symbolizes the establishment that upwardly mobile lower and middle classes typically seek to emulate, one would expect elite music to comprise the basic repertoire taught in the general education of the lower, middle, and upper classes.[45]

This association between the establishment and elite music potentially subverts, marginalizes, represses, and even destroys the common music of ordinary people and devalues it in, or excludes it from, general education. This is the reading, for example, that John Blacking gives the state of affairs in pre-Independence South Africa. As he portrays the situation, Christian missionaries insisted that Venda children learn their hymns rather than Venda traditional music in school, even when such music ran counter to the Venda aesthetic. By privileging Christian hymnody, educators devalued and marginalized Venda traditional music in the school curriculum.[46]

A simplistic response to this problem is to devalue elite musics and plump instead for the elevation of common musics, thereby "inverting" musical values so that common musics are more highly prized than their elite counterparts in the educational process. However, this approach is flawed. Not only is it reductionistic to suppose that the principal factor in creating and sustaining elite musics is their association with privileged persons and classes in society, but history provides ample evidence of less privileged persons and classes in European society who cultivated elite musics and continued to be attracted by them, and members of the establishment who supported and identified with musical countercultures.

The notion of elite music is also difficult to pinpoint. The idea that there is only one elite to serve—namely, society establishment—is simplistic. For example, the rock band Grateful Dead (and its followers) constituted an elite group that was profoundly anti-establishment in its orientation. Rather, the various elites make different musical claims and have various musical interests. Each institution, be it family, religion, politics, commerce, or music profession, makes specific demands on the music that serves it.[47] While the temptation exists to construe elite music to refer exclusively to the Western classical music establishment, this is too narrow a view. The interests of institutions may overlap from time to time, but their powers change over time, they are manifested differently around the world, the musics they promote need not be consistent with those of other institutions, and they may or may not reflect establishment perspectives and practices.

Among other issues, there is the suggestion that education should be about that which students do not know rather than about what they already know.[48] To return to our Venda example, European missionaries might suppose that the Venda already learned their traditional music at home, and school provided the opportunity for Venda children to come to know European music as well. Seeing that students already know vernacular music, they ought to widen their musical perspectives in school by studying the elite music that they do not know. Sticking with vernacular music already known to students is a restrictive, noneducational approach. The inherent ambiguity of musical meaning also makes definitive social readings of music difficult if not impossible to achieve. As a result, it is difficult to prove whether the particular oppressive forces perceived in a given musical piece are indeed in the music itself, or if a social agenda is being read into or imposed on the music by the composer, performer, or listener.[49] It is also possible that elevating common musics over elite musics may create a different sort of tyranny, giving rise to such values as musical accessibility over complexity, practicality over intellectual appeal, functionality over artistry, musical orality over literacy, popularism over elitism, informality over formality, and rawness over refinement. If this is the case, espousing common music alone may prove just as limiting and problematical as the elitist music it is intended to supplant.

Despite these complexities and ambiguities, elite music is generally taken to be that associated with the great traditions, the so-called classical musics of the world. These musics have had widespread and continuing intellectual appeal across cultural and political boundaries. They express a sense of the extraordinary in their formal design and intellectual, emotional, and sensual impact and appeal. They exemplify such values as formality, refinement, restraint, spirituality, dignity, balance, contrast, expressiveness, and intricacy—values that contribute to culture, construed as the refined elements of human society. Even when they are intended to shock or dismay, to express the dark side of life and the evil in humanity, they may be transformative in their effect on their public.

Throughout history, common music has constituted the bedrock for elite music. Out of the ordinary experience of humanity expressed in common music have emerged extraordinary musical compositions and performances, often understood and appreciated by a relative few. This is the case, for example, with jazz, in which the tradition that began as informal music making was transformed into a classical tradition in its own right, appealing to an elite group of practitioners and listeners. Despite efforts to democratize music, particularly in the West throughout the past two centuries, it seems that throughout recorded history, wherever it has been manifested, elite music has been supported by a relatively small public who understood and appreciated it. Talented persons might create compositions and performances that were perceived as artful by a public that acknowledged their genius and gifts as something special and extraordinary even if it did not always take their music as its own.

This notion of elite music bubbling up from its spring in common music underscores the interconnectedness of, and porous boundaries between, common and elite musics and the importance of both to musical and cultural life. Without elite music, common music may become banal, dull, and lifeless; without common music, elite music may become sterile, tedious, and irrelevant.[50] I concur with Rose Rosengard Subotnik, who laments that classical music has lost its connectedness with its traditional and popular roots. Unless it recovers this connectedness, it will become increasingly meaningless and irrelevant to the experience of its public.[51] Likewise, without elite music, common music tends toward the mundane, mediocre, material, crude, violent, and even destructive. Through creating extraordinary things, artists and musicians of whatever genre and practice express a reality of mind and spirit beyond the phenomenal world, thereby refreshing, inspiring, startling, unsettling, affronting, entertaining, educating, distressing, and comforting their public.

To bring these tensions into some sort of reciprocity is a difficult enterprise. It means transforming elite music, especially that in the West, expanding its borders beyond the narrow confines of a rigid canon, repairing links with vernacular music where they have been ruptured, and renewing its connectedness to and rootedness in common music. This is the sort of approach, for example, that Yo-Yo Ma employed in his various crossover projects, the Kronos Quartet took when programming quartets based on rock music along with standard classics, or Vanessa-Mae used in recording both popular and classical albums.[52] It also means resisting pressure to capitulate to popular taste and emphasize only common music. Much recent discourse in music education has focused upon the problems of the plethora of elite and common musics competing for our attention in a multicultural world and the questions about how to build bridges between musics.[53] This position does not go nearly far enough. Transforming musics toward the ends I suggest here includes breaking down dichotomies that insulate traditional thinking, such as notions of self and other, that which is art and that which is not art, that which is inside or outside a musical tradition, music and its context, artist and audience, and elite and common musical traditions. It also suggests revisioning musical traditions in ways that take these dialectics into account, resisting influences that would protect the status quo and silence self and others from making and taking music, forging fresh approaches to music and musical instruction that respect the past yet meet the future, and broadening musical understanding.

Finding a way to break down the many barriers that separate people and enlarge the borders of musical knowing is fraught with practical difficulties. In what ways should this be done? What principles should guide this enterprise?

There are several candidates for guiding principles. First, the ethic of care and carefulness provides a useful guide to action. Contra notions of exoticism, cultural imperialism, and superficiality are the claims of authenticity, integrity, respect, and responsibility toward the musics of others.[54] Second, several interrelated and well-established pedagogical principles may be particularly helpful in deciding when and how to teach what. These include moving from those things nearest at hand to those most distant from the learner's initial understanding, the simplest to the most complex understanding from the learner's perspective, an idiosyncratic to a corporate or public understanding of music belief and practice, and a superficial to an in-depth understanding of a particular music.

Education

Freire distinguishes between banking education and liberating or dialogical education.[55] Banking education refers to the teacher as the active agent in the instructional process who "deposits" information with the student who passively receives it. This unidirectional approach to instruction is predicated on what Scheffler denotes as the "impression" model of teaching, in which the teacher feeds students information that is received by their senses and sorted out by them.[56] Whether one thinks of John Locke's idea of the mind as a tabula rasa (or blank slate), the metaphor of the little cup into which the teacher pours information from her large jug, or the bank vault into which the customer deposits money (and each of these metaphors has different specific implications), the general effect in each case is to empower the teacher and restrain the student, to emphasize the activity of the teacher and the passivity of the student.

Banking education also focuses on a preconceived structure of the subject rather than on the student's psychological mind-set or personal construction of knowledge. That is, instead of forging his or her own knowledge and thereby creating and integrating new understandings within the particular cast of his or her own past conceptions, the student receives knowledge ready made as part of a canon into which he or she is initiated. However, as Dewey points out,[57] there is a dialectic between the rational structure of subject matter and the psychological structure of mind. The way the student grasps a subject may not necessarily be the way the subject is organized, especially at the outset of instruction. On the one hand, the child makes a structure that is integrated within the child's own frame of reference. On the other, the subject matter has its own underlying logical structure predicated upon a range of beliefs and practices that are interrelated one with another and integrated within a whole. In Dewey's view, gradually, over time, the child's structure should begin to approach that of the subject matter.

Dewey's assumption that there is only one structure for a particular subject and that over time the child's structure moves closer to the rational structure of the subject matter seems simplistic today. In a world of multiple perspectives and partial understandings, we are far less sure than Dewey is that there is necessarily a universal structure in subject matter toward which a child's psychological structure would or should move. For example, the field of music presents a variety of possible structures, each focusing on a particular practice or range of practices.[58] Viewing knowledge as personally and corporately constructed suggests that rather than converging toward some underlying rational, universally shared structure, the opposite may be the case—namely, a tendency toward divergent perspectives, each of them partial understandings of a particular subject. The inherent partiality and fallibility of understanding further complicates the picture by suggesting that subject structure is revised over time, as one paradigm replaces another. This state of affairs contributes to the dynamic nature of subject structure and an individual's psychological organization of it, which suggests that structures are themselves processes that are less stable than Dewey may have supposed.

From this perspective, Bruner's early rendering of curricular structure, in which knowledge is construed as a spiral and teacher and student revisit concepts at progressively higher levels of complexity and deeper levels of rational understanding, is inadequate.[59] Notwithstanding his subsequent attempts to stress the cultural basis of knowledge and the importance of personal construction of knowledge,[60] Bruner has yet to explain how to resolve the complexity of the structures operative in the educational process. He has yet to address satisfactorily the question-set: "Which structure(s)?" "How shall the tensions between them be resolved?"

Still, the National Standards movement of the 1990s was predicated on the notion that there is a universal structure against which standards may be measured. For example, the *National Standards for Arts Education* set out nine "content standards" as the rubric for a spiral curriculum in which each is treated at a progressively higher level of difficulty during elementary and secondary schooling. Even though the standards were very general and teachers were at liberty to meet them in various ways, the structure of the subject matter as defined in these standards constituted the benchmark against which teacher accountability was to be assessed. Rather than working from the psychological structures of individual students and starting from the question, "Are teachers and their students engaged in activities that meet the students' specific needs, interests, backgrounds, and talents?" this approach began with the structure of subject matter—what every young person should know and be able to do in the arts. It asked: "Are teachers and their students meeting these standards?" It proposed unilateral standards, general propositions that constituted the yardstick for every classroom. While supposedly voluntary, the standards were treated as normative in that teachers were expected to agree with them, adhere to them, and apply them in some form in every music-teaching situation. Such a universalist approach missed Dewey's observation decades earlier that the psychological structures of students tend only to approximate the rational structure of music toward the end rather than at the beginning of the student's musical study, if they ever do. The possibility of multiple structures, both for the student and for the subject matter; partiality of understanding; fallibility; and dynamic process whereby these structures change through time exacerbates the problem and goes contra to the basis of national standards. When the standards foster convergent thinking and are normative and static propositions that may be irrelevant for a particular instructional situation, they are repressive to teacher and student alike.[61]

By contrast, liberating or dialogical education invites both teacher and student to participate actively in what Freire called "conscientization." This process involves coming to understand the present; seeing how one may be prevented from realizing one's aspirations and dreams; expressing one's own convictions and lived realities by overthrowing oppressive forces; and acting in consort with others to achieve personal and corporate freedom. This is a personal and political process that is potentially liberating to mind, spirit, and body. Education, in this view, is fundamentally about emancipating self and others and achieving a more humane society. For Freire, and I concur, seeing that everyone suffers the effects of inhumanity, all are in need of a liberating education.

Paradoxically, the only way in which individual freedom can be achieved is by working together with others. Liberation is not something that can ultimately be done for another person or for purely hedonistic reasons. It is achieved through individual reflection and action, as one critically evaluates the situation and acts with others to change it. Unless one is in the company of others, one may not perceive a problem, think to change a situation, or feel sufficiently empowered by the affirmation of others to work for change. Achieving liberation requires dialogue, exchange of differing perspectives, and, through posing questions, expanding one's previously limited understanding; comprehending what can, should, and must be changed; and acting to change it. Dialogue is rooted in practice—it contributes to and draws from the phenomenal world. Dialogical learning is, therefore, person-centered, contextual, practical, and transformative as it is also subject-centered, formal, theoretical, and conservative. It cannot stop short of action. As Freire states, theoretical discourse without action amounts to verbalism, and action without theoretical discourse amounts to activism.[62] Neither can be sacrificed in the interests of the other.

Freire's approach relies upon what Scheffler would call the "insight" model of teaching,[63] captured in the metaphor of vision, whereby one sees and understands for oneself and actively constructs personal knowledge. One perceives what one's background predisposes one to notice. This perception is then integrated within one's particular understanding of self, world, and other and results in a unique construction of knowledge that is idiosyncratic in the sense that it need not and probably cannot be fully shared by others.

As Scheffler notes, there is much to recommend this model. It emphasizes the personal commitment of the student to learning, the idea that one cannot deposit knowledge "in" another person as suggested in the impression model or banking approach to education, and the importance of individual perception and construction of knowledge. However, its underlying metaphor of vision not only may be limiting but may be the wrong one. For example, a man might say, "I see your point," whereby a woman might say, "I hear you." The metaphor of hearing, especially relevant not only to the female experience but to that of music, is a different one—potentially more diffused, more immediate, more holistic, more emotional—than that of sight. Whatever the extent of these differences, whether sensory or psychological, they are discrete conceptions of perception and understanding. For example, much of the talk about musical imagination centers on vision, whereas aural imagery is quite a different and complex thing.[64] To say that one metaphor stands for both is obviously untrue. And to talk about musical imagination only in terms of the vision metaphor cannot capture adequately perceptions of sound.

Personal insight also misses the importance of the metaphor of "rule," the notion that human reason underlies beliefs and practices and constitutes the basis for moral judgment.[65] Subject matter is based on rational systems that give rise to rules governing behavior. While its underlying paradigms may shift from time to time, each paradigm is expressed in terms of systems of propositions. To depict knowledge as in a state of constant flux is therefore inaccurate. There may be periods where knowledge and the underlying paradigms on which it is based change rapidly. Such is the case, for example, in the field of astronomy today, as new discoveries challenge past assumptions with great rapidity. At other times, subject matter is more stable, as the basis for a particular paradigm is established over an extended period of time.

Nor is Freire's conception of dialogue uniformly beneficial and benign. Although pointing toward the sort of empathy, reciprocity, and mutual respect that Martin Buber suggests in his book *I and Thou*,[66] Freire's bright picture of liberating education has a dark side. It can tend toward patronage, cultural imperialism, and misinterpretation when a person presumes to identify a problem or fix it for another. As Freire points out, those who seek to educate others carry the image of the oppressor within them, and a fine line exists between assisting students to identify their own particular situations and respond in their own ways and manipulating their beliefs and actions in predetermined ways. People do not always see their own flaws and limitations that may oppress others. Freire hopes that teachers will work "with" students to help them see their real situations. However, his cultural and ideological assumptions color his view. For one, there is the dichotomy he draws between the oppressor and the oppressed, as if one class does the oppressing and another suffers from it. This kind of hard-boundaried thinking overlooks the real complexity of the situation, which Freire also acknowledges, that oppressive behavior has deep roots in human psychology, and all human beings are selfish and thereby potentially oppressive to others. If this be the case, oppression cannot be escaped by naming the "other" as the oppressor. Its roots lie within as well as beyond self or society.

Also, Freire's suggestion that the one-knowing (e.g., a teacher) works "with" others who are presumably less fortunate and less enlightened is easily pressed to suggest that one works "for" others, interpreting the reality they face for them, or manipulating the discourse so that they reach the same conclusion as the one-knowing. There are at least two risks here: first, one regards the other as different and less privileged and, therefore, one is distanced from, or distances oneself from, the other and patronizes the other; second, one misinterprets and misconstrues the other's situation, thereby misleading the other.[67]

Dialogue may also be interpreted as confrontational discourse, as students and teachers challenge each other. Rather than genuinely open-ended conversation, teachers may consider that there are better or worse ways of looking at things and seek to lead their students to what they see as truth by confronting them with obstacles that the students must think through. How can this sort of discourse be liberating for the student? Presumably, it can sharpen students' critical thinking and reasoning powers and, by challenging them, enable them to reflect on their lived realities. However, it may also foster competition rather than collaboration between teacher and student, or student and student, and convergent thinking, whereby students uncritically adopt their teacher's answers to questions as their own. In my view, dialogue can only be thought of as liberating where teacher and student focus on the questions at issue and where the answers are genuinely open-ended. In this sort of dialogue it is not so much the answers as the process of addressing the questions that is of crucial importance in instruction. Even where precise answers are necessarily agreed upon in specific circumstances, the teacher may frame them within the context of larger questions that challenge the received wisdom or the status quo.

Still, a further question-set remains: What is the notion of "liberation" toward which education tends? Will dialogue coupled with collaborative action be enough to turn the tide of oppression and engender freedom in education and society? For Greene, freedom is a dialectic in which individual and community interests are at stake, where reciprocity is secured between these sometimes conflicting interests, and where each person has the opportunity to express himself or herself within the larger community, to have a place and a voice at the table.[68] Freedom is also a process rather than a product, in the sense that people may be becoming free but they have not yet fully realized freedom. There are the marginalized and ostracized ones on the borders of communal discourse, those who have no voice in the collectivity and no place in the public spaces. In Greene's view, the school community can prefigure a larger societal freedom, and the arts have a special place in fostering imagination as a means of envisioning alternatives to an oppressive status quo. I like Greene's metaphor of the school community standing for the wider society and her emphasis on imagination as a means of cultivating divergent perspectives on lived reality. However, I am concerned that the dark side of freedom may suggest another sort of tyranny—one of anarchy, libertarianism, and communalism—pitfalls that Greene recognizes, where logical reason is downplayed in the interests of imagination and intuition, the past is captive to the present, or the interests of the one are subordinated to the many or vice versa.

Confronted with these two potential tyrannies, that of banking education on the one hand and liberating education on the other, it will not be easy to forge reciprocity between them. Given the history of education, liberating education may be the more fragile. Both are fraught with problems when taken alone, and yet finding a way between them is a daunting endeavor.

Tradition

Reasons people give for not wanting to see things in a different way or trying out things that haven't been done before often boil down to the force of tradition, and the fact that the status quo is comfortable for, and protects the interests of, those who have been accepted into a social system. To challenge that system, whether the assumptions that underlie it or the beliefs and practices that characterize it, constitutes a threat to those within and without it.[69] Such a challenge makes people uncomfortable and may even jeopardize their livelihood or way of life. Consequently, many resist change, especially fundamental change, because they are afraid of how those changes may impact them. They may be content with tinkering on the margins of the system, but they oppose its basic change or transformation because they don't want to risk being or feeling worse off than they are presently.

Tradition may be oppressive to those without and within a social system. Those outside the system can benefit from the system's change, even collapse, since they have not bought into the system or been fully accepted by it. They have everything to gain by the hope that a changed system will include their perspectives and interests and be more just and humane as a result. Those inside the system may also be oppressed by tradition as it comes to weigh on the present and restrict their freedom of thought and movement. For example, as a musical group gathers momentum, reaches maturation, and establishes itself as a full-blown institution, its conventions, customs, practices, and rituals become more articulated and compelling. Its gathering history and heritage provide a basis for comparison and an image to preserve, and its past practice takes on greater weight as a means of adjudicating the present and planning for the future. A musical canon emerges to weigh heavily on musical instruction, and its importance grows as the tradition progresses and its repertoire expands and solidifies.

The process of solidifying and even ossifying tradition may continue until a mature musical practice emerges and a canon becomes set in stone. Those within it are systematically and increasingly repressed, even oppressed, by the expectations of them by significant others, and it becomes more and more difficult to break free and change the tradition. When this occurs in cultures and civilizations, if the system is unable to respond to the demands of a changing society, it declines or is truncated prematurely. The only way of continuing a culture or a civilization is to actively resist this process of fossilization and atrophy, and rejuvenate or transform it. In music, this means consciously changing a musical practice to reflect the society of which it is a part or foreshadow an imagined society of the future. In the past, some civilizations, even those that have been relatively insulated from others, have been capable of renewing themselves in this fashion, and others have not. In large measure, the survival of civilizations is due to the openness of their educational systems to change, even if this change is sometimes forced on them by external developments to which they must respond.[70]

Pitirim Sorokin suggests that social systems shift in a cyclical fashion between an orientation to change and an alignment toward tradition.[71] There are times when a society is oriented toward the past and when universally accepted intellectual and moral values and purposes prevail. At other times, a society is preoccupied with change, and sensuality and relativist moral values are ascendant. For Sorokin, these societal swings occur over periods of centuries rather than decades and seem to be more or less predictable. Societies always overshoot the "golden mean," where, as Schiller earlier proposed, sense and reason should be in balance, if also in tension.[72]

This is an intriguing theory, and some see support for it.[73] There can be no doubt that world civilization now faces a time of dramatic and pervasive change in all aspects of life. The pace of this change seemed to gather momentum throughout the past century, as scientific discoveries, technological innovations, and capitalist and international perspectives came to dominate the public arena. Still, Sorokin's view is reductionistic in suggesting that there is a causal relationship between society and its orientation toward tradition and change, this orientation is the basic and principal force driving societal development, and development is cyclical rather than linear or progressive. On the other hand, if one relaxes the deterministic assumptions of his theory, it is possible to rescue parts of it, especially his observation that the societal context of which institutions are a part move over time from traditional to innovative orientations and vice versa. This larger context feeds into and reflects the respective institutional orientations toward change and tradition. Music history, like cultural history more broadly, seems to be marked by periods of rapid and sometimes pervasive change, and it is difficult to find the golden mean between change and tradition, if indeed there is one.

Tradition benefits music and education in important ways. It provides a stable basis for music and instruction by clarifying expectations, establishing policies and precedents, and ensuring continuity of beliefs and practices. Remembering past experience and bringing this memory to bear in analyzing new situations makes it unnecessary to constantly reinvent the wheel. On the other hand, tradition can stifle imaginative action and make it difficult, if not impossible, for musicians and educators to forge new approaches and to adjust and react to societal changes.

Change and innovation is a particular feature of our time. In music, new technologies offer exciting alternatives to traditional ways of composing, performing, and listening to music. They enable composers and performers to collaborate in ways that could not have been envisaged in the past. They make it possible for music to be heard by a large public beyond the particular occasion of its performance, thereby opening musical experiences to many who would otherwise not have the opportunity to hear it. And they afford alternative and effective ways of accomplishing musical instruction in attractive formats beyond such traditional instructional spaces as the studio and classroom, thereby widening the reach of musical instruction and diversifying it.

There is also a dark side to change and innovation. The prominence of commercial and technological values puts a premium on the present and future and emphasizes novelty rather than convention, and the material over the spiritual. Seeing that each new product makes the previous model obsolete, planned obsolescence is a driving force in economic life because it stimulates demand to keep up with the latest development or device and enhances corporate profits. Life cycles of new products shorten as marketing efforts focus public attention on a growing supply of alternatives, the time taken to produce new products diminishes, and the public's attention span decreases because of the expanding range and attractiveness of available alternatives.

For example, the absorption of the "music industry" into multinational information companies that control all aspects of music publishing, recording, performance, and distribution has infused everything from music software, recording artists, and popular songs or genres with a drive toward financial efficiency and profit, change, and innovation.[74] Music has become a product to be marketed, sold, and consumed, rather than a cultural artifact to be enjoyed and treasured for its own sake, irrespective of its economic value. As a pervasive background to everyday life, music shuts out other noise, but it also becomes devalued as it wallpapers people's surroundings, serving as a backdrop and distraction rather than a foreground and object of special interest.[75] The sense of occasional music reserved for particular uses and events is undermined by recordings that sever the links between particular places and times and this music. Also, the connection between music and formality is lost as live performances in formal social settings give way to pervasive hearings in informal and sometimes solitary settings. Musicians, who in the past were supported through patronage of one sort or another, are sometimes silenced and find it increasingly difficult to be heard in the public places. At first, the rise of the Internet fostered a cottage industry of marketed recordings; however, gradually and inexorably, commerce (especially that conducted by large corporations) consolidated its power as gatekeeper and provider. And in the world of commercial values, a few successful individuals and corporations have reaped the majority of material benefits in what has been characterized as a "winner-take-all society."[76]

The widespread availability of customized musical products can foster a sort of musical tribalism in which people retreat to cultural enclaves and participate only in those musics that they identify as their own. Seeing that so many cultures compete for attention, it is comparatively easy to tune out or turn off the musics of others and cling only to one's own music(s). The demise of universal values in the face of this diversity fragments society, reduces the claims of widely held traditions, and loosens the threads that make up the fabric of society and provide a sense of common or shared purpose.[77] The large-scale population migrations that marked the past century, at a rate sometimes so rapid as to dislocate society, contributed to this pervasive multiculturalism of societies around the world. And the spread of democratic and capitalistic ideals internationally stressed such themes as freedom and accountability and not only alienated those who had been disenfranchised and marginalized but prompted them to agitate for the right to participate fully in society and campaign to have their particular cultures respected and included in general education.

In seeking to find a way through the many challenges created by these developments in music and society, music teachers have begun to explore the possibilities of a radically relativist stance in relation to the world's music and, particularly, to focus on the notion of musical practice. These themes suggest profound change in music and challenge the privileging of Western classical music in music instruction. The notion of a plethora of musical practices, each having its own validity and value for study, suggests that the music curriculum needs to be radically broadened to reflect the multiplicity of musical perspectives and practices.

What is less well defended, at least philosophically, is the object of this change. Important questions remain: Is the purpose of this movement to forge new musical practices that synthesize or meld attributes of constituent practices? Is it to create some sort of homogenous world music? Is it to preserve the distinctiveness of extant musical practices, just as animals, plants, and other physical resources are preserved for variety's sake? Is it to make musical practices more humane, inclusive, or whatever, according to presupposed ideals or values? If so, what are the values embraced, and how are they justified? If change is desirable, which aspects of music traditions should be maintained, and which should be changed? In particular, what are the responsibilities of musicians and educators to the transmission and transformation of musical practices? Is focusing on musical practice enough, do practice and belief amount to the same thing, or is it important to also examine the musical beliefs underlying practice? If so, how are the claims of musical belief systems to be adjudicated?

These questions are complex and deeply troubling. Yet well-meaning musicians and educators can bypass them in their enthusiasm for pursuing multicultural approaches to musical and educational practice. Simplistic models and solutions may be proposed, accepted, and adopted without the necessary critical reflection on these and other questions. In such circumstances, the pursuit of multicultural, global, or international approaches to music and education can become a curricular fad embraced enthusiastically without sufficient thought of where it is leading and what it really involves if it is to be accomplished with integrity.[78]

Schiller saw the artist as teacher, one who negotiates the territory between the claims of tradition on the one hand and change on the other.[79] Rather than capitulating to the pressures of traditionalism on the one hand or innovation on the other, the artist-teacher seeks to avoid the pitfalls of these two potential tyrannies. In our time, as in the past, avoiding either extreme requires such attributes as perceptiveness, sensitivity, wisdom, integrity, humility, imagination, and experience to work through effectively. And it may also mean that there are no universal solutions, no one size fits all, no one answer for all time. The answers found reflect the particular and changing circumstances of times and places. How to tackle these challenges educationally is a daunting question.

Mind-Set

Our present time is one in which dystopian visions flourish, and despair, hopelessness, imitation, artificiality, insincerity, and faithlessness abound. Such mind-sets have existed before; however, the realities of violence, poverty, and mental illness reflecting pervasive dislocation, alienation, and loneliness are among a host of problems brought about by the rise of the postindustrial New Economy and the widespread social and cultural changes that have accompanied it. Dystopia is evident in popular culture. Whether it be the portrayal of an inner-city drug gang in the movie *Trainspotting*, growing up black in the U.S. South in Maya Angelou's autobiographical *I Know Why the Caged Bird Sings*, or a window on some of America's schools in Jonathan Kozol's book *Savage Inequalities*, the situation sometimes appears so desperate as to seem hopeless.[80] The fact that those in such disastrous circumstances find some consolation and joy makes their situations even more poignant and tragic. The problems they face appear insoluble because they are also so deeply rooted. A sense of impotence, insolubility, hopelessness, and paralysis drives the dystopian vision where civilization is seen to be self-destructing, human life pointless and worthless, and individuals powerless. Why should one attempt to change the situation when such attempts are doomed to failure? Better to resign oneself to the inevitability of the status quo, find whatever comfort possible in the present, or escape from it by whatever means one can.

Educators having this mind-set may be tempted to believe that the problems they face are beyond them, that the educational system is fraught with difficulties that cannot and will not be changed. They may think it appropriate to take a fatalistic stance to self, world, and other; work within the system wherever they can; and take comfort in the life they have. Seeing that they cannot heal the deep societal and social ills in contemporary life, or breach the injustices and barriers between different others, they may seek to be content to do their own work and leave these problems to others—family, religion, politics, music profession, or commerce—to solve. They may as well not even think about these problems because they are too distressing to ponder, especially when they feel powerless to do anything about the problems. And if things get too bad, they may quit teaching altogether.

It might be easy to condemn such a mind-set out of hand, to see only the dysfunctionality, disjunction, and despair. And yet this perspective can inject a healthy dose of realism into educational plans and programs. It reminds us that music education is fundamentally a social endeavor and that solutions to its problems need to be framed in the wider perspective of society. Nor will quick-fix solutions solve these intransigent dilemmas. It took time to get into the present situation, and it requires time to think one's way through present, pressing issues and act concertedly and deliberately to transform music education. Education is a multigenerational process. Each generation needs to revisit its educational objectives and reframe its purposes in the light of its particular time and place, and this is especially important during the cultural, technological, social, political, spiritual, and economic revolutions of our time. Such a realistic perspective provides some comfort, especially when the predicaments in which teachers find themselves seem insoluble.

Educational and societal dystopianism contrasts with utopianism—the belief in an ideal educational system or society in the future. Utopian visions of education and society stress optimism, joy, hope, faith, and belief that human nature can transcend its past, overcome its dark side, and realize the good. In his book *Pedagogy of Hope,* Freire argues that education has always been an optimistic, indeed idealistic endeavor, and that hopelessness too often condemns people to inactivity, thereby ensuring no or little progress toward the ideal of a civil and humane society. At least a hope-filled pedagogy can help to improve the situation even if it does not reach the ideal.

Utopian visions go further than idealism by positing that through steadfast belief and concerted action the ideal can and will be attained. The ideal does not merely serve a normative purpose, but it comes to constitute an expected state of affairs. Utopian readings of Plato, Rousseau, and Marx presuppose the inherent goodness of humanity. Theirs is a perfect world in which people have a sense of their place in society and delight to share unselfishly their wealth, power, and social status with others. Free from the interference of governmental bureaucracy, educators can rely upon the power of education, human goodness, and natural process to unfailingly produce the citizens of this utopian republic and create the perfect order that characterizes it.

It is easy to dismiss such utopian notions as unrealistic and impractical, therefore unworthy of notice and study. After all, human history is replete with violence, selfishness, and incivility, and the invalidity of these assumptions can hardly be questioned. People are not necessarily content with their place in society, they are not always good, and they do not easily share their wealth and power with others. Good teachers do not always turn out good pupils, and educational experiments grounded in naturalistic and libertarian assumptions, such as that at Summerhill, do not always succeed.[81]

Even though ideals are difficult if not impossible to achieve in practice, their normative value still remains as a source of hope, courage, and inspiration for educators who seek to improve the situation, to make it more humane and civil. Idealism carried to extreme as utopianism may constitute a tyranny, in the sense of overthrowing and revolutionizing present practice in search of an impractical future. Claiming that this particular vision is the only one excludes alternative visions and those who share them. There is always the danger that utopian communities may hold exclusive and elitist views of their place in society and, in the process, isolate themselves or become isolated from the rest of society.

Either mind-set—dystopian or utopian—may be oppressive. Dystopianism loses sight of hope as utopianism loses sight of reality. One is not necessarily better than the other. Yet each has something to offer. Dystopian visions emphasize the dark side of human nature and the problems faced in creating a more civilized, inclusive, humane society. Utopian views emphasize the bright side of humanity and the opportunities for realizing the good, the true, and the beautiful in human life. Reconciling them is a daunting task in which work and play, celebration and tragedy, hope and doubt, present and future must somehow dwell together with tolerance if not acceptance. Developing such a mind-set in a music teacher or educational policy maker is a difficult undertaking and one that is impossible to specify exactly. As with everything else, however, there is no one acceptable mind-set any more than there is one appropriate approach to music education. The practical question remains as to how this can and should be achieved.

Summary

In addressing the reasons why music education needs to be transformed, I have shown in this chapter that along with the effects of generational change, the institutions of music and education are flawed in several ways. Their prevailing ideas and practices have been designed by and for men. Their worldviews represent the old scientific and technocratic paradigm. Their musical and educational values are primarily those of the Western establishment. Their educational values and methods are primarily those of banking education that emphasizes the logical primacy of the subject matter and the active role of the teacher in transmitting knowledge to the receptive student. They are preoccupied with the traditional beliefs, values, and practices of the past. And the individual mind-set of their proponents is pervasively realistic, even dystopian, cynical of efforts toward change, even believing that change for the better is impossible.

A contrasting paradigm offers the prospect of music education that includes the perspectives and practices of women as well as men. It values artistic and spiritual perspectives. It sees musical traditions inclusively and integratively. It serves as liberating education that stresses the dialogical and dialectical character of learning and teaching, and the primacy and responsibility of the learner's active engagement. It constitutes an active agent toward change. And it offers an idealistic, even utopian view of how the situation can be changed for the better.

These contrasting paradigms are in dialectic, and finding ways to bring them together while still keeping the contributions and limitations of each in focus provides a way of showing why music education needs to be transformed. These paradigms also provide a window on understanding some of the systemic problems that afflict music and education, as well as the wider culture and society, and that make such systemic change difficult to achieve in the phenomenal world. I have broached the question of how to address the tendencies toward crudeness, rawness, banality, and violence in contemporary society in a preliminary way by indicating some of the kinds of musical and educational values that might transform music education.

Although I have portrayed such things as gender, worldview, music, education, tradition, and individual mind-set as conceptually discrete, I have also implied that they are, practically speaking, interrelated—for example, in the overlapping gendered views and worldviews of music and education and in the intersection between tradition and mind-set. I have also suggested that solving these challenges is especially complex and difficult because of the many dialectics that defy easy resolution. Music educators are faced with steering a course between pitfalls on either side.

These challenges go well beyond the classroom and studio to society at large, and teachers cannot deal with their particular instructional situations individually or in isolation. Instead, what they think and do is affected by, and spills over into, the society and culture of which they are a part. The issues music teachers grapple with are large and complex as well as specific and particular. In our time, these matters are addressed not only by the teacher acting alone but by educators and those interested in their work acting in consort. As such, the task of transforming music education necessitates corporate as well as individual action.

3

Transforming Education

Successive waves of educational reform in the United States during the past century have met with mixed success, in part because they have addressed symptoms rather than underlying causes of systemic societal and educational problems and because the reforms have not been critically thought through or pursued over the long term.[1] Something more than tinkering on the margins of education seems to be called for, but what? Proposing transformation as a way of conceptualizing these changes raises important philosophical issues. It is ambiguous in the sense that it not only occurs naturally as one generation replaces another but it also can be planned and deliberate, especially when educational aims and means that are unclear or have grown stale become clear, fresh, and relevant to altered circumstances. It also evokes an array of images that depict its character and work. I prefer to think of this transformation in the philosophically hard sense, technically rather than intuitively, and to sketch what does not fully count as transformation before unpacking the notion of what I think it is and how it works in educational practice. In taking this tack, I follow Langer, Howard, Nelson Goodman, and others who have employed a similar philosophical strategy with regard to the arts and education.[2] My interest is primarily in how transformation functions practically, because education is ultimately a social and concrete enterprise. I sketch nine images of transformation, each of which does not suffice when taken alone. I then tease out how these images function dialectically,[3] and I outline some of the implications for educational practice.

Nine Images

Modification

Transformation may be thought of as *modification*, the reorganization of some elements or properties short of changing a thing's central condition or function. After the change, the thing remains essentially the same; it is merely reshaped in certain respects to enable it to survive better in its environment. For example, school—referring literally to the place where general education is conducted—may take a number of specific forms and still retain its traditional function whereby knowledge is passed on from one generation to the next. It may therefore be modified in one respect or another without challenging its traditional role as the means for transmitting knowledge or socializing the young. The changes suggested by certain late-twentieth-century writers do not necessitate a fundamental rethinking of the nature and place of schools in contemporary society but merely suggest modifying traditional aspects of school organization, be it curriculum, instruction, administration, teaching, or learning.[4] Likewise, late-twentieth-century educational reform movements such as Goals 2000 or the national standards and testing movements do not fundamentally challenge the notion of schools and schooling; rather, they work within institutions that remain more or less the same after the reforms have taken place.[5]

While it offers a way of negotiating change to accommodate to particular situations without fundamentally altering the tradition itself, modification contributes to continuity and societal stability by making it unnecessary to continually reinvent the wheel and rethink an entire institution every time environmental circumstances change. However, when the situation changes dramatically, modification may also disguise the appearance of change when more fundamental change is called for. It may excuse unwillingness or inability to invest resources in discovering whether or not the institution has outlived its usefulness or needs to be fundamentally changed or reinvented. History is ripe with the evidence of civilizations that ceased to be because they could not or would not reinvent education when circumstances necessitated.[6] Nor is its definition as clear-cut as some might believe, and its edges are fuzzier than may be apparent at first glance. One might envisage modification continuing to a point over time where a thing's identity is lost and the original object is no longer recognizable—for example, when fact and fiction are blurred, or the cat is modified until it becomes a crow.

Accommodation

Another prospect is *accommodation,* in which one thing conforms to another. Just as the chameleon changes to fit its environment, so social systems adapt to their environments.[7] If they are unwilling to change, they may eventually become incapable of change and fossilized—literally set in stone. Accommodation suggests a willingness to compromise, to let go of things that are regarded as nonessential, and even to change those things regarded as distinctive or fundamental in order to ensure the survival of the social system. Among its advantages, accommodation emphasizes the importance of realism and adaptability, taking into account changing practical realities and being willing to adapt beliefs and values to particular situations. It highlights the integral interrelationship between the social system and its environment; particular ideas and practices are not held in isolation but rub up against others and conform to these others. And it points to the complexity of decision-making and the practical difficulties involved in solving the many intractable problems of human society.

On the other hand, analogies between the social system and biological and psychological accommodative phenomena can only be carried so far and ultimately break down. Accommodation may place undue weight on the environment in which the social system operates, and it leaves aside notions such as the social construction of knowledge in which norms are forged by or within the social system rather than externally given or universally construed principles. It suggests that the social system compromises with aspects of its environment and adapts to these perceived conditions because it takes the external claims on it to be normative; it substitutes external values for its own and ends up exchanging one limited perspective for another. When compromise is the price for accommodation, the institution may lose more than it gains in the change process; compromise is not always a good, nor is it always possible, especially when one value-set contradicts another.

Integration

Yet another concept, *integration,* is employed in Morton's figurative description of an "add and stir" approach to music education curriculum,[8] where elements are combined in a mix that is sufficiently accommodating to enable them to coexist, but where one does not threaten the existence of another. For example, it is possible to forge musical curricula in which male and female, or popular and classical music perspectives, are included but where one does not challenge or confront the validity or sufficiency of the other. Among its advantages, integration suggests the importance of reciprocity and mutuality in allowing each perspective to coexist without enforcing assimilation or threatening the viability of the other. When ingredients are combined, a richer mixture may be created than might exist in the absence of one or other element. Talk of stirring suggests a movement toward some sort of blend of ingredients. For example, in what Morton describes as "add and stir" music curricula, music of women and men is included, although each is examined from the perspective of traditional criteria.

However, while the range of perspectives may be broadened by integration, underlying beliefs, values, and enterprises may be fundamentally unchallenged by the inclusion of divergent perspectives. In the case of the "add and stir" music curriculum, for example, historical perspectives on music developed principally by white, Western males may remain preeminent in examining women's contributions to music. Music by women or popular music may not be taken as seriously as the music of men or classical music, and the appearance of inclusivity and equality may be a facade.[9] Instead of a genuine dialectic, in which masculine and feminine, popular and classical perspectives are in tension—the one challenging, acting as a foil to, or criticizing the other—patriarchal and classical values may remain preeminent and constitute the principal means whereby all musics are adjudicated. Learners' beliefs and practices are not necessarily confronted or challenged, and education may remain, for them, an academic exercise rather than a life-changing experience. Like modification, change of this sort may be superficial rather than deep, apparent more than real.

Assimilation

A further possibility is *assimilation,* in which one thing overpowers and absorbs another.[10] The more powerful social system absorbs or takes another into itself, so that the less powerful other loses its independence and becomes a part of the more potent entity. The weaker may lose its separate identity and become inextricably attached to the stronger. Cultural assimilation is illustrated historically by the Roman Empire's appropriation of Greek culture at the same time that it overcame Greek political power, and the subsequent assimilation and subjugation of other cultures by the Holy Roman Empire, British Empire, and United States of America while maintaining their respective languages, religions, and artistic heritages. Indeed, imperialism and colonization depend on an asymmetrical relationship between powerful and weak, conqueror and conquered, oppressor and oppressed.

Assimilation enables newcomers to a social system to be incorporated as members, and it allows the young to be socialized and enculturated. Just as the Romans benefited from Greek culture, the British colonies were bequeathed a system of public administration, governance, and justice; and Mexican immigrants receive health and educational services from the United States. Nor is this relationship a one-way street. The Greeks benefited from Roman law and defense, British culture was infused with colonial influences, and U.S. culture was enriched by Mexican influences. Freire reads the asymmetrical power relationship inherent to assimilation as paternalistic and oppressive, in that the more powerful person or system can dictate to the less powerful other, thereby removing the opportunity for the other's freedom of choice.[11] Even in situations that seem quite benign—for example, in the case of the benevolent despot who has the interests of his subjects at heart, rules them wisely, and shows them mercy and charity—the dictator restricts the people's freedoms and otherwise imposes his will upon them. I am sympathetic to Freire's enterprise; however, there is a sense in which differences in power are an inescapable part of the human condition, and the situation is more complex than he envisions, especially in today's multicultural societies. It seems that in every society, irrespective of the particular political arrangements, be they democratic or totalitarian, some individuals, groups, and institutions by dint of their nature or environment are better off and more powerful than others. Not only is there no one view of what is oppressive, as Freire seems to suggest, but whether one has the choice to assimilate or be assimilated may make a difference in how assimilation is viewed and whether or not it is indeed oppressive.

Inversion

Alternatively, transformation may be thought of as *inversion*, in which the order of things is turned upside down. For example, some feminist aestheticians wish to replace patriarchal values with matriarchal values as the preeminent artistic values.[12] A sea change of this magnitude suggests profound changes in the individual or social system. Such a reversal of values provides, among other benefits, an opportunity for many more people to participate in self-government and exercise greater personal choice and individual responsibility than in an autocracy. Likewise, if a patriarchal aesthetic were to be replaced by a matriarchal system, artistic life may benefit from the greater informality, inclusiveness, participation, and interrelatedness with life that the matriarchal system might offer.

Notwithstanding its potential benefits, inversion may be restrictive or may not necessarily broaden perspectives; it simply replaces one limited view for another and relies upon a hierarchical arrangement of values that privileges some and tolerates, marginalizes, or repudiates others. Regarding its restrictiveness or narrowness, it is likely, for example, that replacing a patriarchy with a matriarchy will not necessarily improve the situation for everyone, seeing that its values may represent the perspectives of only half of the population. Patriarchy and matriarchy each have limitations, albeit different, and neither perspective is sufficiently broad to benefit all humankind. Regarding its hierarchical assumptions, inversion carries the baggage of privileging some at the expense of others, of turning things upside down so that what was at the top is now at the bottom. Despite this change in position, the thing itself remains essentially the same. For example, because matriarchy and patriarchy are both concerned fundamentally with power, inversion simply affects who has it and whose perspectives will be preeminent— those of men or women. So inversion does not satisfy as the grounds for transformation.

Synthesis

Another possibility is *synthesis,* or the blending or melding of opposites, fusing thesis and antithesis into a new entity. This idea has been attractive to educational philosophers such as Dewey and his followers. The paradoxical nature of synthesis and the underlying tension between thesis and antithesis imply the possibility of an even larger idea, concept, or thing that might encompass both, where the underlying paradoxes and dialectics can be resolved or accommodated in some way, and aspects of the two can be melded. Synthesis accomplishes a resolution of conflict or tension by offering a new alternative; its underlying metaphor of contest suggests that when the struggle between dialectics is solved, peace and tranquility will follow; and its reliance on polarities rather than dichotomies offers the prospect of "soft boundaries" between things in conflict, which complicates and enriches the resulting synthesis.[13]

Although Langer acknowledges that categories are not closed systems and that any category "may spring a leak," she rightly worries that synthesis may become an excuse for sloppy philosophical thinking, where things that should be clarified are not because one rests in the hope that somehow the notion of synthesis will do the trick, and apparent paradoxes may arise in the first place because fine and careful distinctions have not been made.[14] There are other difficulties besides a potential lack of philosophical rigor. Resolving thesis and antithesis into synthesis presupposes the logical possibility and practicality of their accommodation with reference to some broader, more inclusive, even universal principle(s) now hidden from view. One of the contributions of multicultural thought, among other postmodern discourse, is the argument that it is reductionistic to assume that universal principles govern all human conduct in every particular situation, or that each dichotomy is resolvable into a polarity constituting the logical grounds for synthesis; it is simplistic to regard every theoretical synthesis as being practically feasible—witness the complexity and intractability of ethical, political, religious, linguistic, among other cultural and social dilemmas throughout history. Aside from the conceptual difficulties of melding polarities and discontinuities, a host of practical issues surround their implementation—for example, the difficulties in forging and maintaining consistent educational policy in contemporary society.

Transfiguration

Another interesting possibility is *transfiguration,* or the experience whereby the holy person or mythical figure changes into another order or state of being, implying more generally a change in an entity's shape or form. For example, in Jewish tradition, Moses was transfigured when he received commandments from God; in Christian tradition, Jesus was transfigured before his crucifixion; in Kaluli myth, a male ancestor was transfigured into a *muni* bird; and so on. Transfiguration indicates a profound and internal change, a heightened state of consciousness and physical being that may or may not be accompanied by or result in a permanent change in form or shape. This notion is potentially rich. It denotes a profoundly internal change within the individual that can be detected readily by others, suggests a change that begins with the individual's experience and radiates outward to be caught by others, focuses on a convictional moment of insight that dramatically changes those who witness or hear about it, and devolves from a charismatic figure whose profound change acts as a catalyst to inspire commitment on the part of his or her disciples. It is the stuff of myth and story that seeps out from an event involving a few people into the larger society. And it provides the impetus for a groundswell of social change that bubbles up from below rather than being imposed from above.

Emphasizing the dramatic element of personal transformation, however, negates change that seems to creep inexorably onward, gradually reshaping personal and social life. Centering on a charismatic figure or event, and relying on the impact of this personal drama on others, like the outward ripple of waves, takes insufficient regard of the power of institutions, their resistance to change, and the fact that the force of a transfigurative moment may be blunted by those who stand to lose by a change in the status quo. That transfiguration may be momentary pays insufficient regard to the importance of continuing reinforcement and support throughout subsequent life. One may look back to a dramatic experience in the past as a source of inspiration for present living; however, unless this is fed in the present, its impact gradually dims. Given that educational changes often transpire over the course of decades, even centuries, transfiguration seems too limited in scope and too transitory an experience to sustain educational transformation by itself over the long term.

Conversion

Likewise, the idea of *conversion* is employed in religious understanding to denote an inward change in conviction in which one intellectual perspective or worldview replaces another. Like transfiguration, it highlights the nature of personal experience and its contribution to social change. Rather than focusing on an ecstatic or dramatic experience that is visible to others, conversion concerns the nature of knowledge and truth claims. One's conviction goes beyond reason; it is felt rather than simply thought about, emotional and physical as well as rational, intuitive or imaginative. It is a profoundly spiritual experience approaching the overlay of corporeal, emotional, and cognitive elements captured differently in Langer's conception of "feeling," Scheffler's notion of "cognitive emotion," and Yob's idea of "emotional cognition."[15] The advent or settling of this conviction may be dramatic (as in James Loder's example of Paul's conversion to Christianity) or evolutionary (as in Loder's view of stages of faith development). For Loder such transformative convictions have several characteristics: they occur within the context of environment, entail a sense of selfhood, include a sense of "void" or of not being, and involve a sense of "new" being, of beginning again.[16] Whatever their particularities, these transformative convictions deal with such fundamental questions of existence as "Who am I?" "Where did I come from?" "Where am I going?" "What is the significance of my life?" As such, they are potentially life-changing events.

The idea of conversion offers a great deal to educational transformation. Like transfiguration, it highlights the importance of individual experience as a prelude to communal and societal transformation. Focusing as it does on conviction rather than the appearance of something extraordinary or magical, conversion highlights the importance of mind and body in the educational process, of a holistic experience or feeling that goes beyond reason to invoke imagination, intuition, emotion, and bodily sensation. Because conversion represents a more-or-less permanent change in one's state of mind or body that affects the way one thinks about oneself, the world, or whatever lies beyond, it suggests something more than a transitory altered state of consciousness, or reliance on miracles or other extraordinary events. As such, it offers a continuing basis on which transformation might be accomplished. However, it does not contain mechanisms to ensure social as well as individual change. Like transfiguration, its reliance upon changes in personal experience in order to achieve societal transformation is probably too optimistic regarding the willingness of people to change, individually or collectively. In including intuition, imagination, emotion, and physical sensation, it may also downplay reason as the basis for discourse and judgment. Notions of embodiment of knowledge, imagination, intuitive thought, and the interplay of emotion and intellect, while drawing attention to holistic and diverse ways of knowing and although constituting various sorts of rationality, also potentially overlook the contributions of logical discourse to human knowledge. The impact of some postmodern thought has been to undermine the importance of logical and propositional thought in favor of more holistic perspectives and procedural understandings. While some of these insights have enriched and challenged our understanding of human rationality, reason construed as logical and propositional thought also offers a legitimate and important way by which humans think about themselves, the world around them, and whatever lies beyond.

Renewal

The possibility of *renewal* invokes the metaphors of rebirth or reincarnation, in which something is revived, resurrected, rejuvenated, or revivified. It is reanimated, rekindled, and brought back to life. This suggests that there has been some sort of loss of energy, vitality, and purposefulness, that the original animating vision has dissipated. Renewal captures the notion of recovering what was lost and in the process reenergizing the organism or institution. In their formative phases, group members are enthusiastic, purposeful, and optimistic about their future.[17] Renewal invokes a return to the self-same enthusiasm, purposefulness, and optimism that characterized members at the outset. As such, it has fundamentally to do with matters of attitude on the part of a group's members and with the manner in which the group goes about its work so as to engender growth, expansion, and development.

This idea offers much to educational transformation. It relates particularly to the tendency for social groups to lose their focus, purposefulness, and enthusiasm at various times throughout their history. Without such renewal, groups may regress and eventually cease to be. When renewal takes place, the group is rejuvenated, the enthusiasm of its members is rekindled, its goal orientation is clarified and pursued with passion and determination, and it evidences growth typical of organizations at an early phase of their development. Its focus on the spiritual dimensions of being is in opposition to the pervasive materialism of our time and acts as a corrective to it. And its invoking of the birth metaphor highlights the role of imagination in grasping what now is and recreating what might be. On the other hand, besides being less relevant to youthful persons or groups, this metaphor suggests that what is new is normative or better than what is old. In the West, where youthfulness is valued over old age and where novelty is esteemed over tradition, the metaphor may have more force and validity than in the East, where the opposite has historically been true. And its view seems backward looking and simplistic in that one seeks to recapture the past rather than also focus on the present and future.

Images in Dialectic

Each of the foregoing images of transformation is insightful yet flawed or limited in one way or another, and none suffices as the sole conception of transformation. My own dialectical view sees "this is with that," so that various elements and perspectives are in tension with each other, one or another coming to the fore at a particular time and place as actors might move about on a stage.[18] Combining these images is sometimes difficult if not impossible, and tension, even conflict, cannot be avoided. Modification, accommodation, integration, assimilation, inversion, synthesis, transfiguration, conversion, and renewal have differing contributions and limitations as images of transformative education. Each image provides a useful yet limited perspective on the complexity of transformation and informs particular aspects of educational transformation in this time and place. One may constitute the focal point in a given situation, but others are also considered, if only peripherally. And the possibilities inherent in each image are not prematurely foreclosed before deciding which image is most relevant to the present state of affairs.

Among the dialectics that arise out of these images and their functioning together, transformation is *metamorphic* and *incremental*. It is metamorphic in the sense of transmutation, transfiguration, and renewal that extend beyond accommodation, assimilation, or modification to a radical and fundamental reshaping, even rebirth of the social system and the individuals within it. There is a change in the state or the stuff of the social system, its core values, beliefs, and mores, even its raison d'être. Figuratively, its very genes—the gut of its makeup, guiding principles, and blueprint for the future—are altered. It exists for new purposes, in a different state than before the transformation occurred. The transfigurations of its founding mothers and fathers, the visions of its heroes, and the insights of its prophets and seers are sources of inspiration to its members as it undergoes this profound change, faces in a different direction, and pursues its new goals in a fresh way. Yet even as it does this, it also retains the features of, and is forwarded by, accommodation, assimilation, or modification. Seeing that system elements change at differing rates, some being more progressive than others, accommodation, assimilation, and modification are needed to keep the system working together. Education may change little by little, gradually accommodating to changed realities, assimilating new ideas, and modifying elements to meet altered conditions. Sometimes, change may be so incremental as to be imperceptible. And the extent of the transformation may only be apparent over the long term, be it decades, centuries, or even millennia.

Transformation is both *systemic* and *particular*. On the one hand, it extends across an entire educational system and impacts every aspect of the group's function and operation. On the other, it affects particular individuals and groups within the system. Assimilation, integration, synthesis, inversion, modification, and accommodation are essential if reciprocity is to be found between differing individual and collective beliefs, values, and mores. Assimilation involves the willingness of members to accept beliefs and practices that are different from one's personal wishes in order to share membership in the group; seeing that people within a group differ, some assimilation is desirable if a group is to work cohesively and effectively as a single unit. Integration suggests that members are willing to respect the views of different others and allow them to coexist in the group without pressuring them to change; this mutual tolerance allows the group to experience unity of purpose while at the same time recognizing that unity does not equate with homogeneity of procedure. Synthesis invokes the idea that polar opposites in the system may be fused or melded in some respects to produce a different perspective than either polarity taken alone; it also suggests the idea of finding a path midway between extreme positions, reminiscent of the balance implicit in Aristotle's "golden mean." Inversion highlights the fact that transformation is a mixed blessing, that there are those who stand to lose, as well as those who stand to gain from systemic change. Modification entails structural changes as well as in the appearance of the system to those within as well as without it; transformation not only involves substantive change but the appearance of substantive change. And accommodation suggests that the system must respond to practical realities in the phenomenal world, and this recognition may help preserve it against unrealistic and impractical strategies and temper the radical and impetuous elements within the system. The working together of these images underscores the particularity of transformation. Individuals or groups within the system may seek to subvert otherwise conservative elements and forward radical ideas and practices that challenge and even destabilize it.

As a functioning entity, transformation involves *reflective action* and *active reflection*. Reflective action focuses on the thoughtful quality of practice; active reflection centers on the practically oriented nature of thought. One is not prior to or more important than the other, and practically speaking, they are inseparable. Donald Schön distinguishes between reflection-in-action and knowing-in-action; reflection in the midst of action occurs as a person must make procedural decisions and judgments while doing or undergoing an activity while also understanding what is going on, whereas knowing-in-action may occur when the performer knows what he or she is doing without being able to say why or how the performance is being accomplished.[19] In my view, reflective action is like Schön's reflection-in-action in that it also incorporates procedural and propositional knowledge in the midst of the activity. However, it goes further to include reflection-on-action, which may occur outside (either before or after) the activity and constitutes imaginative, intuitive, and rational thought about it.[20] Freire's emphasis on active reflection points to the eminently practical quality of knowledge that is intended to be transformational.[21] He is right that a transformational idea must be put into practice if it is to improve the lot of humanity. Ideas, attitudes, values, and beliefs presage human action; they constitute the bedrock on which human activity is predicated and from which it draws. This plethora of philosophies, paradigms, theories, and beliefs forms the basis for assumptions about human behavior and expectations of self and others; ultimately, educational ideas need to be put to the test in the phenomenal world. Theory and practice, reflection and action are therefore interconnected, and transformation reflects and contributes to this relationship.

Transformation is also an *individual* and *collective* enterprise. In earlier times, educational change may have been a relatively straightforward undertaking. Given a person with sufficient power, an idea that resonated with the public, a relatively unified culture, and political savvy, quite profound educational changes could be wrought by individuals in relatively short periods of time. Today's world presents a very different picture. Aside from the institutionalization of contemporary cultural life, the pervasive impact of mass media and technology, and widely shared values, societies are often culturally heterogeneous, and people are so aware of their rights and their differences from others that it is more difficult than ever to find common ground for collective action. These "multiplicities" and "pluralities,"[22] or the plethora of distinctive groups and perspectives that characterize these societies, have their own distinctive visions of what transformative education is or should be, and it is difficult to reconcile, even meld, aspects of them, beyond merely tolerating them. The idea of creating spaces where all these disparate groups and individuals can sit down together, as Greene suggests, is a daunting one. And the notion of creating a schoolhome, as Jane Roland Martin urges,[23] is difficult because so many different visions prevail of what home should and can be.

The impetus for change comes from *within* and *without* the social system, from individuals as well as indicated to them by the group as a sort of common sense. As such, it can be profoundly democratic when individuals form a community in which all have a voice. In the absence of the individual engagement on the part of all its members, systemwide changes are perfunctory and superficial; the system may appear to adapt or respond to changed circumstances, but there is not a deep and abiding commitment to different shared purposes or a real change of heart and mind on the part of all or most of its members.

Forging an educational community also constitutes an important challenge, especially seeing that it has a *dark* as well as a *bright* side. Greene suggests that liberatory education can only take place within the context of community—that without community, individuals may never discover personal freedom from oppression. In this view, communities may provide the spaces in which, together with others, people can gain the courage to break out of the silence either forced upon them or in which they have been complicit.[24] I agree that the task of educational transformation needs to include building the kinds of communities that will foster such liberation. Scott Sanders also writes of the importance of community in a society in which mobility and isolation are features of contemporary life.[25] In deciding to stay put, to participate in the community of the place he calls home, Sanders reminds us that the American search for individual freedom need not be bought at the price of losing a sense of community, of being anchored to a physical and spiritual place. Being in a community, even a community of fellow travelers or kindred spirits widely separated by physical distance or time, is to have a sense of place, of where one is in relation to others. It is to be comforted by the fact that one is not alone, that there are others who share in the joys and sorrows that are a fact of human existence. In light of these potential contributions, the educator's challenge is to create, together with others, the kinds of communities in which justice, civility, and humanity abound, and in which liberatory education may flourish.[26] Notwithstanding these possibilities for liberation, individuals, groups, organizations, and institutions may be reluctant to give up or share power, and provide opportunities for the sorts of dialogical action that Greene envisages. Human selfishness, ambition, and disregard for different others are resilient qualities in public life and are so deeply ingrained as to surface even in the midst of communities forged for liberatory purposes. There are many differences of opinion about particular beliefs and practices, and these differences make achieving freedom for all the members a daunting task. Such forces can counteract, undermine, and even destroy the potentially positive contributions of community.

Transformation is *state of being* and a *dynamic process*. Even where a climactic event seems to characterize transformation, there is still a preparation for that particular moment or state of affairs and the process of working through the implications of that event for the future. Although there may be several theoretically distinctive phases in the transformative process,[27] practically speaking, one blurs into another as transformation unfolds. Beyond a single event that occurs at a particular time and that seems to participants in it to be immediately and virtually complete, transformation is also in the process of becoming. As such, it possesses a quality of livingness and vitality. Irrespective of whether it appears to be climactic in the sense that there seems to be a central moment, a single experience that stands apart from or above the ordinary, or imperceptible in the sense that it is difficult to tell exactly when and where a change occurred, the experience of transformation is felt as a living, vital thing. As such, it seems to rise and fall against the backdrop of ordinary experience, and yet afterward it is clear that a profound change has occurred. Its dynamic quality makes it difficult to observe because in its unfolding there may be no single defining moment in the dynamic process of change. It seems to carry the seeds of change within itself and it takes time to evolve. Even where the social system responds to its changing environment, the impetus for change comes from within as well as without; it is not only enforced from the outside but evolves from within the social system. There is a willingness and ability to be transformed on the part of the system itself, quite apart from any external pressure on it to do so, and this internal volition to change energizes and enables the transformative process. While there are limits to the degree to which an analogy with the physical world may be pressed, a social system's evolution may also reflect the impact of physical and human catastrophes, and the particular political, economic, religious, artistic, and other policies that shape social and cultural environments in which it exists. This evolutionary quality suggests that transformation is profoundly internal not only to the social system taken as a whole but to the particular individuals it comprises—that is, the transformation of a social system cannot occur in the absence of the transformation of the individuals it comprises; it involves a deep and abiding commitment to different shared purposes and a real change of heart and mind on their part.

This dialectical view broadens as it also problematizes the concept of educational transformation.[28] It may be useful in understanding the nature of educational undertakings, but it may be less successful in excluding what does not count as transformation. Taken together, these images suggest that transformation is accommodative and revolutionary, form and function, superficial appearance and deep structural change, hierarchical and egalitarian, subversive and conservative, centered on a transformational moment and de-centered from it. These dialectics are not easily reconciled, and the paradoxes they raise contribute to the theoretical and practical complexities of educational transformation.

A nest of related questions remain unanswered: How broadly should this notion of transformation apply? What values are implicit in this view of transformation? What are the ends toward which education should be transformed? I want to leave aside these questions with the prospect of an answer to them later. For the present, with a more philosophically robust if also problematic notion of transformation, one is in a better position to evaluate its usefulness as both an idea and a descriptor for educational transformation. How does such a transformative view of education play out in practice? In particular, what kind of individual and collective action is needed to transform education?

Educational Transformation in Practice

A useful approach to understanding how educational transformation functions practically is to take a symptomatic approach. By symptomatic, I
mean that various characteristics when taken together suggest that educational transformation is under way in practice. What are these symptoms?

Imagination

As a "*way* of seeing and feeling things as they compose an integral whole,"
in which "old and familiar things are made new in experience,"[29] imagination constitutes a central mechanism by which transformation works.
Although the nature and function of artistic imagination have been explored
by philosophers of the arts and education,[30] I am thinking here of its role in
the broader social context. As Mary Reichling explains, imagination has several facets: intuition, or the ability to holistically and immediately grasp the
nature of things and see them in different relations than the ordinary; feeling, or a sense of things as they have been, are, or could or might be,
whether cognitive, emotional, or physical; perception, or the ability to see or
conceive mental images, be they aural, visual, spatial, or whatever; and
thinking, or the capacity to conceptualize, or reason things through analo-
gously, inductively, or deductively.[31] These images form various types of
imagination, whether pure fancy, heuristic or abstract imagery, aspect perception, or thinking analogically, metaphorically, or paradoxically.[32] This
creation of images of various sorts and seeing of mental visions is the stuff
of imagination. Without it, transformation fails.

Before one can accomplish systemic change, one must first imagine how
things could be different and how such change might be accomplished.
Freire rightly observes that people only hope when there is a fleshed out
dream or vision to hold onto, and transformation relies upon the presence
of hope and faith in its realization.[33] Imagination enables the articulating of
a vision. It makes it possible for people to hope for something that is intellectually satisfying and emotionally compelling, about which they are con-
victed as well as passionate, and it motivates them to press toward this
imagined goal.

Working imaginatively involves taking advantage of fresh ways by
which to forge links and reciprocities between disparate individuals and
groups; using novel approaches to rethink problems and challenges that
the social system faces; and devising alternative strategies for meeting the
needs, interests, and desires of students. In education, curricular ideas are
typically recycled and have a way reappearing in different guises in each
successive generation. A teacher who has taught for more than thirty
years—a rarity in public elementary and secondary schools in the United
States these days—has seen ideas come and go and may have become jus-
tifiably cynical about educational developments masquerading as "new
trends." For example, integrating school subjects, multicultural awareness,

national assessment, school restructuring, and the like have all had their day before. During the past century school music curricula have swung back and forth between an emphasis on performance and on listening, and the self-same claims for music technology today were advanced earlier in the twentieth century. What goes round in education seems to come back round. If educators are to escape this merry-go-round, this continuing recycling of tired industrial ideas in postindustrial societies, it is necessary to ask probing questions, challenge the status quo, and have the courage to re-vision education in genuinely novel and imaginative ways that meet the present information age. Rather than discarding all that is old and embracing only that which is new, educators need to reevaluate old ideas, including those that have been discarded in the past, to see what they offer for the future, decide what should be preserved, and devise new approaches that meet the needs and challenges of the present world.

Spirituality

In recent years, writers have begun to examine the notion of spirituality as it applies to music education, to distinguish it from religiosity, and to unpack some of its characteristic dimensions.[34] As breath signifies the living person, spirit refers to that which is quintessentially alive and human, to which the arts, the religions, and all the other ways in which people make meaning appeal. It is spiritual in its involvement of a deep sense of "otherness," mystery, awe, and reverence in the face of the fragility and shortness of human life, the inevitability of death, and the possibility of new beginnings full of promise; it is felt cognitively, emotionally, even physically.[35] Indeed, its spiritual quality comes closest to notions of conversion and renewal in the sense that one's life is reoriented due to a change of attitudes, beliefs, and habits, and one is figuratively reborn. This sense of mystery, reverence, and awe seems akin to Loder's observation that a convictional change such as occurs in conversion necessitates the individual's coming directly into contact with the central questions of life, with her or his mortality, and the importance of the present as a moment to be treasured and used wisely.[36] And it evokes Alfred North Whitehead's reference to the spiritual quality of education as "religious"—that is, without confronting issues surrounding human existence, students study "inert" or "dead" facts or ideas, and education loses its vitality and livingness.[37]

This spiritual quality of transformation is a feature not only of the individual's experience but of the corporate experience of the social system; the group and its members share in a collective sense of mystery, reverence, and awe. Spirituality moves within the system both inside out and outside in— that is to say, from the individual members of the group to its corporate beliefs and practices and back again to the individual members, thereby providing a unifying force for the group and a source of inspiration for its members.

Particularity

One of the important insights of postmodern thought has been a realization of the importance of place in meaning making, the recognition that, ultimately, education is carried on by individuals or in groups by a particular teacher and student(s) in the context of the wider community.[38] Each comes to the instructional situation with a framework of expectations, assumptions, beliefs, attitudes, values, knowledge, and habits shaped, in large measure, by the particular place and time in which she or he lives. Educational policies rely on the willingness and ability of teachers and students to abide by them, and they only work insofar as they are perceived to apply to these particular instructional units. Where they are seen as irrelevant, they are subverted, co-opted, or ignored by teacher and student alike.[39] They are subverted when teachers and student undermine them by disavowing them or by colluding with each other to do what they wish in spite of external mandates. They are co-opted when teachers and students invoke them to cover what they wish to do, whether or not their actions are really in accord with these mandates. And they are ignored where they do not fit teachers' and students' perceived realities, especially if their actions fall within the bounds of willingness of external authorities to tolerate some degree of noncompliance. The more powerless the jurisdiction, the greater its toleration for noncompliance, even if for no other reason than it lacks the ability to enforce its mandates. The nature of education is such that subversion and collusion in the face of external mandates are relatively common, and this also seems to have been the case in the past. Teachers adjust their activities to the situations in which they find themselves. For example, the history of national tests in England, among other countries in which such tests have been used widely, shows that these tests did not necessarily raise educational standards. Rather, teachers taught to the tests, thereby subverting their intended purpose of widening and deepening educational understanding. This was also the case in private musical instruction where studio teachers prepared their students for conservatory examinations by teaching just the specified test pieces rather than the wider repertoire they were supposed to sample.[40]

One approach to the problem of formulating expectations to fit the host of particular situations in a social system involves framing statements at a high level of generality so that they can be interpreted in many specific ways.[41] Such statements typically focus on the objectives to be met rather than on the specific methods by which objectives will be reached or the assessment criteria by which performance will be evaluated. Lacking specific methodological and assessment criteria, these statements cannot serve as rigorous standards in any but the soft sense of qualities that are either present or absent; they do not constitute standards in the hard sense—that is, normative assessments of whether something was done brilliantly, satisfactorily, or poorly. Such propositions are often couched as self-evident truisms; taken-for-granted, commonsensical notions; or vague generalizations whose very ambiguity provides opportunity for their co-option and subversion.

For example, according to the national music education standards formulated in the United States, every student will be "singing, alone and with others, a varied repertoire of music," "performing on instruments, alone and with others, a varied repertoire of music," "improvising melodies, variations, and accompaniments," "composing and arranging music within specific guidelines," "reading and notating music," "listening to, analyzing, and describing music," "evaluating music and music performances," "understanding relationships between music, the other arts, and disciplines outside the arts," and "understanding music in relation to history and culture."[42] There are no commitments in these "standards" to the particular range of repertoire or particular levels of difficulty, among a host of other specific, normative issues. Rather, these activities are characteristic elements among the things that Western music teachers have been doing since antiquity, accepted for decades as criteria for reputable school music programs in the United States and around the world. They may be present in such varying degree that, practically speaking, they are all but meaningless normative statements. The advantage of these statements to music teachers, of course, is that they can be construed in many different ways. Teachers can appeal to them to show that their curriculum has the requisite breadth meanwhile doing more or less what they please; they can use them for political purposes by showing that musical instruction is academically and musically rigorous even though teachers' musical and intellectual expectations of students may remain quite low; they can ignore them, especially where they know that administrators do not know the difference or are not interested or in a position to enforce them; or they can co-opt them by teaching to ensure that their students demonstrate the prescribed standards while at the same time ignoring other issues in musical education that are not directly mandated.

Even if standards are commonplace in the educational literature, they will not necessarily transform educational practice. For example, during the height of what has come to be known as the "aesthetic education movement" in the United States, during the 1970s and 1980s, many music educators invoked aesthetic rationales as a basis for their teaching.[43] Few could have defined the word *aesthetic*, much less have gone on to articulate principal ideas in the field of aesthetics. Yet "music education as aesthetic education" became a convenient slogan around which to muster the troops and convince the public that music was worth including in the curriculum for its own sake. Regardless of the rhetoric, teachers did pretty much what they wanted to do, whether or not it was actually "aesthetic education." I suspect that the same thing might also be said for the practical results of national standards in music education. Such standards provided political cover for musical education in schools at times when the public was preoccupied with matters of educational accountability.

To transform teaching and learning, the community of educational policy makers needs to address the particular situations in which teachers and learners find themselves. Rather than sidestepping these specific issues and problems, as has often happened in the past, teachers and their students need to grapple directly with them and address them head on.[44] These issues have fundamentally to do with the nature of music and education and with the appropriate purposes of, and approaches to, music education in a multi-cultural, internationalized, information-driven world. I suggest that they cannot be addressed monistically and universally. Rather, they will need to be worked out cooperatively, consensually, and dialogically in ways that reflect the particular places in which musical education is carried on.

A particularistic approach to educational transformation offers several advantages. It draws upon the cultural richness of the places in which it is conducted and provides a sense of connectedness of people to the places in which they were born and live. It respects the many ways of teaching and learning music. It constitutes a mechanism for evoking transformation that is individually motivated rather than being imposed as a top-down solution on the social system. And it is realistic in acknowledging that a unilateral and monistic approach will not necessarily be transformative. On the other hand, it may downplay, even ignore, the shared characteristics of musical experience, teaching, and learning in favor of their differences. It may negate the importance of policy decisions on behalf of the public; the claims of shared values, beliefs, and expectations; and the power of political realities within the social system. Rather than denying these shoals, however, the educational policy maker needs to remain vigilant in steering clear of them insofar as possible.

Embodiment

Musical knowledge is not only taught conceptually or formally but is also caught informally by the singer repeating the song over and over until the learner eventually "gets it" and is able to do it. Being "caught" captures the ancient idea of breathing knowledge and vitality into another person.[45] Where an example has normative value for its public, as an exemplar that represents the ideal or best practice, those who do not possess it may admire the skills and know-how that produced it and wish to possess this knowledge themselves. The exemplar in its very being serves as a source of motivation for others to acquire the means to possess it whether by imitating it, in the sense of copying it, or in creating something like it, based on it, or going beyond it. The very fact that ideas are embodied or expressed in a practical or physical way causes others to want not only the activity but the ideas associated with it; other witnesses wish to seek it for themselves.[46] These witnesses seek not only to do as the exponent does by way of action and practice but to be the sort of person that he or she is by way of character and demeanor. Through this mechanism, transformation spreads between and among individuals and groups.

One of the most persuasive ways in which to influence educational expectations is through the "demonstration effect."[47] Here an idea is translated into a model, or exemplar, which is then examined and evaluated by educational policy makers and the public and emulated elsewhere. Many music education methods were introduced in this fashion.[48] As Howard points out, learning by example is particularly important in the arts, where knowing how to go on or do an art is as significant as knowing about it.[49] Demonstrations not only provide an expression or exemplification of a theoretical principle, but they also show how to go about putting it into practice. As such, they are crucial in educational transformation.

The word *model* is frequently misused and overused in the educational literature. Howard unpacks some of the possible ways in which this word can be construed: a sample or "typical instance"; a scaled representation; a simulation or approximation to the real thing; and an exemplar or ideal instance.[50] I do not wish to tease out each of these types here so much as to make the point that a demonstration may fall into one of these categories or yet others, and it is necessary to know what is intended by and in the demonstration before one can safely interpret it. Failing to make these distinctions runs the risk of mistakenly and uncritically emulating an example in ways that were not intended.

This raises the practical problem of determining how examples are used and interpreting them appropriately. To use an historical example, in the early nineteenth century William Woodbridge, Lowell Mason, and their followers assumed that the Boston Academy of Music would demonstrate the efficacy of music instruction in the Boston common schools.[51] The academy was a private music school administered by professional musicians, whereas the Boston common schools were administered by a School Committee comprising people who were not necessarily musicians. These were very different environments. Yet the academy was intended as an exemplar. The musicians attempted a sort of performance contracting when music was first introduced into the Boston common schools, and in the early years there was a tug-of-war for control of musical instruction between the musicians and the School Committee. It may have been the fear of loss of control over musical instruction that led such musicians as Elam Ives Jr. to part company with Lowell Mason and the common-school model of music education and stick with their own privately operated music schools, community music schools, and conservatories. In the minds of these musicians, public school music education didn't or couldn't come up to the mark. Similar pitfalls in interpreting examples exist today in a world in which education is an increasingly global rather than local, state, regional, or national endeavor. It is tempting to look abroad and see a rich array of educational examples that on first glance may appear promising. These examples need to be carefully and critically evaluated before being emulated in another place or at another time under very different conditions than those for which they were designed.

Fallibility

The incompleteness of any particular perspective provides the basis for the view that at some future time one may come upon a richer, truer, fuller, better idea or practice than one espouses at present.[52] One may accept provisionally an idea or practice, recognizing that one may be wrong. Later it may become apparent that the alternative not chosen might have been the better choice. There is always the possibility of the road not taken, the idea not pursued, the practice not selected; at some time in the future roads may intersect, or one may opt for an alternative route. Fallibility occurs because one is not omniscient or in possession of perfect knowledge. As Howard suggests, the artist both knows and does not know what she or he is up to; one may foresee some things but not others, and there is always the prospect of the unexpected consequences of ideas and actions, even where the artist or craftsperson is quite sure at the outset what the outcome will be.[53]

Discontinuities and ambiguities between the worlds of theory and practice also give rise to incomplete knowledge. For example, a particular idea may suggest several alternative practical solutions, and a particular practice may be spawned by various ideas.[54] Because of the partiality of a particular practice or theoretical perspective, there is a sense in which each offers one facet of what may be a larger idea or reality. Negotiating one's way through these possibilities necessitates what Schwab calls the "arts of eclectic," the idea of grasping the inherent ambiguity and multiple perspectives of theory and practice, the partiality of understanding, and the difficulty of moving between the worlds of theory and practice and of deriving complex solutions that take these difficulties into account. While going some way with Schwab, Scheffler challenges Schwab's characterization of the discontinuity between theory and practice, arguing that there is a greater overlap between the two than Schwab allows and suggesting that reason provides a basis on which reciprocity may be forged between them.[55] Notwithstanding the importance of these specific criticisms, Scheffler and Schwab agree that theory and practice are ambiguous constructs.[56]

Educational policy makers and those interested in their work need to negotiate and communicate between the different interest groups within any social system. Because education is conducted in the public spaces, educational policy makers require political acumen, wisdom, prudence, persuasiveness, integrity, intellect, trustworthiness, veracity, and determination, among a host of other personal and professional qualities and skills. Politics in the best sense is the art of government. In a democracy, the public entrusts certain individuals with the responsibility to act on its behalf in order to carry out particular tasks for its benefit. Public education is one of these activities, and it cannot avoid being a profoundly political process. Nor is the state the only institution that is politicized educationally. In other institutions, such as the family, religion, commerce, and the music profession, transformation also takes place publicly and is forged by the institution's officials and policy makers in the public arena.

Once a transformative vision is applied in the phenomenal world, the task is very much messier and more ambiguous than its theoretical ideal might suggest. Unexpected consequences flow from human action, alternative visions compete for the public's attention, vested interests jockey for power and prestige, and the task of realizing a transformative dream is a daunting one. This task is made even more problematical at a time when institutional power is pervasive and ordinary individuals must join together if they are to be heard in the public spaces.

Given these realities, ideas need to be examined critically before implementing them, and actions undertaken and reviewed carefully and thoughtfully. Rather than being pretentious plans that are implemented without adjustment and afterward evaluated, plans need to have a somewhat rhapsodic or improvisatory feel because they probably need to be adjusted and fine-tuned while they are being implemented. This kind of dynamic and flexible administration, like teaching, requires skill and confidence to execute and is more difficult to accomplish successfully than a static approach with its specified inputs, production processes, and outputs planned ahead of time and executed according to a preconceived plan. Nevertheless, it fits nicely the qualities of the present information age in which such flexibility and nimbleness are valued.

As one moves to higher levels of generality, from the psychological to the institutional and societal nexus, problems of foresight and unexpected consequences multiply and conclusions become more tentative. The larger the group, the more difficult it is to correctly read the situation, assess the operative causal relationships, and accurately forecast the impact of policy decisions. In large social systems, the relationship between *a priori* theory and its practical application is much more complicated and problematical than in the case of a single individual or a small group such as a teacher-student dyad. Many variables are interconnected in complex ways, and each actor in the system has a unique perspective on and incomplete knowledge of it. Designing and implementing social policy are therefore fraught with difficulties, including the theoretical assumptions made, policies formulated, expected effects of implementing these policies, ways of assessing whether expectations have been met, and means of evaluating what future changes should be made. All along the way, it is possible that policy makers could be wrong and that some other approach would have been more effective if only they were omniscient.

Advantages accrue from undertaking educational transformation in this spirit. Educational policy makers attempt to make the best judgment in light of the situation that presents itself, remain open to the possibility that a better idea or solution may be found in the future, and understand that policy forged for the present need not necessarily hold for all time. Where knowledge is presumed to be incomplete, they search for valid and reliable data on which to base and formulate their assumptions, expectations, and practices. Rather than attempting to manipulate evidence to fit their preconceived ideas and persuade others of their points of view,[57] they carefully analyze the situations they face and take as full an account of them as possible. Research grounds and drives policy rather than vice versa, and policy is formulated carefully, cautiously, and sensitively. In the educational arena, rather than being preoccupied with ideologically driven transformation, the educator is concerned to do careful research, find out where the people are, and work for consensus with them so that the policies developed fit, as nearly as possible, the situations in which those affected by them find themselves.

This principle is not without its detractions. Among other things, recognizing fallibility may excuse a lack of steadfast purpose over the long term. It may mask educational faddishness, in which educators accept uncritically every latest idea and hottest trend. It may seem insufficiently strong minded to those used to authoritative and strident voices in the public spaces, and it may not inspire confidence in educational policy makers. It may underestimate the power of the status quo, the resilience of institutions and their resistance to change. And it may overinflate the potency of research and downplay ideology as the basis of educational transformation. Notwithstanding these potential pitfalls, I cannot see how educational transformation can be undertaken in an intellectually honest way other than by admitting that well-meaning persons are fallible and that even the best-laid plans and procedures are provisional.

Dialogue

Educational policy makers require the skills to negotiate and forge practical plans that are consonant with their analyses of the particular situations they face. As Dewey notes, such an education is probably more difficult to carry out than in the absence of such conflicting, competing, or diverging interests and challenges.[58] Freire and Greene are right that the only way around the multiplicities and pluralities in contemporary society is for dialogue to occur between those holding disparate and sometimes antithetical perspectives, even though this invites a messy, sometimes difficult, and even painful process. It takes time to talk; to genuinely, respectfully, and humbly hear the other; to figure out what bridges might be built between different and well as similar points of view; and together to forge ways to solve the practical dilemmas faced in working together.[59] Dissent must be a possibility in this sort of dialogue. Without it, voices are silenced or marginalized, and all cannot participate in liberatory education. Dialogue suggests that ideas need to be interrogated and that participants need to be open to criticism of their ideas and willing to criticize constructively those of others. An ability to be able to separate one's own feelings of self-worth from the ideas one is propounding is essential if one is to undertake such a conversation. Consensus is difficult to reach under the best of circumstances. Sometimes one agrees to disagree with another, to live and let live.

Too often, educational dialogue has been carried out within the context of hierarchical organizations that strangle, truncate, and otherwise thwart this dialogical process. There may be an appearance of dialogue in a process that is actually quite anti-dialogical in its thrust. For example, a mandate is handed "down" by an educational committee appointed by the state, groups form to discuss it and offer their input, and this conversation is allowed to go on for a few months. At the end of this prescribed time, an editorial committee summarizes what has been learned and hands it back "up" to the originating educational committee, which then develops the final policy. Too many administrators are unwilling to receive criticism of their ideas or actions. Conversations conducted within the framework of such mandates or constraints cannot be truly open or educationally liberatory. No administrative action may be better than ill-advised or hasty action. Better that alternative mechanisms be developed to let ideas genuinely emerge from those most affected by them—a process that is doubtless more time-consuming and difficult to achieve but nevertheless can result in a more humane, civil, and inclusive community. Or better that adjustments in response to criticism of administrative actions be made along the way than that unintended or negative consequences of actions be permitted to go unchecked.

Dialogue toward liberatory education requires that the stranglehold of top-down, hierarchical thinking be broken and bottom-up, egalitarian thinking be fostered. This is especially the case because education is by nature dialectical. Because tensions exist between aspects that are difficult to reconcile, if at all, and must often be lived with and worked through on a continuing basis, ongoing dialogue is necessary in the attempt to forge understandings between disparate interests, find common ground wherever possible, and solve unavoidable conflicts through peaceful means. Sometimes dialogue may constitute a safety valve to prevent violence. By attempting to throw bridges across chasms of misunderstanding, mistrust, and alienation, one hopes to build mutual respect and better understanding of the differences between people and what these beliefs, values, attitudes, and understandings mean to those who hold them. Even when resisting or rejecting the ideas of different others, one can still learn to live with them, respect them as fellow human beings, and know how to tolerate or repudiate the expression of beliefs and practices that counter one's own. Nor are justice, freedom, and civility won for all time. They need to be continually reaffirmed and reforged in each dialogue, in every time and place.

Agency

Organizations provide a means whereby transformation is undertaken and undergone. Collective action necessitates creating and sustaining educational systems whereby activities on behalf of the public or the community can be conducted. Among the many ways of envisioning organizations, Gareth Morgan suggests images of machines, organisms, brains, cultures, political systems, psychic prisons, flux and transformation, and instruments of domination.[60] The ways in which administrators and members of a social system envision the organization affect how they think about it and others within it and impact their consequent actions. For Morgan, no one organizational image suffices; each has advantages and disadvantages, and every participant is in the process of constructing his or her own particular reality. Among the theories accounting for administrative behavior, Douglas McGregor's theory X and Y have achieved particular importance.[61] Theory X assumes that people are inherently lazy and must be directed and controlled by management through the exercise of authority. Theory Y assumes that people are naturally industrious and that conditions should be created such that the workers can achieve their personal goals through working toward the collective success of the enterprise. Theory Z assumes that both of these views are too simplistic and that a more complex situation obtains.[62] In theory Z there is a place for leadership, for recognizing the complexity of human nature, for engaging a diverse community of workers, and for fostering self-fulfillment while also ensuring that collectively shared goals are met. Goals and processes are important, and reconciling these aspects is more complicated than either theory X or theory Y assumes. Among the leadership qualities that promote imaginative, diverse, cooperative action are faith, courage, consensus building, listening, empowering those closest to where the decisions must be made, and ensuring accountability for personal and corporate action.[63]

If this multidimensional view of organizations is on the mark—and I think that in postindustrial societies, such organizational characteristics may be even more pronounced than in industrial societies (even to the creation of virtual organizations, those fluid and nimble alliances formed for the purpose of achieving particular ends)—then educators need to fundamentally rethink the sorts of organizations they build. This view offers the prospect of catering to the multiplicities and pluralities of contemporary society, accommodating to the fast-paced technological, social, and cultural changes of the present world in which access to information and the mass media have profoundly altered the way people see the world and what they know about it. Its complexity necessitates that leaders and led are willing to share the burden of forging collective policy and administering the organization and able to work out honestly and civilly agreed-upon processes for sharing power. This may be more easily said than done, especially where institutions are inherently flawed, people with power do not wish to share it, certain individuals and groups are marginalized or silenced, and consensus is difficult if not impossible to achieve.

Freire's cellular mechanism for organizational change—his notion of discussion/action groups that infiltrate the social system—may be too simplistic because such groups are often outside regular institutional structures.[64] Rather, educational transformation seems to require complex multidimensional or multifaceted strategies that transcend a particular organizational image; take into account the needs, interests, and wishes of a diverse constituency; encourage a variety of solutions; and occur inside as well as outside the social system's structures. Such a complex model should be within the scope of an environment rich in technology and information to derive and implement, and it is unlikely that there will only be one solution.[65] Rather, various solutions may be worked out, each of which may apply particularly to a specific time and place.

Among the difficult practical issues to be addressed is the matter of
choice, the degree to which teachers, students, administrators, parents, and
other educational stakeholders are able or encouraged to choose among a
diverse array of educational possibilities and environments.[66] Compulsory
public education is a comparatively recent phenomenon in educational history, and the ideal of the common school available to all, regardless of race,
color, gender, creed, economic or social status, or cultural background, is
still a relatively fragile one. Proposals for school and curricular choice have
been viewed in some quarters as controversial because they seem to
undermine the common-school ideal. As such, they carry a lot of negative
political baggage. However, the publicly supported school as it now exists is
a nineteenth-century institution, more or less geared toward the demands
of an industrial society and in need of re-visioning for a postindustrial
world. Transforming the institution of the school need not necessarily
mean repudiating ideals for which it stands, including education for all citizens at public expense; curricula that foster such values as mutuality,
inclusivity, civility, respect for different others, humanity, and love of learning; and promotion of peace and tranquility in human society. Forcing a
diverse constituency into a single mold goes contrary to the principles I
have sketched in this chapter, but allowing or promoting choice also opens
the Pandora's box of how to do so while at the same time retaining some
values from the past, especially democratic ideals. Although, practically
speaking, this is a difficult matter to resolve, it is one of the important challenges of our time. And people of good will should be able to figure out
practical strategies to meet the claims of educational choice on the one
hand and inclusiveness on the other.

The school curriculum, construed as what is intended to be learned and
what is actually learned, constitutes an important means by which educational transformation occurs. This is the point where theory meets practice,
where ideas, beliefs, and values are actualized in the phenomenal world.
During the past twenty years, especially, curricular thinkers have grappled
with how to transform the learning process from a linear, static, subject-
driven, goal-oriented, industrial model to a multifaceted, organic, experiential, process-oriented, postindustrial entity. Gender studies, theology,
psychoanalysis, sociology, anthropology, and aesthetics, among other fields,
have strongly affected curriculum studies.[67] Reconceptualists, including
Michael Apple, Maxine Greene, Herbert Kliebard, and Philip Jackson, have
challenged traditional curricular ideas by emphasizing such ideas as the
individual and social construction and experiential quality of knowledge. In
so doing, they have exposed and criticized the establishment's political, religious, and economic interests underlying the traditional curriculum in general education, particularly in state-supported schools. By highlighting the
individual's interaction with subject matter and the importance of
contextualizing curriculum, they have de-centered subject matter and re-
centered the individual at the heart of the school. Yet, notwithstanding

their potential to transform education toward liberatory ideals, these writers too often are marginal dwellers in educational theory and practice.

Among the school subjects, Greene believes that the arts are particularly positioned to transform education. As she explains, the arts rely on and foster imaginative thought and action.[68] Artistic communities can provide spaces where diverse groups can come and dialogue together. They are models and metaphors of what school communities can become. Deanne Bogdan also writes of the transpositions among the arts, of the rich interplay between music, art, and literature in awakening and fostering imaginative learning.[69] And Donald Arnstine posits the value of the arts in creating the sorts of dispositions needed by citizens of a democracy.[70] I am sure these writers would agree that the arts are not alone in developing imaginative thought—the dispositions, values, and attitudes of character that will allow a democracy to succeed—and that other subjects can be approached in imaginative ways or promote democratic societies. Still, they are right in observing the particular importance of artistic imagination and intuition for validating as well as acquiring knowledge. Imaginative and intuitive thought and the ability and willingness to see others' perspectives, value them, and care genuinely for others as one also cares for wisdom are also particularly important in a technology- and information-driven world. In such a world, multiple perspectives and individually tailored strategies are especially important; lockstep, standardized processes and products are outmoded; and new ways for working together with others must be forged.

Schools are public institutions charged with educating the young, and as the central institutions for mass education, they are integral to the process of educational and societal transformation. In *In Search of Music Education* I describe various images of school and schooling. Others abound, including Martin's notion of the schoolhome inspired by Maria Montessori's *casa dei bambino*.[71] Martin argues that pervasive societal conditions necessitate the school's becoming a home and fulfilling roles that once might have been filled by the home. In her view, rather than being an impersonal institution, the school needs to be a place where the student is and feels cared for, where love and mutual respect ground social interaction, where a child-centered curriculum motivates students to want to learn, and where the school reaches out into the community to touch the hearts and minds of students' parents and family members. Her vision of school resonates with Madeline Grumet's feminine view of teaching and Noddings' idea of school as a caring community.[72] Rather than thinking of school as one's father's house, one sees school as one's home, in the best sense of the word—a place where reciprocity, inclusiveness, and love form the basis for moral behavior; where power is shared; where different others are accepted, valued, and loved; and where people, not procedures, are at the center of the educational process.

Teaching *through* imagination by accessing metaphors, analogies, and other heuristic devices designed to enable students to do something as well as learn about it is also consistent with transformative education. Techniques such as improvising strategies, looking for "openings," as Greene puts it, or opportunities by which to connect with the student and bring student and subject matter together, are helpful in this kind of teaching. Howard's example of Birget Nilsson evoking the metaphor of the tree planted in the earth in one of her master classes shows how particularly appropriate metaphors are to music instruction.[73] Imaginative teaching not only takes advantage of students' interests and perceived needs, but it deliberately cultivates divergent thinking and provides opportunities to develop the aptitudes, skills, and habits needed to carry thought into self-directed action. Opportunities for imaginative reflection-in-action and reflection-on-action, both individually and collectively, have the further advantage of forging links between the worlds of theory and practice, thereby suggesting openings through which theory might be translated into practice or vice versa, toward a more humane world.

Developing imagination need not come at the expense of critical thinking and reasoning. Rather, higher-order thinking skills such as analysis, application, synthesis, and evaluation would seem to go hand in hand with imaginative and intuitive thought—a relationship that arises from the nature of the aesthetic and artistic enterprise born out in the lives of outstanding scientists and artists.[74] This being the case, a curriculum that fosters imaginative thought and activity would also demand intellectual reasoning, passion, commitment, and care by teacher and student alike.

Nor is it enough to think of curriculum only in intellectual terms. If education is to be transforming, it needs to go beyond the things of the mind to focus on an inclusive view of the person.[75] Dispositions such as love of learning, self-discipline, honesty, carefulness, patience, fidelity, curiosity, empathy, determination, and open-mindedness are among the values that citizens of a democracy need to possess and are the hallmarks of transforming education. These attributes of character lie beyond the learning of facts or information— no matter how valuable—and affect how people behave. Through focusing on things of great value and shaping the ways in which people are disposed to think and act in humane, honorable, compassionate, and intellectually honest ways, arts curricula may promote the conduct of a civil and democratic society. Without developing such dispositions, curriculum falls short.[76]

The curriculum may not be enough to guarantee educational transformation. Greene may have overemphasized the power of the arts curriculum in effecting change and relied too heavily on the strength of example, a cellular mechanism similar to that invoked by Freire, in which transformative communities become catalysts for change in their surrounding environments. Greene may have been too optimistic regarding the willingness of educators and other educational stakeholders to change. Practically speaking, some systemic organization would seem to be helpful, even essential, if widespread change is to occur. A key question is how to devise the sort of institutional leadership that eschews top-down, hierarchical thinking; fosters individual as well as collective transformation; and empowers teachers to create the kinds of learning environments that meet the particular needs and interests of their students and foster more civil societies.

Expectations

The expectations of all those involved in the educational enterprise have a profound effect on teaching and learning.[77] Expectations of self and others are grounded in notions of human potential; they are influenced particularly by one's social and cultural environment, by what reference groups or significant others expect. These expectations are internalized and reinforced over a lifetime. They harden as beliefs, values, attitudes, and habits that resist change, and they ground social interaction. As such, they form the basis of common sense; they are so internalized that they may not be consciously thought about or questioned. Instead, they are taken for granted as normative.

Scheffler interprets potential as "the *capability of acquiring* new learnings."[78] He posits various ways in which human potential can be viewed. The *capacity* notion suggests that such-and-such is physically possible—that is, John can become a pianist because he has the strength, endurance, aptitude, and physical characteristics to play the piano. He may not yet be a pianist, but he can reasonably be expected to become one because no physical or other impediments stand in his way. The *predictive* notion suggests something else, that "*if* he has the chance *and* is not prevented" he will learn to play the piano. Not only does John possess the attributes to play, but he is likely to want to do so, and it can be reasonably predicted that he will do so. The *decision* notion further stipulates that "the agent's own decision constitutes a critical factor in acquisition." That is, John must decide for himself to become a pianist and must dedicate the time and effort required to acquire the skills and knowledge he needs. Ultimately, then, predictions of potential are conditional; their realization is determined by the individual's choice and active engagement.

This being the case, expectations constitute a bridge between past and future. They emerge on the basis of past beliefs and practices, are amenable to change, and precede practice. People are prepared, or even love, to act on the basis of expectations. Changes in expectations make feasible changes in action. They ground action in reasoned, intuitively, and imaginatively construed assumptions. The conditionality of human potential means that expectations are vital in determining that potential. For example, as Blacking shows, musicality is fundamentally a matter of societal expectations that either nourish or neglect musical potential.[79] Psychological studies also confirm that while heredity plays an important part, considerable weight falls on environmental factors as the basis for musicality.[80]

Conversion, or what Loder would term the "transforming moment," results in profound changes in expectation-sets of self, world, and what lies beyond. Expectations go beyond assumptions to predict or commit to action. Conversion implies not only an altered mind-set, or a spiritual sea change, but also a holistic phenomenal experience, a profound change in dispositions to think and act and in one's way of life. Likewise, paradigmatic changes such as those described by the Tofflers, result in profound societal shifts that parallel the individual experience of conversion. Whether viewed individually or collectively, expectations are the seeds of actions, and changing them is at the core of educational transformation. The fact that expectations are grounded in the past makes them resistant to change. This may be fortunate because society depends on the stability of expectation-sets. In the absence of stability, the lack of continuing basis for social interaction results in anarchy. Changing expectations may therefore take some time and require persuasive evidence. In educational history, it is not unusual to encounter changes that take years, decades, lifetimes, even centuries to undergo—witness the history of publicly supported education in Europe and the United States.

Summary

In sum, this view of educational transformation has rich possibilities for envisaging and undertaking educational change. It is a complex and ambiguous construct construed in a philosophically hard or technical sense. Focusing on what cannot fully count as transformation—modification, accommodation, integration, assimilation, inversion, synthesis, transfiguration, conversion, and renewal—allows one to see how each concept can contribute to an understanding of transformation yet is flawed or limited in some way(s). The multifaceted and dialectical nature of transformation results from a "this is with that" working together of images, each of which has a potential role to play. Sketching the resulting dialectic properties of transformation shows how it functions metamorphically and incrementally, systemically and particularly, as a reflectively active and actively reflective undertaking, an individual and collective enterprise, in which change originates with and without the social system, that has a potentially "bright" and "dark" side, at once a state of being and a dynamic process. And describing the various ways in which transformation functions practically—including its imaginative, spiritual, particularistic, embodied, fallible, and dialogic properties; its reliance on organizational and curricular agency; and its dependence on expectations—reveals how it may be undertaken and why it is a daunting endeavor for educational policy makers and public alike.

As an ongoing, creative, and social process, educational transformation is never complete. It requires, among other things, continuing, thoughtful, and critical analysis and persistence in following through educational objectives and approaches over the long term. In the face of unforeseen circumstances, it demands flexibility; it means admitting mistakes candidly and rethinking curriculum as a principal agent of educational transformation. And given the particularity and social nature of educational transformation in place and time, it necessitates working collaboratively in politically astute ways to forge goals and methods for, and change the expectations of, all of the stakeholders in the educational enterprise.

4

Transforming Music

What is meant by the word *music*? How is music transformed? And what are the practical implications for music education? In previous writing I suggested that music was a social phenomenon and examined some of the ways in which groups form around particular beliefs and practices.[1] While these insights are helpful, they constitute part of a complex and ambiguous phenomenon. As a way of teasing out some of these ambiguities and tensions, I sketch five images of music that together illustrate the many ways in which musicians and music educators conceive of and practice music.[2] I then outline three ways in which music is transformed. The chapter concludes with the practical implications of this analysis for music education.

The word *music* is a Western construction, and some societies do not have an equivalent word in their vocabularies. While they might do what we in the West call music, they do not think of what they do in the same way. If we could go back to the ancient Greeks, we would find the same situation, in that their notions of music were far more integrative with other arts and quite different in emphasis than ours. Still, one is a creature of one's time and place. If one is writing from the perspective of, and position in, Western culture, it is perfectly appropriate to ask what is now meant, at least in the West, by the word *music*. The question of whether this Western word ought to be used in societies for which there is no equivalent word is quite another matter that lies outside the scope of this writing. I neither claim nor deny that my analysis relates to other musical and cultural traditions and perspectives. The relevance of these ideas to different musics suggests commonalities as well as differences between musical traditions and practices.

The word *music* is used variously as noun, verb ("to music"), and adjective ("musical"), in both the singular and plural, and is associated with other notions on which it is contingent such as ability, perception, understanding, skill, symbol, and sign. This ambiguity necessitates clarifying the different ways in which the word is understood and used. My own approach to this ambiguity is a dialectical one that invokes different images to suit particular purposes. Analyzing the various ways in which the word *music* is understood by musicians and teachers alike is an important step in developing a conceptual framework that can be compared to other approaches, fleshed out, criticized, expanded upon, or modified in the future. Beyond this theoretical interest is the important practical matter of how teachers invoke these images in music instruction. For this reason, my examples come mainly from various music curricula that indicate the intentions and instructional practices of music teachers.[3] Focusing on the practical ways in which teachers use these images also reveals how teachers reconcile musical dialectics in their own teaching.

The story of Western classical music has been told principally in regard to the specific styles that characterized music of a particular time and the people who made it. Less has been said about the social process of musical transformation, about how and why music changes in the context of its practitioners and public, and why some music has been preserved more or less unchanged for long periods of time while other music has changed rapidly.[4] Rather than offering a detailed account of the ways in which Western classical music transforms itself, a project that lies outside the scope of this chapter, my central point is to show that whether they realize it or not, music teachers are engaged in the process of musical transformation. In earlier writing I discussed the impact of cultural institutions—family, religion, politics, music profession, and commerce—on musical ideas and practices and the effect of music, in turn, on the nature of those institutions.[5] Rather than traveling over this ground again, my present focus is on the work of musician-teachers, who are at the very center of the musical enterprise and whose efforts are crucial to preserving and transforming musical traditions. Whether a musical tradition lives or dies depends on the effectiveness of the process whereby music passes from one generation to the next, and on those in the position to shape future musical beliefs and practices.[6] Not only is this an educational matter, but the musical challenge for music educational policy makers is profound.

The Western classical music tradition has come under close scrutiny and criticism for its historical association with the upper classes or society establishment, its role taken to be symbolic of upper-class or establishment values and an agent through which the lower or economically and politically disadvantaged classes are oppressed. Its repertoire has been viewed as obsolete, sexist, racist, ethnocentric, and anachronistic; its performance venues regarded as sonic museums where people come to gaze with their ears; and its values largely ignored or rejected by the public at large. Its preoccupation with preserving a canon of masterworks has been seen to reify, stultify, and restrict the classical repertory, thereby making it less interesting and unpredictable to performers and listeners alike. Its composers, often employed

by university and other authorities and not dependent on earning a livelihood through their compositions, have been regarded as isolated from the
general public, their works criticized for their irrelevance, esoteric quality,
intellectualism, and lack of popular appeal. And its Western roots have been
seen as too limited and limiting, and criticized by music educators and others for constituting too restrictive a view of music in a multicultural society.[7]

Efforts to include popular and classical music in general education and to
broaden the range of repertoire studied to vernacular and classical musics
around the world have met with mixed success. Stemming particularly from
such initiatives as the Tanglewood Symposium in the United States,[8] some
policy makers in the West have embraced contemporary music of all sorts,
blurred the lines between classical and popular music, extended their study
to vernacular musics globally, and thereby subverted the supremacy of classical music, even largely ignoring it. Others have been reluctant to let go of
the comparatively narrow focus on classical music and have taken a much
more conservative view of their educational role.[9] Still, even where definitions of music have been broadened beyond the Western classical tradition,
the concepts underlying musical study in general education remain largely
those of Western classical music.[10] Some music teachers take popular music
less seriously than classical music, and classical and popular musics systematically prejudice women and minorities, among other marginalized groups
in society.[11] Thus, while outwardly espousing inclusiveness of many musics
in the curriculum, music teachers of all stripes still practice the profession in
exclusive ways, and the musics taught are systemically flawed, affirming or
alienating to women, people of color, ethnic and linguistic minorities, the
young, the elderly, the uneducated, the poor, and the disenfranchised.

I am particularly interested in Western classical music because it is my
own heritage, its wealth of historical evidence is helpful in understanding
the process of musical transformation, and it constitutes an important tradition among many others also worthy of study. My focus on this tradition
should also be read as symptomatic of pervasive challenges in all of the
musical traditions of which I am aware. Even in those musical traditions
that some writers have viewed as supposedly more humane, inclusive,
egalitarian, communal, and cooperative than Western classical music, there
is an undercurrent of pervasive societal sexism and patriarchy, men are
unwilling to share power with women, and ethnocentricity and exclusivity
are evident in musical beliefs and practices.[12] This is not to say that all
musics are the same in terms of their specific practices, but they all reflect
these underlying social and societal tensions.

The idea of Western classical music is ambiguous. At present, the descriptor "Western" is probably a misnomer, and I use the term for lack of a better
word and because of its widespread use. In reality, it is an international tradition forged by musicians on every continent, drawing from vernacular and
popular musics around the world, whose roots, while developed in the West, are

also Eastern.[13] While it should be distinguished from other eminent classical traditions, such as the Persian, Indian, and Chinese, it also intermingles with them to some extent as it does with other musics such as jazz and rock, which have not been considered classical in the past. Its boundaries are indistinct. In its etymological sense, the word *classic* refers to works judged to be exemplary or typical instances of a particular genre. It may describe a particular style of late-eighteenth- and early-nineteenth-century European music, a formalistic approach to music, or the musical tradition associated with high European culture, and its description typically hinges on nineteenth-century conceptions of music. Now, it is also being applied to notable works from other Western traditions such as jazz and rock that historically lay outside its purview. As a multicultural tradition, Western classical music evidences a wide range of styles, genres, forms, scales, and timbres ranging over the two millennia of the Christian era. It varies from a mixed-media event serving various social functions to a pervasively sonic event experienced in concert halls.[14] So great are these differences that it may be more difficult to generalize about it than to note its particularities and variations.

Still, a few generalizations can be made about this musical tradition. Among these, it arose principally in Europe during the Christian era and thence spread internationally; it was traditionally cultivated by privileged and educated classes and spread later to the middle and lower classes; its canon is chiefly the work of white European men; it is composed mainly for formal social and musical occasions; it is a literate musical tradition in the sense that it is notated and transmitted via musical scores, texts, and recordings as well as orally from teacher to student; and it has formal interest and functional purpose. One cannot go much beyond these generalities without important caveats. This tradition is far broader than the notion of "common practice," the elite music cultivated in Europe in the three centuries between 1600 and 1900 C.E. It encompasses early Christian music and its development throughout the High Middle Ages; music associated with the renaissance of the secular arts in the fifteenth and sixteenth centuries; music associated with worldwide nationalistic movements; atonal and electronically generated music; and music that crosses over into other traditions—popular, vernacular, and classical. And it cannot be fully understood without considering its Western, Eastern, and Southern roots in the musics of ancient Greece and Rome, the Near East, and northern Africa.

Five Images

Music as Aesthetic Object

The image of music as aesthetic object is one of the most prevalent philosophical perspectives on music, especially since it draws on a large literature on aesthetics, a Western philosophical specialty devoted to the study of the arts. In the West its focus has been on the Western classical tradition; however, philosophers are now joined by ethnomusicologists, anthropologists, sociologists, and others in exploring the various musics of the world, their different aesthetics, or the systems of thought and practice whereby judgments are made about the arts, thereby opening the prospect of comparative studies of them. So this view need not be restricted narrowly to include only the Enlightenment views of Immanuel Kant or his successors such as Eduard Hanslick, who sought to describe a universalistic view of the aesthetic judgment and the musically beautiful.[15]

Its focus on the work of art values the product or end result of a process of music making that is underpinned with assumptions about what constitutes an exemplary performance and how music should be made and sound.[16] Whether it be a piece of composed Western classical music, a rock song, an Indian raga, or a Kaluli lament, the music can be thought about, described, understood, and judged by its public in terms of particular ideas about the nature of its beauty and construction, and in terms of how well a performance meets these assumptions or the criteria of this practice.[17] In the Western classical tradition, for example, certain specific elements are employed in a performance or composition, and the whole presents an articulated form or structure that more or less exemplifies the underlying aesthetic assumptions that govern it.[18] People initiated into this aesthetic perceive import or meaning in the composition or performance and are able to distance themselves psychically from the "work" or performance in order to make dispassionate judgments about it.[19]

Understanding music, in this view, necessitates grasping the underlying assumptions that determine what is heard and seen in the phenomenal world and its formal structure in order to see how it is made. And this understanding is arrived at through making, hearing, and seeing music performed and reflecting upon it. The majority of music history, theory, and music appreciation courses, and score analysis classes in the preparation of choral and instrumental conductors in which representative musical works are studied structurally and in depth, are based on this musical image. Structural listening is assumed by many expert musicians, although listeners often do not hear music in the way these musicians think they should.[20]

This view of music has much to recommend it.[21] In focusing on music's formal properties and examining its structures, one gains a deeper understanding of music as a creative work, and one gains a greater respect for the human achievement that this composition or performance represents. Nor need one necessarily hear the composition in the phenomenal world to imagine how a musical score should sound beforehand as a "sonorous image."[22] The emphasis on the particular rule systems that govern this music also enables initiates to grasp its function as a way of thinking rationally through and about sound. And its objectivity highlights the shared understandings of music that are common to its public and about which there is some measure of agreement.

On the other hand, its focus on the formal structure, musical elements, and rule systems that govern it may be too theoretical and may fail to attend sufficiently to the social and practical realities of music making and taking, with which there is not a one-to-one correspondence. Nor does it challenge the Western notion of music as a specialized art form or account satisfactorily for situations in which music as construed in the West integrates with other art forms within human rituals and for which there is no equivalent or specialized conception.[23] In its emphasis on musical products or works, it may pay insufficient attention to the unfolding or flow of sound through time and the process whereby the product is made. Seeing how something is made (or the process of creation) is not the same as seeing what is made (or the product or art work).[24] Nor does such a study or structural analysis of the end product (or drafts thereof) attend sufficiently to music that is improvised or created in the present as opposed to music that is composed ahead of time and brought to life later by the performer, where reflection-*in*-action rather than reflection-*after*-action is a primary consideration, or for which there is no score. And in its dualistic, either/or thinking, in its dichotomizing subject/object, inner/outer, reason/emotion, process/product, and so on, it may take insufficient account of the dialectical nature and interrelationship of these entities and the fuzzy boundaries of what is generally known in the West as music.

Music as Symbol

Related to the notion of music as aesthetic object is another view that achieved prominence in the latter part of the twentieth century and signifies how music is perceived and has meaning for its creators and publics. Writers who take this view of music include psychologists of music interested in studying how people listen to, perceive, think about or in, learn about, develop specific abilities and skills in, and make music, and philosophers who are interested in musical thought as a symbolic process and how music functions as a symbol system.[25] Articulating the nature of the musical symbol also requires acknowledging the importance of imagination and intuition as a means of understanding what is an inherently dense and ambiguous symbol system.[26]

Among the more recent symbolic interpretations of music is the idea of music as narrative. This view draws from literary criticism and history to see music as analogous to or expressive of myth and story through which music is understood, enacted, interpreted, criticized, and subverted. Viewed conservatively, narrative is perceived or read in the music, and it cannot be interpreted correctly without the benefit of particular narratives that constitute the particular perspectives through which music is interpreted and help shape what is created and understood.[27] As such, its approach "is subjective in that it depends on the education, intuition, and talent of the individual critic-interpreter" and thereby constitutes "a branch of hermeneutics."[28] Deconstructed as "a myth of the inner life," music informs one's deepest self, be it thought, felt, or otherwise inexpressible through ordinary discourse, and presents in a manner analogous to narrative.[29]

Postmodern writers go further to claim that the makers and takers of music literally endow it with the qualities of narrative as they challenge the power of the "dominant regimes" of "musical composition and reception," provide "a vehicle for both acculturation and resistance to acculturation," and deploy "narratographic strategies" or perform "narratographic rituals," often as an accompaniment to story which music sometimes overpowers.[30] The process of deconstruction invoked in these undertakings "aims at minimizing the authority that may be invested in potentially monolithic structures" and undertaking a creative, critical, and careful analysis of the musical situation that *"affirms"* as it also energizes.[31]

Going beyond figurative (be they metaphorical or analogical) constructions of music as narrative, music is taken to literally *function as or with* narrative. Whereas "musical works" remain the focus of music theorists (even in this more liberal view of music as narrative), recognizing musical rituals goes some way toward challenging the supremacy of the musical work over the process whereby it is made and blurring the boundaries between music and the other arts and social events with which it is associated. In contrast to the conservative position regarding music as narrative, which seems like the image of music as symbol although it is "read" mainly through the lens of literary criticism and historical scholarship, the postmodern view seems akin to, although it stops short of, the image of music as agency to be discussed below. Music of the Western classical tradition sometimes serves the explicit purposes of narrative—for example, instrumental, opera, and film music; however, the claims of music as narrative are particularly compelling for musics of other traditions. For example, Native American musics draw from, enact, and nourish the stories and myths of Native American peoples and can only be understood in terms of these narratives.[32]

The particular conceptual lenses, narratives, and discourses that frame music shape the specific meanings uncovered in musical study or expressed in music making. For example, Susan McClary and Catherine Clément deconstruct Western opera in the light of feminist theory in order to apprehend meanings traditionally hidden from view or taken for granted rather than examined critically; Philip Brett and his colleagues view music from the perspective of queer theory; Jacques Barzun and Ernst Fischer see music within Marxist thought; and James Martin understands art in theological terms.[33] Proponents of this image argue that every view of music is inherently particularistic and partial and that the interpretation of a musical piece or event reflects the ideological assumptions of its maker or taker. There is no such thing as "music alone" in the phenomenal world, and the perspectives, discourses, and narratives by which it is constituted or with which it is associated provide keys in unlocking musical thought and practice. And so the task of musical education in this view is to critically explicate these narratives, understand their wider significance in human life and culture, and even actively subvert the dominant discourses.

This view of music has several important strengths. Not only does it focus on how music functions rather than its ontological quality, but it also interprets what is heard and seen in the light of theoretical ideas through which these practices can be understood. It is a very cognitive view of music in its assumption that humans make music rationally and intentionally for reasons that may be understood in the light of the symbols and signs employed or referenced in music. In its emphasis on musical meaning, it recognizes music's role as mediator between the music maker and taker and that which is signified within the music. The variety of ways in which musical symbols function, whether as denotation, connotation, reference, or expression, helps to explain the relationship of music to other things with which it may be associated and provides a contextual perspective on the music that is broader than and different from the view of music as aesthetic object. Indeed, the possibility that music may refer to things beyond itself suggests that music may not be the focus of attention, as it is in the image of music as aesthetic object, but rather a means or accompaniment to other ends outside or beyond itself. Moreover, the perception of the musical symbol as affected by physical phenomena and apprehended psychologically opens the prospect of discovering how humans perceive musical sound, the reasons for particular musical preferences, and ways that incoming sensory data are processed, stored, and retrieved in memory, thereby prompting scientific investigations of musical perception and cognition. And although some writers take a quite narrow psychological or semiotic view of musical meaning, the image can be interpreted quite broadly to take account of the musical symbol as social and cultural construct.[34]

A narratological perspective recognizes the partiality and fallibility of knowledge, the contribution of discourse and narrative to framing perception and impacting understanding, the role of music as a part of and resistance to the dominant culture, and the interconnectedness of the various cultural elements. In its cultural and ideological focus, it points to the inherent subjectivity and interconnectedness of knowledge and seeks to explicate some of the grounding metaphors, stories, and discourses by which self or society as well as music are to be understood. That narrative is often chaotic and presses the frames in which it is constituted, as Lawrence Kramer observes, focuses on those tendencies in music and society that lie beyond the norm and are chaotic, subversive, and idiosyncratic. In cultures where the arts are fragmented, music as narrative may soften the sometimes artificial boundaries between the arts and provide a more holistic perspective on the arts in general and music in particular. And in de-centering musical beliefs and practices, it also re-centers the study of human nature and culture as an appropriate focus of musical study.[35]

On the other hand, the excessively cognitive thrust of this image may value and attend insufficiently to the practical activities of doing music and overlook the subjective and physical experience of music. Not only may this search for musical meaning overemphasize theoretical constructions that lie outside or beyond this music, thereby de-centering the music in the music curriculum, but it also may privilege music that is highly intellectualized and intended to be contemplated deeply and at length (typically the great traditions) over that which is purely entertainment and created for present ephemeral enjoyment (some little traditions).[36] And the fact that much music serves as an ordinary part of life to be felt or experienced ephemerally as an accompaniment to other activities, rather than as the focus or means of intellectual contemplation or a direct source of meaning making, challenges and subverts the ideal of musical profundity implicit in the view of music as symbol, at least within the Western classical tradition.

Its theoretical and critical perspectives presuppose the validity of the ideologies and narratives that constitute or frame music and can presumably unlock its beliefs and practices. In so doing, it may take insufficient cognizance of the flaws in these perspectives as ways of making, apprehending, and being in music or the claims of changing traditional beliefs and practices when necessary. In its more conservative view, music viewed as narrative risks the interpreter "reading into" music explanations that are fictions, or finding what one is predisposed to find within the music. For his part, Peter Kivy cautions that more philosophical work is needed on what "narrative" and "musical narration" really mean.[37] Notwithstanding the efforts of music theorists in the meantime, these definitions remain sketchy, somewhat uncritical of the literary criticism and history from whence they come. Even through this image blurs distinctions between music and other cultural elements, the music itself nevertheless remains in the foreground as a distinct entity more or less separate from other aspects of the culture in which it resides as a thing apart from the rest of life.[38] When music as narrative privileges the study of the musical work, it may fail to attend sufficiently to the acquisition of techniques and skills that enable one to go on practically as a musician or the blurred boundaries of what constitutes music. Just as it may be guilty of Eurocentrism if it applies Western musical perspectives to the analysis of other musical traditions, it may also misinterpret Western musics that have become specialized and separate from the other arts if it uncritically applies musical and other narratives that imply interrelated arts. In "softening" the boundaries between the arts, one also runs the risk of an ideological crusade on behalf of the more integrated arts of the past, romanticizing past fictions, or failing to be sufficiently true to the specialized art forms that Western musics have become and to the uniquely musical as opposed to narratological perspectives that characterize them. And given the unintended consequences of all human action, deconstructing and reconstructing music carries with it the possibility that one may be wrong and one's efforts may privilege a new ideology that may turn out to be just as oppressive or restrictive as those it seeks to replace.

Among the music curricula predicated on this musical image are many courses in the history and theory of music in which the search for musical meaning is undertaken with reference not only to the musical score but to evidence beyond the music, and courses in musical interpretation for performers.

For example, a pianist such as Alfred Brendel or Glenn Gould might study the extant evidence in the search for the best performance practice regarding this piece or pieces.[39] There are also school curricula that seek to integrate the arts and other school subjects construed as symbol systems.[40] Examples of music curricula that have explicit narratives include: Claire Detels' curriculum to cultivate the "soft boundaries" between the arts; courses intended to rectify gender imbalance in music by focusing on and integrating the music of women within the terms of feminist theory; Andrea Boyea's suggestions for a music curriculum that includes Native American musics understood in terms of Native American stories; courses in music anthropology in which the myths that ground the music provide frames of reference for music that expresses or refers to them; and ethnological or ethnomusicological approaches to music in which music is understood critically, comparatively, and contextually with reference to particular narratives without which it cannot be grasped.[41]

Music as Practical Activity

For the majority of musicians throughout history, music has been an activity, something done in the phenomenal world rather than thought about, and for the greater part of Western history, references to music were to the verb "to music" or to doing or making music in the phenomenal world through performing mainly improvised music. Despite the fact that Western classical music was regarded as a branch of philosophy in the medieval university, studied with the benefit of theoretical treatises by Boethius among other scholars, most musicians went on doing or making music in their homes, guilds, and churches, in private and in public, and the preparation of musicians was an inherently practical endeavor. Of course, the notion of "practical activity" is broad, and philosophers vary in their description of the nature and imperatives of music making. Among these views, Theodor Adorno examines the various practices of Western musicians and listeners; Howard treats these practical activities as matters of thought and action, governed by rule systems that are interpreted by performers; Francis Sparshott, Philip Alperson, and their colleagues focus on the systems of beliefs and practices that describe and prescribe what music makers and takers actually and should do; Small views music making as social rituals played out according to well defined rule-systems; Marie McCarthy and David Neuman think of these practical activities as traditions passed on orally from one generation to the next; and David Elliott thinks of musicing or the making of music at the center of musical education.[42] Musicians need to possess procedural knowledge in order to go on to do music; since the technical and critical skills acquired by experts are used primarily to make music in the phenomenal world rather than to theorize about it, the challenge for neophytes is to acquire this practical knowledge and be able to use it in making music. While practicing musicians think about music abstractly and theoretically, their primary focus is on what and how a song is to be sung, an instrument is to be played, and a dance is to be danced, and on satisfying the particular expectations of its exponents and public concerning when and how this should occur. Among the curricula exemplifying this view of music are those of the Associated Board of the Royal Schools of Music in the United Kingdom, the Royal Conservatory of Music in Canada, and the Australian Music Examinations Board, which are practical and performance-oriented (although they include theoretical and historical elements), and where students are examined on their ability to play their instruments before a jury at progressive levels of advancement. Indeed, the European conservatory was designed primarily in the interests of preparing performing musicians who also possessed a theoretical and historical understanding of music.[43] There are also the pervasively performance-oriented high school music programs in the United States in which teachers seek to pass on to their students the critical and technical skills required of exponents of particular musical practices.

The view of music as a practical activity highlights many different ways in which people make and take music throughout the world. Viewing music as a practice or a system of things that musicians and their publics generally do moves away from abstract ontological or metaphysical questions of music's significance toward the traditions and skills that are exemplified in the phenomenal world. Rather than looking beyond the actual practice to find some deeper theoretical or abstract significance, musical interest inheres in the practices and techniques themselves. Evidence of many musical systems that are more or less discrete and that may also overlap reveals a wide variety of ways in which people play with, create, and do interesting things with sounds, making meaning with and through them. They employ sounds along with visual means such as body painting, masks, costumes, and dances in rituals that mark significant life events such as birth, puberty, marriage, and death as well as informally for enjoyment and entertainment. In stressing music's part in culture as a communal as well as individual act, this image shows the human imagination at work and the many ways in which humanity is expressed. And in our time when things intellectual are often divorced from and regarded more highly than things practical, this image focuses on and validates practical activities as inherently rational and valuable.

On the other hand, emphasizing the practices that make up particular musical traditions may underplay the importance of the ideas and conceptions that give rise to or follow from them, or to which they refer. In focusing on the particular technical and critical thinking skills that need to be employed in a music's creation, performance, and reception, proponents of this view may overlook the underlying and theoretically perceived commonalities and generalizations between them. In its tendency to dichotomize the theoretical and practical worlds, this view may be as fallacious as is seeing music as aesthetic object when it creates false dichotomies between theoretical/practical, inner/outer, making/undergoing, generalization/particularity, and so on. Nor may this view take sufficient account of notions of music as sound imagined in contrast to sound heard in the phenomenal world, the experience of Western musicians who are able to hear a musical score imaginatively in advance of hearing it or without being able to physically hear it, or speculative or figurative views of music and music education evidenced in the recent writings of Joscelyn Godwin and June Boyce-Tillman, among others.[44] And where one's perspective is uncritical—for example, when instead of challenging or subverting a music practice, a teacher accepts it as it is and seeks to pass it on largely unchanged or unadulterated to one's students—one fails to take sufficient cognizance of practices that are flawed, oppressive, and in need of change, even transformation.

Music as Experience

The notion of music as experience is contingent on the idea of "experience," an idea mined particularly by Dewey.[45] Although the word *experience* is so philosophically problematical as to have become unfashionable in recent philosophical literature, Wayne Bowman has reclaimed it in his image of "music experienced."[46] If one takes a philosophically "hard" definition of experience, such as that described by Dewey in which when various symptoms are present (symptoms such as its inherent subjectivity, an interaction between the person and the environment that is significant and potentially life-changing so that the impact of the present situation leaves a permanent trace, in which the interaction with the environment in the present situation is linked inexorably with those that precede and follow it), experience can be presumed, it is possible to reclaim the word *experience* as the basis for a musical image. Writers in music and music education in the phenomenological tradition following Edmund Husserl include Alfred Schutz, Alfred Pike, Douglas Bartholomew, F. Joseph Smith, Lawrence Ferrara, Judy Lockhead, Arnold Berleant, and Harris Berger.[47] Among the music educators to articulate the artist's subjective experience, the nature of musical feeling, a sense of musical unfolding and musical "flow," the role of play, and the nature of the thinking that constitutes a key to musical experience, one thinks of the recent work of such writers as Yaroslav Senyshyn, Eleanor Stubley, Mary Reichling, Iris Yob, Anthony Palmer, and David Elliott.[48] Still other psychologists seek to discover scientific laws that help to explain processes of musical perception, cognition, preference, and development.[49] All of these views emphasize the person's subjective grasp of music in a variety of ways either described and catalogued philosophically or tested empirically and descriptively. So while specifically phenomenological assumptions may constitute too restrictive a view of this image, the various ways in which experience is construed focus on the individual's interaction with music in whatever role, be it composer, performer, or listener. That this experience is inherently subjective makes it less amenable to scientific investigation, although music psychologists presume that individual behaviors regarding music are sufficiently robust to serve as indicators of subjective experience. Music curricula predicated on this image typically emphasize opportunities for students to interact actively in the process of music making and taking whether as composers, performers, or listeners, in ways that are very accessible. Instead of focusing on the acquisition of technical and critical skills as evident in the view of music as practice, this image allows for the possibility for people to articulate the nature of their specific musical experiences through such means as journals, conversations, and musical artifacts (for example, solo and ensemble performances in traditional settings, recordings, Web sites, and electronically generated performances). Whether it be through improvised music making; mixed media; composition; or experimental, computer-based, Internet-driven, and interactive music curricula employing compositional software, sound sampling and generation, and the like, the objective of such curricula is to get past the sometimes tedious acquisition of techniques to experience music directly through acting as musicians.[50]

Among the insights of this view, its emphasis on the direct and actively personal albeit subjective experience of music highlights music's expressive role as a means of communication and the importance of creative thinking and play as a way of being human. Schiller, among others, sees play as the highest level of human existence in which reason and imagination, mind and body are involved.[51] The notion of music as play elevates music making and taking, doing and undergoing as ways of knowing. Going beyond traditional music perspectives to forge new ones validates the creativity of thought and practice integral to music among the other arts and pushes back the frontiers of belief and practice. Emphasizing the inherent subjectivity of musical experience verifies other ways of knowing that are not scientific or objective and fosters divergent thought and practice. And utilizing means that bypass the acquisition of techniques standing in the way of access to musical experience, whether as composer, performer, or listener, can make musical experience more immediate and broadly accessible and can overcome the barriers between expert practitioners and neophytes. For example, the fact that it is no longer necessary to perform a Bach piece live in order to hear it and that one may now program a computer to play the piece, change Bach's score, and synthesize the desired sound of the computer realization in ways that Bach may not have imagined makes it possible to get around acquiring technical skills required in the past and, through various means, directly compose, perform, produce, record, and listen to music.

On the other hand, this view may not sufficiently attend to the widely held traditions that a musical practice comprises, or the acquisition of technical skills needed for live musical performance without which a tradition eventually dies.[52] In emphasizing the subjective nature of musical experience, it may overlook the more objective, dispassionate judgments and assessments that are regularly made about music by such persons as music critics, competition adjudicators, or concert audiences. As such, it may attend insufficiently to the formation of widely held social perspectives that seem more objective and on which there is often considerable and widespread agreement. The assumptions underlying this musical image also make it difficult to observe and test reports of musical experience. Phenomenological observations may be difficult to verify or refute because they are, by definition, inherently subjective, and scientific observations may be suspect because they rely on unrealistic assumptions about the musical event that cannot be finally validated. One is therefore left with a musical image that is fallacious in the sense that it is predicated on circular reasoning and on assumptions that cannot be challenged, verified, or refuted.

Music as Agency

The image of music as agency refers, among other things, to the instrumental value of music as a means of attaining certain political, social, religious, psychological, educational, or economic ends and moral virtues, thereby oppressing or liberating people, transforming musical and educational traditions and society at large, and foreshadowing the future society.[53] Here musical value arises because of the importance of its instrumental purposes rather than from its intrinsic merit as music for music's sake. Like music as narrative, music as agency serves other ends beyond itself. Unlike music as narrative, music as agency constitutes a means of attaining these other ends. As a social, political, religious, economic, and psychological force, music both reflects institutional and personal values and helps shape the institutions of which it is a part and the individuals that make up its public. It may be used to oppress and to liberate, as an agency of domination and a means of subversion, as a way of silencing some and giving voice to others, for good and evil. Its power as a means of effecting change in the individual and society arises from the fact that it is intuitively and imaginatively known and felt, even before beliefs and practices are worked through and reflected on logically. As it is played and sung, it constitutes a means of educating mind and body that is direct and holistic, its significance felt before it can necessarily be explained. And it acts, in the individual as well as in society at large, as leaven in the lump, infusing the whole gradually and imperceptibly. For those with particular agendas, such as the attainment of democratic ideals, moral virtues, social change in particular directions, equitably distributed and publicly supported education, and specific standards of musical practice, music is judged with reference to its efficacy in the realization of these agendas rather than by virtue of its artistic or specifically musical qualities. Among the curricula that embrace this image, there are those based on religious or liturgical music designed to serve the Christian church, such as in the Church of England choir schools; the songs of the labor movement in the United States used in some labor-supported colleges; marching band programs that benefit athletic programs; and ideologically driven music courses that expose and seek to rectify racism, sexism, homophobia, and classism, among other prejudices that the music teacher may seek to expose and root out.[54] The belief that music is a powerful agency in affecting individual as well as social beliefs, moral values, and behaviors for good or evil leads teachers to censor musical repertoire deemed

undesirable and to emphasize songs that in their texts and styles exhibit particular desirable beliefs and moral values.[55] Hence, school music textbooks
are selected carefully and reviewed critically to ensure that musical materials
accord with the purposes of those responsible for the education of the young.[56]

Among the contributions of this image is the notion that music is dynamic,
in process of being transformed, and integrally related to the society of
which it is a part. Also interesting is the insight that as a powerful educational agent, music can be both oppressive and liberating, and much hangs
on the particular purposes of those who use it and the specific uses to which
it is put. The idea that these socially construed meanings may not be immediately apparent and require explanation and criticism allies this image to
notions of music as symbol or narrative and draws particular attention to the
beliefs and practices of the makers and takers of music. Justifying the
instrumental values of music in societies preoccupied with economic and
material rather than artistic values is also likely to be more persuasive than
justifications based on its inherent or intrinsic value expressed as "music for
music's sake." In such societies, not only are these other things more readily
observed and counted, but they are valued more highly than music. Also,
such views open the door to polemics that emphasize music's instrumental
value and forward such notions as "strong arts" develop "strong schools" or
musical study develops social skills and improves intellectual capacity or performance in other school subjects—views that may be persuasive for those
educators or members of the public who would otherwise not value music
and musical study for its own sake.[57]

Notwithstanding its insights, this view is also flawed. Not only may it over-
state the power of music to effect social change or prophesy the future, but
also its claims may be difficult to test, especially since the psychological and
sociological aspects of music are subjectively apprehended. Researchers, as
creatures of society, cannot observe people objectively, because their posi-
tionality or relation to the particular individuals and social systems being
studied affects their perspectives or "assumptive frames of reference," which
are always partial and biased.[58] So refuting the truth claims of proponents of
this musical image is difficult if not impossible to achieve. As with the image
of music as experience, the observer may need to be content to *describe* rather
than *explain* what is seen, because explanation, at least in the scientific sense,
is impossible, and claims to the contrary are fallacious. In emphasizing the
agency of music, proponents of this image may not attend sufficiently to the
nature of music itself or recognize sufficiently its sometimes static as opposed
to dynamic quality. Musical traditions are not always in process of dramatic
change, as periods of musical history in which the rate of innovation was
quite slow clearly demonstrate. Time scales in which this process of agency
and transformation are conceived or the speed of musical change—for example, the transformation of Gregorian chant into the electronified music of
today—over a period of hundreds of years[59] are also disjunct from those of

human lives lived in a matter of decades. This musical image may be useful in describing historical events, but it may be less helpful in predicting future changes. And the demonstrable resilience and power of institutional mores even in the face of "grassroots" changes in the particular perspectives of individuals challenges the notion that through changing the intellectual perspectives of one's students, one can thereby guarantee change in their behavior and in musical and social practice. Thus, when pressed to put their visionary ideas into practice, advocates of educational transformation such as Freire and Parker Palmer may start with a cellular "grassroots" approach but inevitably wind up calling for concerted political and institutional action.[60] And music teachers seeking to transform music, education, and society require institutional as well as individual change.

Mechanisms of Musical Transformation

At least three mechanisms are involved in musical transformation. The first centers on the cultural context in which music making and taking transpires and its impact upon music and music instruction. The second is grounded in the nature of music; particularly, the symbolic nature of the music and its interpretation, the nature of the musical event, and the character of musical taste. And the third relates to the musical transmission process; notably, the ways in which musical beliefs and practices are passed on from one generation to the next. While conceptually distinct, these mechanisms are practically interrelated; however, for expository purposes, they need to be sketched separately. Leaving aside the discussion of cultural context, which I have taken up at length elsewhere, I focus here on mechanisms relating to the nature of music and the ways in which music is transmitted from one generation to another.

The Nature of Music

The five dialectical images of music that I have sketched—aesthetic object, symbol, practical activity, experience, and agency—could each be systematically teased out to show how musical ambiguities and tensions contribute to musical transformation. However, it suffices for my present purpose to highlight elements of these images to show how musical change is inevitable over time.

The ambiguous nature of music conceived as aesthetic object and musical symbol and the role of imagination in interpreting it are useful places to start. In taking this tack toward the arts, Goodman suggests four "symptoms of the aesthetic"—namely, syntactic density, semantic density, syntactic repleteness, and exemplification—which provide philosophical grounds for explaining why artistic transformation is likely to occur.[61] Syntactic and semantic density refer to the highly nuanced structural characteristics and meanings of artistic symbols. Respectively, syntactic repleteness refers to the richness of artistic symbols and the fact that they seem not only complete in themselves but apart from ordinary life, and exemplification refers to the fact that import tends to inhere in the art work and cannot be divorced from it, although I prefer the word *expression* to denote the relationship between the art work and its significance, seeing that it invokes a transformative quality that goes beyond exemplification.[62] These qualities not only contribute to a high degree of ambiguity in certain respects and precision in others, but they require imaginative thought to interpret within artistic experience.

As a notated tradition, the musical score in Western classical music, while containing precise note marks, also possesses elements that are open to divergent interpretation, and this ambiguity sparks the imagination as the musician brings the score to life.[63] The possibility of differing readings and interpretations contributes to the dynamic quality of musical transformation, its metamorphosis from one expectation-set to another, and its imaginative quality. This precision of the score in some respects and its ambiguity in others, and the fact that it presages, accompanies, or follows a live performance, undergirds the dialectical and active-reflective nature of musical transformation. Its spiritual and inspirational value as a record of the composer's intention, insofar as that can be determined, and its role in preserving past practice not only grounds musical transformation and serves as a check on it but also clarifies the extent to and directions in which it occurs.

Metamorphic changes may seem relatively subtle, such as the progressive changes in concert pitch or tempi expectations over the past four centuries, or more dramatic, such as the changes from the suggestive notation of the seventeenth-century figured bass to the more prescriptive notation of the late nineteenth century and the graphic notation of the mid-twentieth century, or from tonal to atonal music in the mid-twentieth century. And the systemic quality of musical transformation arises in the score itself; the score is an expression of human feeling through marks that denote dynamic, timbral, rhythmic, pitch, and formal elements of music, which are interpreted variously by composer, performer, and listener. For example, composers may take for granted certain aspects of musical practice and therefore not notate them. If a common practice is lost, for one reason or another, the score may be interpreted differently, or changes in performance practice may be made deliberately that may transform music more dramatically. Alternatively, seeing that the score clarifies specific aspects of a musical style, it also enables a new style to be readily distinguished or demarcated from an old one.

Take the well-known case of J.S. Bach. His sons studied his scores yet set off to distinguish themselves from their father and to write in new, different, and more popular styles. Over time, the elder Bach's music was gradually lost, and when it was revived in the nineteenth century by such musicians as Felix Mendelssohn, some of the knowledge that Bach would have presumed his musicians to have possessed had disappeared. For example, thorough bass realization and improvisation had been largely replaced by virtuosic performance and score interpretation in which the composer left relatively little to the performer's discretion. New instruments had been invented and were in common use. The sound of Bach's music (as realized from available scores) was very different from what Bach would have heard and would have sounded strange to audiences accustomed to other musical sounds and practices. It wasn't until the latter twentieth century that the extent of differences between eighteenth-century and modern performance practice came to be more fully appreciated, and the degree to which music had been transformed in the interim more clearly evident.

In oral traditions, without the score as a guide, musical performance must rely on human memory, and one might expect oral traditions to be more fragile than those that are notated. However, this need not be the case. Music is an eminently practical and oral/aural art, and even in literate traditions, the musical score serves mainly as an adjunct to the orally transmitted details of performance practice. Music's vulnerability arises from the fact that it must be brought to life or realized in or through performance. Scores and audiovisual recordings may be aids to preserving knowledge about performance, but they do not constitute procedural knowledge or knowledge gained from doing the music, whether composing, performing, or knowing "how to go on in" it.[64] Nor should one underestimate the human memory. For example, Roman chant was preserved for centuries before being written down. Even then, it continued as an oral tradition, notwithstanding that particular versions were preserved for posterity in musical scores. Despite the evolution of Roman chant between the fifth and fifteenth centuries of the Christian era, the rapidity and extent of musical transformation during this time seems to have been less dramatic than that in succeeding centuries, when there was greater recourse to musical scores and when sacred repertory broadened to include many styles and forms. Somewhat paradoxically, it seems that the greater the use of scores and recorded performances, the faster and more dramatic was the musical transformation. An explanation of this paradox may lie in the role of the score and recording in clarifying past and present practice, inviting diverse interpretations of it, and prompting divergence from it toward new performance practices, forms, and styles, and the rapidity of changes in the environment in which it was made, seen, and heard.

Whether music is notated or not, the nature of the musical event—specifically, the functions of composition, performance, listening, production, marketing, and distribution—fosters musical transformation. Historically, and in other musical traditions outside the West, these roles seem to be less specialized than they are typically in Western classical music, although their independence may have been exaggerated by some contemporary writers.[65] My point in distinguishing them here is not to suggest that they ought to be so specialized but to focus on them as ideal or theoretical types that may, practically speaking, overlap one another. Nor do I see them in a linear order of priority, from the composer who is the architect of music and the source of musical creativity, to the performer who mediates the composer's intention, to the lowly listener who takes it all in. Rather, the composer, performer, and listener, along with the host of other actors in the musical event, including sound and recording engineer, impresario, marketing agent, stage director, set and lighting designer, marketing executive, and distribution agent, are necessary actors in contemporary musical practice. All are involved in the making and taking of music. Although their particular interests and tasks differ, all participants in the musical process have something important to offer, and they each may bring an imaginative and creative perspective to the process. Changes within any one of these elements can lead to musical transformation.

The possibilities for musical transformation through composition and improvisation are self-evident. The composer works through a musical idea, either before or during performance, through improvisation guided partly by expectations on the part of a public and also by a human desire to create something extraordinary. I see this activity as motivated by the desire to play, to celebrate, and to invent and by the urge for immortality, transcendence, and otherness that fuel human aspirations to excel, to create things of meaning and worth that are admired by others, and to be remembered not only as persons but for their work. These human qualities and aspirations seem widespread. It is small wonder that the ancients thought that to play was to be like the gods and associated music with the supernatural because of its playful and spiritual significance and power. The resilience of ideas concerning the relationship between music, play, and spirituality is so ingrained and widespread as to be almost commonsensical.[66] Seeing that the composer wishes to create music that can be interpreted by the performer, responded to by the dancer, or grasped by the listener, she or he must take into account the performer's, dancer's, or listener's expectation-sets while at the same time tantalizing, daring, and stretching him or her with the unexpected. As Nicholas Cook notes,[67] failing to take into account what listeners are able to hear leaves the composer out of touch with the audience, and failing to interest them sufficiently results in listener boredom. The composer's role in bringing a musical idea to life while keeping the performer, dancer, or audience in mind is key to the transformative quality of music. Whether it be Margaret Bond, Cécile Chaminade, Libby Larsen, Ethel Smyth, Joan Tower, or Ellen Taafe Zwillich, each composer brings her own unique perspective to bear on the task of fashioning a musical train of thought that is realized in performance and delights, entertains, or is grasped by listeners.[68] The process of musical transformation continues as some of these innovations gradually become incorporated into standard practice while others are abandoned.

Distinctions between composition and improvisation hinge on differences between reflection before performance and reflection in the midst of performance.[69] The composer, on the one hand, has the opportunity to work out an idea more or less fully and in a personally satisfying way before the performance; she or he has time beforehand to shape a musical piece, develop a musical train of thought, and work out intricately, if she or he wishes, all or most of the salient details of the musical piece. The composer's imagination, intuition, and reason are involved in planning the piece in advance of hearing it in live performance. The improviser, on the other hand, while possibly sketching a performance ahead of time, seizes the moment and capitalizes on serendipitous opportunities offered in the performance itself; in the midst of the performance, he or she brings past experience and a repertoire of ideas and techniques to bear in playing imaginatively and intuitively with musical ideas and evolving a musical train of thought that draws from the live performance as much as from ideas in advance of it.

The performer also plays an important role in musical transformation. Along with obligations to a particular musical practice, and, in literate traditions, to the musical score, the performer brings a personal interpretation influenced by her or his personality and the ambiguity of the musical practice or score.[70] In literate traditions, a composition obligates the performer to be faithful to the musical score and to what the performer knows of the composer's intentions, qualities of sound, performance practice, and personal sense of how to interpret it so as to reveal it in the best possible light for contemporary audiences. An improvisation, on the other hand, frees the performer to compose in the midst of performance although bound to some extent by listeners' expectations and the performance practice in which he or she works. There is a wide variation in the amount of leeway the Western classical performer is afforded. For example, the early-seventeenth-century operatic singer could ornament the melodic line quite freely, whereas the early-nineteenth-century singer typically had much less freedom in this respect; the eighteenth-century instrumentalist was permitted to improvise to a far greater degree than her or his nineteenth-century counterpart; and a late-twentieth-century chorus might have freedom to improvise graphic notation, while an early-twentieth-century choir had few such opportunities for improvisation. Within these limits, ambiguities of tempo, instrumentation, dynamic, articulation, timbre, and pitch make possible individual readings or interpretations of musical compositions. The performer approaches the score or musical practice with an assumptive frame of reference influenced by various psychological, social, and cultural factors.[71] These bear both on the musician's particular take on the score or musical practice and on the risks he or she is willing to take in performance. As a result of this complex array of factors, musicians will interpret the score or musical practice more or less individualistically. Depending on how these performances are received by their public, some innovations are accepted while others are ignored or rejected, thereby contributing to musical transformation.

Musical transformation also occurs through the related medium of the dance. Historically, much Western classical music was intended to be danced; witness the array of social dances preserved from ancient times and formalized in choric dramas, suites, and ballets.[72] Langer takes the dance as her metaphor for the livingness, expressiveness, and dynamic properties of the arts.[73] The dancers not only respond to the musical sound through creating an array of formally choreographed or improvised movements, but they inspire the creation of music to fit their movements. The ambiguities of dance and music are mutually reinforcing, contributing over time to musical transformation.

The listener likewise contributes to musical transformation. Listening lies along a continuum between active and passive, active when music forms the center of focal awareness, and passive when it is heard as background in peripheral awareness.[74] The degree to which music is in the foreground or background of perceptual awareness affects the way the listener is receiving and thinking about or through it. I see each of the distinctions between active and passive listening and between focal and peripheral awareness as weak syndromes in which one runs into the other, and I like Howard's distinction between the awareness that can be articulated discursively and awareness that remains inarticulate through ordinary discourse, although I suspect that this distinction likewise constitutes a weak syndrome. Some may wish to impose stringent conditions on the listener, including the necessity of active musical listening, qualities that Copland's "gifted listener" possesses.[75] Historically, however, it seems that musical events have more often than not included the entire gamut of active and passive listeners. This phenomenon can be explained simply in terms of the role of music as a social event and by the fact that people have different motivations for participating in a musical event, active listening being only one of them. Being seen to be present on a particular occasion, enjoying the company of another person who enjoys this music, and employing music for relaxation or worship or while doing other things are all motivations for musical listening. Kivy's example from E. M. Forster's *Howards End* of Mrs. Munt, who taps "surreptitiously when the tunes come"; Helen, who sees "heroes and shipwrecks in the music's flood"; Margaret, "who can only see the music"; and Tibby, who "is profoundly versed in counterpoint, and holds the full score open on his knee" illustrates the varied ways in which listeners hear music.[76] Each person is imaginatively listening, although the images and associations this music evokes and the degrees of concentration upon it differ from one person to another. All are listening "respectably"—Mrs. Munt responding physically to the melodies she hears, Helen to the associative images this music conjures up, Margaret to the musical sounds themselves, and Tibby to the musical elements conveyed in the score. Even the musically educated Tibby may find his attention wandering away from the music in the midst of a performance. Kivy's example is interesting because it suggests significant differences among and between listeners in response to musical ambiguity. These divergent listening experiences (like those of composer and performer) not only destabilize the musical experience but contribute to musical transformation as listeners gradually come to value some music or ways of listening to it over others.

Music production has come to be an important aspect of contemporary musical life, and it likewise serves as a transformative agent. Through such means as instrument manufacture, sound recording and amplification, acoustical engineering, and set and lighting design, technology has radically altered the nature of musical events by providing new and different means of music making—for example, more powerful instruments, higher volume, computer-generated sound, and mediated music or music propagated through mass media.[77] Whereas music might once have been heard only in live performance, the possibilities for hearing recorded music are ubiquitous; where music might once not have required amplification in the relatively small and intimate concert spaces, sound is now generally filtered and amplified electronically in today's large concert halls and opera houses. Likewise, recording engineers play a vital role in generating and capturing a performance, and through sound sampling, splicing, mixing, microphone placement, and other sophisticated technical means, engineers literally "produce" the recorded performance. The invention of digital audio and video systems has significantly changed the sound quality of recordings and broadened the physical and situational characteristics of venues in which classical music is heard to include the home, workplace, park, business, and vehicle. Changes in production technologies, among others, have contributed to musical transformation by making possible new and different musical events.

In an era when music is commercialized and repeated,[78] marketing constitutes an agent of musical transmission as a principal way by which music makers reach the takers of music. This is especially true in our own time, when music has become an internationalized commodity and a few multinational corporations control the vast proportion of music distribution internationally.[79] Such companies are often highly integrated in the sense that they can supply the entertainment and the means of accessing it. For example, Sony owns recording contracts with artists; recording studios; film-making units; television, radio, and cable stations; and movie houses, and it manufactures radios, televisions, and other audiovisual equipment. Artists are dependent on marketing themselves and their music, and marketing is crucial in determining which musicians will become stars. The tastes and preferences of those in the music industry are often driven by a desire for financial reward, and thereby by popular demand, and marketers help shape the music that is pitched, heard, and otherwise promoted and, ultimately, public musical taste. For example, the media hype surrounding appearances of the "Three Tenors" or stars such as Wynton Marsalis, Yo-Yo Ma, Jessye Norman, or Kiri Te Kanawa reveals the important role of marketing in late-twentieth-century classical music. The public's memory is also fairly short. Shortly after their retirement, twentieth-century operatic stars Joan Sutherland and Janet Baker were superseded by other rising divas with different voices, interests, and talents. The process of transformation goes on as one generation of musicians replaces another and each in turn is marketed to the public in changing ways that reflect the specific means available and that emphasize the particular gifts and personalities of musicians and the public's changing tastes.

Besides the nature of the musical symbol and the various functions of music makers and takers sketched above, musical taste also contributes to the transformation of the musical experience. In his classic study of musical taste, Paul Farnsworth outlines general principles that he believes have universal application; these are extended in recent research and worth revisiting.[80] Farnsworth suggests that musical taste is a social-psychological phenomenon and that groups understand the musics with which they identify in more or less common ways. Taste is like fashion in that it changes, sometimes slowly and incrementally, sometimes quickly and dramatically. The more deeply it is ingrained in social mores, the more it resists transformation. Farnsworth's documentation of the resilience of musical taste and its susceptibility to change over time is reinforced by John Mueller's landmark study of the American symphony orchestra, in which he likewise evidences changes in orchestral composition and repertoire, popularity of composers, and musical taste over the latter part of the nineteenth century and early part of the twentieth century.[81]

During the twentieth century, popular musical taste cycles shortened significantly, from years to months, weeks, and even days. Whereas in the past an artist or a piece of music might remain popular for a long period of time, popularity became quite ephemeral. I think, for example, of Elton John's Grammy award–winning song, "Candle in the Wind," rewritten for the occasion of Princess Diana's funeral, which sold millions of copies in a matter of weeks and continued selling well because of its connection with the tragic death of a public icon. While its influence lingered, newspapers soon went on to record other musical events such as the Rolling Stones' *Bridges to Babylon* world tour and the opening of Paul Simon's musical, *The Capeman,* among a host of other events that diverted the public's attention elsewhere, to be superseded in turn by others, until they all sank eventually into the background of public consciousness.[82] Likewise, recordings and performances of the musical *Titanic* (which opened several months before the film of the same name) captivated the public's attention for several months. The story of the sinking of the Titanic, a twentieth-century myth, and music's role in supporting, capturing, and expressing this myth help to explain the musical's comparative longevity. Part of the reason for this reduction in the length of musical taste cycles may lie in the massive marketing and promotion of artists required in today's music scene and in the fact that the public's attention is constantly distracted by a rapidly changing array of musical events being promoted in the media and on the Internet.

This situation also exists in classical music. It too must be marketed, and fashions come and go. In the late twentieth century, for example, I recall the media interest in Gilbert Kaplan's conducting of Mahler's Symphony no. 2 (*Resurrection*), the popularity of the albums *Chant* and *Chant II*, the appearance of William Bolcom's *McTeague*, John Corigliano's Symphony no. 1 inspired by the AIDS crisis, duets between Placido Domingo and John Denver, the film soundtrack *Shine,* and Steven Hough's electrifying performance of Lowell Liebermann's second piano concerto dedicated to him, among a host of other events. Some classical artists have great resiliency; witness twentieth-century pianists Annie Fischer, Alfred Brendel, Artur Rubinstein, and Vladimir Horowitz; conductors Sarah Caldwell, Leonard Bernstein, and Georg Solti; and film composer and conductor John Williams, to name a few. Likewise, some musical repertoire remains popular for decades, even centuries; witness the programming in late-twentieth-century opera houses still dominated by nineteenth-century repertoire,[83] and the longevity of music by such eighteenth-century composers as Handel and Bach.

In explaining why some music seems to last while other music is quickly forgotten, Charles Ives distinguished between musical substance and manner, substance referring to music's inner spiritual quality, and manner its outward sensuous style.[84] At first glance, Ives's hypothesis that musical substance contributes to musical longevity because style is more closely tied to a particular time and place, whereas substance seems to transcend time and place, is intriguing because it seems true that some music more easily transcends particular places and times than others. For example, Mozart's music appeals to Eastern musicians; its qualities of elegance, precision, balance, inventiveness, and melodic interest seem to resonate with traditional values prized in the East.[85] Likewise, Western classical composers have been fascinated by other musical cultures and have incorporated them into their compositions; witness Claude Debussy's and Carl Orff's fascination with the Balinese gamelan, and Leonard Bernstein's and George Gershwin's use of jazz. The fact that composers perceive a music's substantive quality and import it into another music or musical style might seem to support the idea that musical substance is a potent quality determining the ability of music to transcend a particular style.

I am less sure, however, that substance and manner are as discrete as Ives believed them to be or that he is right in explaining musical longevity mainly in terms of this distinction. His thesis is problematical for at least two reasons. First, if substance and style constitute a weak syndrome, it is difficult, practically speaking, to determine the vanishing point of substance and the starting point of style. For example, the jazz idiom and style are imported along with its melodic, harmonic, and rhythmic features into Gershwin's *Rhapsody in Blue,* Duke Ellington's concert pieces, or Bernstein's *West Side Story,* and rock music into performances by the Kronos Quartet. Second, if musical syntax constitutes the primary interest in musical meaning making, Ives's notion of musical substance (which carries with it the connotation of musical semantic) may be questioned on the same grounds on which notions of musical semantic have been challenged. Semiotic analyses of music and studies of classical music's specific semantic inevitably flounder on the shoals of music's inherent ambiguity, abstract quality, and subjective appeal.[86] If one allows Kivy's point that musical interest is more likely to be syntactical, especially in the case of absolute music,[87] and if syntax is inevitably tied to style, then music's longevity and transferability must also be explained stylistically, and the practical grounds for distinguishing substance and manner are weakened. For these reasons, while it may be useful to retain the substance-manner distinction as a weak syndrome construed figuratively rather than literally in order to conceptually map various sorts of musical interest, I doubt that musical substance holds the key to musical longevity that Ives believed it possessed or to the intermusical transference to which I have alluded. Instead, as I have indicated, a complex set of psychological, social, and cultural factors seems to come into play.

Much of the time, musical interest is not formal but functional. It serves primarily as a means of agency. It entertains, brings pleasure, constitutes a diversion, and accompanies ritual and dance. In these cases, the connections between music, psychology, and society are especially important in explaining why some music has longevity and other music is of passing interest, if any at all. For example, the continuing popularity and appeal over decades of the Titanic myth to which I have referred—a tragedy that highlights inhumanity, greed, and the failure of technology in the face of natural disaster— may help to explain the continuing popularity and appeal of the film soundtrack, musical, and other literary and artistic expressions of this myth.

Even allowing for the fuzzy edges of what is music, and for the bias of this analysis toward Western classical music, I have suggested that each of the musical images is prone to ambiguity and imaginative transformation as it is brought to life from time to time and place to place. To the degree that it is conceived of as aesthetic object, symbolically, experientially, as practical activity, or agency, music is a living, vital *thing* that is prone to change just as it is also prone to be preserved for posterity. The notion that music is not a "thing," as Small claims, is philosophical nonsense.[88] Each of the foregoing images may be thought of as a "thing"—even Small's own image of music as social ritual—and, as I have already shown, there is plenty of philosophical and empirical evidence for music's being thought of in these varying ways, and any number of people around the world who believe they know what it is.

Musical Transmission

I have suggested in earlier writing that musical groups coalesce around particular musics, are more or less identified with them, and share a particular musical taste.[89] Such groups tend to become institutionalized, as does the music with which they are associated. The fact that these musical groups and institutions are dynamic contributes to, and acts as a brake on, musical transformation. One of the ways in which musical taste is shaped is through the process of musical transmission, whereby musical knowledge is passed from one generation to the next. Agents of musical education selectively transmit traditional beliefs and practices and frame new ones; their reach extends far beyond school-age musical instruction to include the musical activities of the various societal institutions such as the family, religion, state, music profession, and commerce. The nineteenth and twentieth centuries also witnessed the emergence and institutionalization of a classical music profession, which took increasing responsibility for the systematic transmission of classical music from one generation of musicians to the next. Alongside the universities, which provided academic musical training, conservatories emerged to prepare professional performers for the concert stage, opera house, symphony orchestra, and choir.[90] The classical music profession also became involved in preparing music teachers for elementary and secondary schools as well as fostering systematic private instrumental instruction for the young. Recitalists, opera managers, orchestra and choral conductors, and critics sought to educate their public through their repertoire, program notes, and published critical commentaries on compositions and performances. In these and other ways, the music profession emerged as a principal agent for musical transmission in our time.

Howard's analysis of the ways in which artistic learning takes place through means of instruction, practice, example, and reflection forms an excellent starting point for examining the process of musical transmission in the context of formal education.[91] Seeing that musical transmission goes well beyond formal education to encompass informal education, however, I extend his taxonomy to include osmosis, participation, observation, and sensibility–types that serve as counterpoints to and in dialectic with his and collectively map some of the attributes of informal music education. This dialectical view serves as a broader basis on which to understand the transformative nature of musical transmission than Howard's focus on formal instruction.

In learning by *instruction*, Howard refers to the teacher's formal or didactic exposition by which the student grasps knowledge. This exposition and explanation is of two sorts, although, practically speaking, one melds into the other; the first concerns the transmission of propositional knowledge, or Gilbert Ryle's "knowing that" such-and-such is the case; the second refers to passing on of procedural knowledge, or Ryle's "knowing how" to do something in the sense of being able to do it.[92] Howard is careful to distinguish instruction from teacher instructions, which are specific directions to the student and often, although not always, procedural in nature. In musical instruction, for example, one thinks of a music historian lecturing about the symphonies of Giovanni Battista Sammartini to her class, or a flautist instructing his master class on breathing technique. This is in contrast to the teacher giving instructions about how a term paper is to be prepared or how students are to practice breathing exercises in the context of their practice sessions. Howard does not seem to be saying that instruction is limited to exposition; rather, it may also include questioning and discussion. Whatever the specific method, the teacher is intent on imparting certain information or wisdom to students and on inculcating rules that govern behavior, whether individually or in groups, in an organized and formal way. Given the limitations of time and space, and the costs of musical teaching and learning, instruction provides an efficient means of musical transmission.

The student's task is to grasp the ideas and practices being taught, know about and how to do them, and integrate this knowledge within her or his emerging musical understanding. Learning by this means involves the application of reason, coming to understand the logical and practical rules that undergird particular beliefs and practices and gradually acquiring a formal as opposed to idiosyncratic grasp of the subject matter in question. For example, the student gradually comes to see that musical ornamentation is a systematic array of turns, trills, mordants, slides, and the like; that there are systems of rules for each particular practice and each particular ornament; and he or she comes to know when to apply each and when to bend a rule or ignore it in a particular situation. Because musical knowledge is highly nuanced, instruction provides a convenient way whereby the student grasps its complexity and acquires a comprehensive and systematic musical understanding.

By contrast, *osmosis* entails absorbing knowledge without the benefit of direct instruction or learning through indirect or informal instruction. In its literal sense, osmosis refers to the physical mechanism whereby one thing absorbs elements of another; for example, an egg boiled in salt water literally absorbs salt through its shell. In its figurative sense, however, osmosis refers to the process whereby the student, even if in a context not intended to be overtly or primarily instructional or educational, nevertheless acquires propositional and procedural knowledge through observing or participating in musical events. For example, a music student attends a recital or performs in an ensemble, thereby acquiring knowledge about literature, performance practice, and rehearsal and performance decorum without necessarily being formally instructed in these things. This knowledge is intuitive in that the student may grasp it holistically, rhapsodically, and idiosyncratically. It is also imaginative in that the student perceives an event and feels, senses, or reflects on its significance. As a result, osmotic knowledge may be unsystematic because the student selectively gathers that knowledge in which he or she is most interested or that seems most immediately relevant or interesting.

Each approach has its strengths and limitations. Instruction, as conceived by Howard, benefits from the teacher's organized presentation of information to the student and from the student's acquisition of a comprehensive, systematic, and logical grasp of the subject matter and the rules that undergird practice. However, it may be dogged by passivity or resistance on the part of the student when the teacher seeks to pour information into the student, and it may stunt individual initiative, divergent thinking, and transformative action on the student's part. On the other hand, osmosis may take advantage of a student's initiative, imagination, and intuition in grasping subject matter in the context of a wide array of musical events. However, it may result in an unsystematic knowledge of the subject matter that relies too heavily on the student's initiative and insight in the learning process. Taken together, however, instruction and osmosis suggest many ways in which the student acquires musical understanding and wisdom, although reconciling, melding, or combining them, or some aspects of them, may be difficult to achieve in practice.

According to Howard, *practice* (or "an established or customary way of doing things") encompasses more than the notion of the verb *to practise*, or "repetitive practise involved in training or drill." It also refers to "exercising an occupation or profession" as might a doctor or lawyer. Howard would like to distinguish between the medical student who *practises* medicine and the fully qualified doctor who *practices* medicine. To become a fully competent musician, one must practise and hone one's technical and critical skills as one strives to arrive at one's "vision of mastery," or imagined end-in-view. Howard views practise, in the sense of "repeated trial or performance," as "ambiguous as between drill and training," both of which involve imaginative decision-making and thoughtful action. Moreover, through imaginative action, the artist grows into and beyond a particular artistic practice; indeed, Howard goes further to suggest that "we grow into [the traditional demands of our chosen disciplines and professions] *precisely in order to grow beyond them and maybe alter them for future generations* [italics mine]."[93] Therefore, whether practice is viewed in the more restrictive sense of acquiring skills and knowledge, or construed more globally as the way things are generally done by competent practitioners, it is inherently ambiguous.

Although Howard emphasizes the studied acquisition of a particular artistic practice through practise, he infers but does not underscore the importance of *participation* as a means of coming to know a particular practice or of changing that practice. By participation, I mean taking part as a member in the activities of a particular musical group regardless of whether they are intended to be educational. Participating in musical activities need not imply direct instruction about a group's practices or initiation into its beliefs or explicit practise in the formal sense that Howard implies.[94] Rather, knowledge is intuitively gained when one is engrossed in a ritual of one sort or another in which music plays a part. Much musical knowledge is gleaned this way. Children watch adults playing music or singing and "pick up" knowledge intuitively and informally as they participate in the social group's activities. Through doing this, they come to know a "way of life" that encompasses more than possessing knowledge passed on through direct instruction. Participating in religious rituals, jazz jam sessions, or concerts; watching television; and listening to recorded music while traveling with family members are all ways that the young come to know a particular musical practice informally. This participation is ambiguous, seeing that it is imaginative, and it likewise not only leads to knowledge of a musical practice but prompts one to go beyond it. For example, realizing that informality is valued in contemporary American society, symphony orchestra managers now design outdoor concerts where people can come dressed casually and picnic in family groups while listening to orchestral music. This informality carries back to the concert hall, where musicians and audience may dress informally and popular musical taste is taken into account in concert programming.

Through participating in these events, people come to admire certain music, learn how they should behave, imagine how things might be different, and demand change when they think it necessary. Concert patrons may be encouraged to provide their opinions of the musical programming, and these opinions are taken into account in planning the next concert season. Generational changes among musicians also reflect and feed changes in musical taste, exemplified by the repertoire changes between the eras of Arthur Fiedler, John Williams, and Keith Lockhart, conductors of the Boston Pops Orchestra during the twentieth century.

Practice and participation, while obviously interconnected, each have their strengths and weaknesses. Practice is directed toward the formal acquisition and practise of the technical and conceptual skills associated with a particular way of music making and taking while participation focuses on the informal acquisition and use of musical knowledge picked up through taking part in the musical events encompassed in that way of music making and taking. Both are inherently ambiguous, and this ambiguity prompts musical transformation. Each without the other constitutes too narrow a view. In its focus on systematic instruction and practise, practice, as Howard conceives it, overlooks informal and indirect musical learning, while participation, as I have envisaged it, neglects formal and direct musical learning and may result in idiosyncratic and unsystematic knowledge and skills. Practically speaking, music teachers invoke both aspects to varying degrees; they encourage students to practise and to participate in master classes, recitals, and other social events where music is heard. Both perspectives enrich understanding of how musical knowledge and practical skills are acquired and developed.

Howard's notion of *example* covers informal and formal instruction and focuses on showing something as opposed to simply telling about it—allowing a continuum between showing and telling that "requires a convergence of attention by instructor and learner on the relevant details in order for the demonstration to 'speak for itself'." Even though Howard admits unconscious intention, his focus on learning through example clearly privileges intention and falls mainly within the rubric of formal instruction. He invokes, for example, Ryle's notion of the intelligent "follower" who knows what to look for, thereby bypassing the efficacy of example where the condition of conscious intention on the part of instructor and student is not present. I like his "polychromatic" view of learning by example—through "*sample* or typical (exemplifying) instance," "*model* in the sense of a scaled up or scaled down design of structure, pattern or function," "*simulation* which approximates in varying ways and degrees to the real thing," "*exemplar* taken to be a perfect replica or 'ideal' realisation," and *overemphasis* or the caricature of prominent features. I would extend his list to include *anti-example*, or the opposite of a desired action. The learner's task, then, is to seek deliberately to follow or imitate the salient features of the example (or in the case of caricature or anti-example, studiously avoid them), although

Howard allows that there are "many cases of 'unconscious' or involuntary imitation" that are picked up by the learner. Learning doesn't stop here because the learner extrapolates, reaches beyond present knowledge, and escapes "the bonds of received knowledge and precedent"; his or her imitation is "selective and interpretive, requiring an exercise of judgement and choice" and, as such, is inherently imaginative and ambiguous.[95]

By contrast, *observation* focuses on the perception of an event. In contrast to example, which requires learners' active participation and imitation of a particular skill, observation refers to the process whereby they receive information through their senses, process it, and reflect upon it without the necessity of physically demonstrating what has been noticed or learned. Observation is also ambiguous in that it may or may not translate into imitation. Learners may choose to ignore an example that they observe and act in a divergent manner from it. For example, in mid-twentieth-century North American homes, children, having observed the swing and jazz music of their parents, sought out a different musical expression for themselves in rock and roll music.[96] Their children embraced a variety of other rock and popular styles, and their children's children rediscovered swing and jazz. Observation, therefore, can be said to have resulted in musical differentiation and changes in musical taste as each generation reacted to its parents' music and sought another expression for itself.

Example and observation each have something to contribute to musical transmission and are limited in one way or another. Example focuses on showing, on doing as well as telling, whereby observation relies especially on receiving information from the phenomenal world. Both involve selective judgment and imaginative thought. Taken alone, example pays insufficient attention to subjective perception and reflection and unintended learning, while observation places insufficient emphasis on directed attention and active participation as means of musical transmission. Together, example and observation enrich our understanding of how the musical transmission process works and why it is so inherently unstable and dynamic.

Howard's concept of *reflection* hinges on the importance of grasping the significance of an artistic symbol system. Taking his cue from Goodman's symptoms of the aesthetic, he notes that the structural, semantic, and expressive aspects of art grab one's attention and provoke reflection about what has been heard, seen, or otherwise felt. Acknowledging that the exercise of reason in intellectually working through these aspects may also be emotional in quality (consonant with Scheffler's "cognitive emotions" such as the joy of verification or surprise), Howard proposes that reflection focuses on "'rethinking' or 'reconsideration'," mulling things over after the fact, giving them "a second, longer or deeper look," and recognizing the particular "signature and style" of the achievement.[97] This intellectual quality of the aesthetic experience underscores reason and its role in making artistic judgments or in working through the significance of an artistic event afterward.

Alongside reflection after action, there is the thought or reflection in the midst of action stressed by Schön, or what I call *sensibility* for want of a better term.[98] Howard recognizes its role in artistic reflection; however, I want to bring it into the foreground in tension with reflection as he sees it. This thinking is less logical and analytic than intuitive and holistic, more felt than consciously thought about or through. In the midst of making music, for example, one relies instinctually on one's sense of what should be done in this particular situation rather than on a conscious working through of an idea from cause to effect in the abstract. Like reflection, sensibility is grounded in a mastery of style and technique, allowing the performer to make adjustments intuitively along the way while relying on experience to determine how things should go. Sensibility relies not only on formal training but also on the entire experience of one's informal observations of how something should be done. One senses that this tempo is right for the acoustics in this hall, one should play or sing this phrase in this way or take these particular risks on this occasion, because one knows that such-and-such is possible on the basis of past experience. As one performs, one may see or hear something new that one has not seen or heard before, and in the act of performing or executing a musical piece, one may play imaginatively, intuitively, even emotionally with a musical idea. Sensibility seems to be close to Langer's concept of feeling in that it relates to the perception of movement and arrest, tension, and release that is evoked in the work of art. It is also akin to Yob's notion of emotional cognitions in that intellection seems to center on an emotion rather than vice versa.[99] And it invokes a range of intuitive, imaginative ideas, emotions, and sensory impressions that lie beyond reasoned discourse.

Reflection and sensibility each contribute to an understanding of the musical experience and to the inherent ambiguity of music because they each emphasize the inherent subjectivity and particularity of a musical event. They are open-ended activities that may result in changes in the future. Reflection, in this view, emphasizes the importance of mulling over what has been created after the event, critically examining aspects of its significance and style, applying one's reasoning powers to understand the meaning or significance of music and its larger cultural context. Sensibility underscores the lively role of imagination, intuition, and sense in the midst of the musical event. Either taken alone is too narrow a view: reflection pays insufficient attention to the role of sense, and sensibility gives inadequate credence to the role of reason and critical analysis. Both aspects are essential in making and taking music, and both contribute to its vitality and dynamism.

Musical transmission generates musical transformation as it also contributes to the preservation of past beliefs and practices through such means as instruction, practice, example, reflection, osmosis, participation, observation, and sensibility. Insofar as musicians and music educators are agents of musical transmission, they are faced with the practical challenges of reconciling the dialectics of transmission and transformation, with forging new music as well as transmitting musical knowledge from the past.

Practical Implications

Every musical image provides valuable insights and is flawed or limited in some ways. None suffices as the sole perspective on music. Rather, each typically interacts in dialectic or tension one with others. Faced with this reality, my guess is that other teachers, like me, want to preserve them all, even if this means the prospect of reconciling the tensions, conflicts, and apparent contradictions between them in order to create a program of study. How might these dialectics work in practice? I envisage them, for example, as actors on the stage, each coming forward as the particular role demands and being applied as needed within music curricula that are more or less eclectic.

A dialectical view of musical images challenges the notion that there is only one right way of coming to know, thinking about, and doing music and that there is only one right way of being in music. No one image satisfies as the sole basis for curriculum, but the music teacher draws on one and then another as the need arises.[100] This may be particularly the case in North American schools, where local control of education may permit teachers greater freedom in designing and carrying out their programs. Even in nationally or centrally organized music curricula, such as in the United Kingdom, the comprehensive nature of musical study suggests that music teachers typically draw from various musical images.[101] Opening the prospect of "multiplicities" and "pluralities" of musical thought and practice can enrich music curriculum and give voice to those who have been silenced.[102] And it broadens the ways in which music can be construed and fosters diverse ways of making and taking music.

Still, the needs of exposition require teachers to focus sequentially first on one thing and then on another. Thinking very practically and developmentally, Swanwick and Tillman suggest that music teachers might visit one point and then another on their music curriculum spiral.[103] A "this with that" dialectical view, as sketched in Chapter 1, does not require synthesis in the sense that all of the images are somehow melded or synthesized into one transformed entity. Such an approach would be far too simplistic and take insufficient account of the tensions and paradoxes involved in melding aspects of these images. Instead, teachers move between these images from time to time as the needs and interests of their students and their own mandates and objectives demand.

Educational policy makers may also need to think in terms of instructional objectives and the means by which they can be achieved in general terms that allow individual teachers the freedom to select the specific ends and means that meet their specific purposes but are more or less consonant with the broader purposes and methods. There needs to be sufficient flexibility or what I have elsewhere termed "zones of tolerance," wherein some degree of dissension from these purposes and methods on the part of individual teachers is permissible and encouraged.[104] Teachers also need to have a part in the construction of these broad purposes and methods. In music, for example, teachers have long recognized this principle, and the "national standards" read as general purposes and dimensions of music learning are formulated very broadly, allowing a multiplicity of ways in and degrees to which they can be realized. It is tempting to dismiss such broad statements as meaningless because they are couched at a high level of generality. Nevertheless, when combined with specific instances that exemplify certain desirable ideas and practices, they can be useful guides for teachers, students, and public alike. What should be particularly remembered is that in their zeal to specify these general principles, educational policy makers may come to treat them as specific prescriptions. Such a move would be to the detriment of creative and productive teaching and learning because it demeans the teacher's role as creator of the curriculum and diminishes individual choice by teacher and student alike.

A dialectical view of music may reveal gaps and fissures in music curricula that have been insufficiently attended to in the past. It challenges tradition as it also preserves elements of it. Music can be studied as formal construct and inseparable from the society and culture of which it is a part; artistic process and product; and religious, political, or whatever agency of societal and cultural change. Such a seemingly paradoxical view commits the music teacher to work toward particular ends that may have been regarded outside the traditional scope of music instruction—representative of values having to do with the betterment of society and the enrichment of cultural life and experience. Solving these paradoxes, practically speaking, entails a "this with that" approach to music; that is, invoking differing images as each situation warrants. In problematizing music, it also permits and encourages a rich mosaic of particular instructional solutions appropriate to each individual situation. And in making music "one's own," it clarifies notions of self and other and opens up opportunities to surmount or accept the boundaries and differences between human beings. Such a broad view of music enables teachers and their students to come to understand the many similar and different ways in which people around the world express themselves musically and in other ways, and the importance of cultural practices, expressions, and artifacts in enriching all human life.

This view of music underscores the importance of a comprehensive approach to musical education. Notions of "comprehensive musicianship" have been very resilient historically. The Bach family practiced such an education in their day, and in the intervening centuries, while the particular starting points and approaches to achieving it have varied from one teacher to another, music teachers have long recognized the importance of providing a wide array of musical, artistic, and cultural experiences for their students. The same is true in our time. Read as dimensions of musical education, the national standards embraced by the MENC continue this tradition of providing opportunities for singing, playing instruments, composing, improvising, reading music, coming to know a wide array of musics, and integrating music with other aspects of culture. And this ideal of comprehensiveness is also seen in educational systems around the world. Transforming music education from this perspective suggests reaffirming the objective of a broad program of studies that eschews narrow, parochial, and ethnocentric interests and seeks rather to open the worlds of music and culture to young and old alike.

The integration of music with the other arts and school subjects is a matter that also has a long-standing tradition. Good teachers have long recognized the importance of linking one subject to another wherever possible, and Detels' plea that the borders between music, the other arts, and school subjects be "softened" makes excellent sense and deserves reaffirmation.[105] Thinking of all the subjects we teach as parts of a wider heritage of wisdom, knowledge, and skill encourages students to seek interconnections between the things they learn and broaden their views. Subject matter distinctions are largely a matter of tradition, conceptual entities that are helpful in organizing knowledge. Encouraging students to explore, cross over, and challenge these boundaries stimulates imaginative thinking and practice and opens further frontiers of knowledge. Coming to understand music, along with all the subjects, as an aspect of human inventiveness that is manifest around the world in a myriad of ways dignifies humanity and helps the learner to better understand self and society.

In the past music teachers have focused on their curatorial role of preserving particular musical traditions. They have intuitively and sometimes explicitly recognized that unless they take this role, the musical traditions they follow will die. Those who wish to keep a musical tradition alive need to pass it onto the next generation. Bridges need to be built to the past as well as to the future, especially in an age in which technological invention and information explosion seem to have put a premium on the present. Without a sense of traditional beliefs and practices, there is an enormous loss of a sense of rootedness in and wisdom from the past. Still, the above analysis suggests the importance of what Austin Caswell has termed an "ethnological" approach—one that is comparative in its view of musical belief and practice and contextual in its view of music as an element of culture and humanity.[106] And it also goes further to call for a critical view of music and culture. This approach is consonant with Henry Giroux's concern about the role of education as a site for interrogating and contesting culture, calling the received wisdom into question, engaging in dialogue about it, and transforming education toward a more humane society.[107] And it resonates with calls for a more critical stance in regard to received belief and practice in music education.[108] My own dialectical view of the tensions between the curatorial, ethnological, and critical suggests that it is incumbent on educational policy makers to work out practical resolutions for their particular circumstances. To take this approach, however, means that music teachers and those interested in their work must look beyond a narrowly focused curatorial view of the tradition(s) they practice toward the claims of a more culturally contextualized and critical view. This may lead them to actively transgress the taken-for-granted to, as Giroux puts it, focus on "ruptures, shifts, flows, and unsettlement."[109] Transforming music requires careful and critical reflection concerning those aspects to affirm and transmit or repudiate and jettison.

Such a broad view necessitates significant changes in teacher preparation. Music teachers along with teachers of other subjects need broad preparation in the humanities and sciences. A broad and liberal education can enable them to think critically about various subjects; grasp the interrelationships between the arts, humanities, and sciences; and make connections beyond their own subjects to other subject specialties. This need not mandate integration of all the arts or of music with other subjects. But it ought to enable teachers to interrelate music with other subject areas and thereby soften the hard boundaries of specialized subject matter that have become the hallmark of contemporary thinking. Such a perspective necessitates that a considerable amount of time in music teacher preparation be devoted to the study of other subjects beyond music and education. Critical thinking and reflection about music teaching and learning can also be fostered through a dialogical approach that fosters independent and reflective thinking by teachers. Rather than fostering a prescriptive approach, those charged with teacher preparation can employ a variety of techniques that teach for openings, foster self discovery on the part of the neophyte teachers, critical examination and analysis of the particular instructional situations they face, and an ability and confidence to develop their own approaches to those situations. While past methods and approaches may be useful guides, they ought not be the ends of education or regarded as the best or only ways to proceed. More important is the development of the teacher's independent thinking and professional skill as a craftsperson and artist.

Adequate resources are essential to support the work of education in music and the arts. If music education is to be comprehensive and sound, music teachers require the allocation of sufficient time, money, space, and administrative support to accomplish their objectives. A subject ought to be included in general education only if it can be approached with integrity. Yet, all too often, musical study at the elementary and secondary levels is hampered severely by the lack of teachers, instructional time, space, and administrative support and understanding of music among the other arts. And at the tertiary level, music is frequently excluded from the academic programs of the majority of students. One might posit broad instructional objectives of musical study, but in the absence of wider public support, objectives—no matter how laudatory—cannot and probably will not be achieved. It therefore falls to musicians, educators, and the public at large to work to provide the support that can facilitate a comprehensive and sound approach to musical education. The supporters of music and artistic study in general education in the nineteenth century understood this imperative. They also understood that securing this support was as important as demonstrating the effectiveness of their programs, that their mission was a political as well as an artistic and a cultural endeavor. Music educators today forget this fact to their peril.

What can music teachers do to transform the musical traditions they profess? In *In Search of Music Education*, I suggested that they first need to realize that musical transmission and transformation occur under the auspices of such societal institutions as family, politics, religion, music profession, and commerce.[110] Transforming music involves the action of all of these institutions, not just the school or the music studio, among the other places that teachers have historically taught. Music education is first and foremost a societal and cultural undertaking, evoking the ancient Greek notion of *paideia*, in which education equated with cultural ideals and practices and music was a central element.[111] In every age, music policy makers need to think broadly about how to bring together a variety of societal institutions toward musical transformation. In the eighteenth and early nineteenth centuries the clergy led the way in promoting mass musical education within schools and churches. In the late twentieth century the MENC formed and led consortia of various organizations committed to educational and cultural renewal, to help forge public policy supportive of the arts. Whatever the specific means, musical transformation relies upon a broad coalescence of support by societal institutions. And public policy is imperative in achieving it.

My focus in this chapter has been on the role of the music teacher working within an array of such societal institutions, whether as a music teacher in a publicly or privately supported school; an independent music teacher in a performance studio; a church musician; an orchestra, choir, or opera house artistic director; or a music software developer. What can the teacher do in transforming music? In briefly sketching a reply, I focus, first, on the ambiguity of musical belief and practice and how this implicates change and, second, on the ambiguity of the transmission process whereby knowledge is passed on from one generation to another.

At the risk of being labeled a "formalist" and an "essentialist"—terms that in recent postmodern discourse have taken on a negative valence—I suggest that in the Western classical tradition (and other classical traditions, too), music is both object and symbol, process and product. In musical traditions in which the music is a part of a ritual, an oral practice rather than written or notated, improvised rather than composed, the ritual itself is objectified and symbolic for its practitioners. Judgments are made about its rightness and about the achievements of its performers on the part of music makers and takers alike. As a thing, it is rightly studied for its own sake and for the contributions it makes to the particular contexts in which it is made. It has meaning that is corporately understood—whether it be for the sheer joy of the sound or the sight, the celebration it affords, the virtuosity of its performers and the enjoyment of their risk taking, or the intellectual games it manifests, or for what it contributes to events that may be solemn and full of pathos. Much would be lost by abandoning the study of music for its own sake—especially when in the West, at least, there is such a rich tradition of works, old and new, that have survived over the ages or have recently captured our attention. Notwithstanding the imperative of a contextual and ethnographic analysis of music, there is the structure of the musical works themselves (shot through as they are with references to other things).

Once one begins to dig within the notated score or recording, or to understand how to improvise in a particular style or genre, to understand the rule systems that undergird the work or its performance, the sense of rightness of occasion, performance practice, and reception, one comes to understand the many nuances and multiplicities that emerge when the rules are applied in the phenomenal world. Artists understand that rules are broken, bent, as well as followed sometimes freely and other times strictly. "Thinking in" a particular musical practice means coming to know how rich are the syntactic and semantic elements of the symbol, how replete and expressive is the superb performance for composer, performer, and listener alike.[112] And the more one studies a particular piece, form, genre, or musical practice, the more multifaceted and rich it seems to become. This ambiguity fosters experimentation, pressing the limits, breaking some rules and forging others.

Music teachers need to know deeply the music they seek to teach. How is it constructed? What makes it what it is? How ought it be composed, performed, and listened to? What are the specific contexts that shape its interpretation and performance? What are the myriad skills comprised in its performance? This means studying the music itself as aesthetic object and symbol. And it means knowing how to translate ideas into practice in the phenomenal world, whether through singing, playing instruments, or performing a ritual dance. Thinking in this music means immersing oneself deeply in it and being able to think in action as well as reflect afterwards. One cannot teach music effectively if one is not first a musician—one with a broad array of understanding and skills in the particular music(s) one wishes to teach. Putting classroom teachers to work teaching music in elementary schools is only as effective as the musical knowledge and skills that those teachers possess. Music is unlike history or mathematics, in that one must not only be able to know about the subject but one must also possess practical skills and be able to do it. And as many musicians will attest, learning about music is sometimes far easier and less time consuming than is knowing how to make music skillfully. If we really want to transform music, we shall need skillful musicians teaching music from babyhood to old age. People with little knowledge, interest, or skill in making music ought not be entrusted with music teaching in the preschool and elementary grades.

And bringing about this change would require a wholesale change in thinking on the part of educators who assume that an elementary school teacher
should be capable of teaching every subject in the curriculum, including
music. Either we shall need to follow Martin Luther's injunction that we
should not consider a classroom teacher if he or she is not also a musician,
or we shall need to appoint music specialists to do the music teaching in elementary schools. But to rely upon people who are uninterested in music or
who know little about it for the musical instruction of young children is to
guarantee that most people will not have a superb musical education, and
relatively few will succeed as musicians (whether amateur or professional).
Transforming music would involve dramatically changing this reality so that
many people know about and make music throughout their lives from
babyhood into old age. In his book *For the Love of It,* Wayne Booth describes
his experiences as an amateur musician and what teachers and the amateurs
they foster have to bring to the life of music in society.[113] Understanding the
benefits that amateurism could make to transforming musical culture
underscores the importance of elementary education in music for all people. No wonder musician-educators such as Jaques-Dalcroze made so much
of the importance of placing musical instruction in the hands of skilled
practitioners from the very earliest levels of education.[114] To do this, we
need skilled music teachers at every educational level who also make and
teach music for the love of it and of the students they teach.

Understanding aesthetic objects or symbol systems that are dense (whether
semantically or syntactically), seemingly whole and replete, and expressive, and
thereby ambiguous, requires the development of imagination. Imagination has
various faces. Beside the inherent rationality of the art work and practice are
its requirements for perception, intuition, and feeling. All these aspects
taken together necessitate that students develop their musical and artistic
imaginations. And to do this requires that teachers provide opportunities for
this development to take place. Cultivating the imagination does not invite
a "free-for-all" in which students play without particular ends in view or
parameters within which they can create. Rather, it requires opportunities
to systematically develop musical skills, open-ended problems to be solved
that foster divergent musical solutions, and growing and broadening horizons of musical knowledge to explore. Teachers need to be leaders in providing opportunities for their students to develop their musical imaginations. And one would expect that the preparation of teachers would nurture
the kinds of beliefs, attitudes, and skills needed to accomplish this end. In
short, teacher preparation also needs to be imaginative, as it exemplifies the
characteristics desired in a teacher and as the means exemplify and express
the ends in view. Rather than having "inert" ideas be the focus of education,
music transformed through imaginative thought and practice is a "living"
thing—the sort of end Whitehead was at pains to develop.[115] Broadening the
music transmission process to include informal as well as formal instruction,
and active as well as passive means, as I have suggested, can also transform

music education. Taking Howard's analysis at face value suggests the importance of instruction, practice, example, and reflection to musical learning. This quartet is very rich, practically speaking, because it suggests the importance of telling as well as showing, explaining as well as inquiring, the teacher's living example as well as knowing about a particular field, and reflective thinking after action as well as in the midst of action. Teachers need a broad array of techniques to foster these approaches to learning. And the means by which they are prepared, in turn, need to reflect this breadth of skills, from practical skills and habits to critical thinking skills at a high level of mastery.

This breadth of teaching and learning musical skills models the self-same range of teaching and learning skills needed in other subject areas. As Howard points out in the subtitle of his book, *Learning by All Means*, these are "lessons from the arts." Notions of ambiguity and imagination have roles to play in knowledge broadly construed. And artist-teachers need to be foremost in modeling these skills in their classrooms, studios, and all of the other places they teach. Such a broad array of learning through formal means can renew not only music but other fields of study as well.

If one extends Howard's analysis more broadly to include notions of osmosis, participation, observation, and sensibility, as I have done, the prospect for transformation is even more dramatic. When teachers also understand the importance of the learner's informal absorption of knowledge by being in a situation for an extended period of time, of doing music among the other subjects as opposed to learning about it, of watching and listening as well as doing, and of the power of emotional life and feeling in acquiring knowledge, their work can be transformed. Learning cannot be hurried. It takes time to absorb, to be in the midst of music making, to be an observer watching musicians do their work, to come to love what one does as a musician, and to appreciate the efforts and achievements of others (even if one does not particularly identify with that music making). In a time in which efficiency is at a premium in the learning process, it is well to learn patience and persistence and to be willing to undergo the learning process for as long as it takes to master one's particular skill or practice. And the neophyte musician needs to acquire a broad background, including an appreciation for the other arts, the humanities, and the sciences. Accomplishing this in practice—for example, in the pre-service and in-service preparation of teachers—means ensuring a broad, well-rounded education; a love of learning; a commitment to one's specialty; and a realization that education is a lifelong process. Becoming a music teacher is a vocation—a life's work. And this model of teaching prefigures the teaching of other subjects as well.

The tensions of forming and preserving imaginative approaches to music and education that utilize a variety of approaches to teaching and learning need to be worked through in particular circumstances. Here, music educational policy makers need to forge plans to be carried out in the phenomenal world. It is well to realize that the educational project is a political undertaking because plans are often imperfectly realized, they have unforeseen circumstances, and they are challenged by those with other vested interests. Knowledge is contested, and educational undertakings are the sites of this contest. Unless one takes into account the sometimes messy business of political persuasion and power, it is difficult to envisage music and education's being transformed. And because knowledge is contested, and what is deemed valuable may change, if not in general purpose but in specific nature, from time to time, and from generation to generation, teachers of all stripes need to be politically astute. Just as did their predecessors, music teachers today need to understand the political process, how to be heard and heeded in the institutions of which they are a part, and how to effect change institutionally. Here, social and political knowledge are invaluable and need to be a central part of music teacher preparation.

An aspect that is, perhaps, one of the most detrimental to securing and keeping the services of outstanding teachers of almost any subject is the support they are given; in particular, the financial rewards they receive. Even within the field of music, performers (especially those that achieve success in their instruments) are often remunerated more highly than teachers. And given the low level of salaries, particularly in the United States, it is no surprise that the work of teachers is held in such low esteem, and the revolving door to the profession means that many school teachers are relative neophytes, most leaving within a few years. The breadth and depth of musical preparation envisaged above merits full-time employment and higher salaries than are often paid. Salaries (and respect) will increase only as teachers work together politically to demand and expect that their efforts and work be properly recognized and compensated. In other countries in which I have worked as a teacher, teachers are treated as full-time workers, the school year is longer than in the United States, teachers' salaries are much higher than in this country, they receive a high level of respect in the communities in which they work, and the work of education is accorded greater importance than it is in this country. I am often struck by the exploitative salaries of young teachers and professors, or of those of more mature years who by dint of their devotion to the young work for otherwise unacceptable remuneration. Taking music seriously means investing significant public resources in the future of musical culture and paying teachers properly. We cannot expect to transform musical culture otherwise. And what we learn from music education can just as well be applied across the field of education, generally.

Summary

In this chapter I have examined these questions: What is meant by the word *music*? How can music be transformed? And what are the practical implications of this analysis for music education? I have sketched five musical images, namely, music as aesthetic object, symbol, practical activity, experience, and agency. These are in dialectic and are invoked by musicians and teachers on a "this with that" basis, as actors might move about on the stage.

I have suggested that musical transformation is a complex phenomenon that arises not only out of the cultural context of which music is a part, expressed through such societal institutions as commerce, politics, religion, family, and music profession, but also out of the ambiguity of music, its engagement of imagination, the dynamic nature of the transmission process, and its informal as well as formal dimensions. In the Western classical tradition, musical ambiguity can be explained by reference to the highly nuanced qualities of the symbol system—for example, a musical score that may be precise in certain respects and ambiguous or open to individual interpretation in others. Ambiguities in musical belief and practice also contribute to transformation over time. Because music is brought to life through performance, it is particularly susceptible to change. And as a social art involving composers, performers, listeners, producers, marketers, and distributors, among others who make and take music imaginatively, change takes place more dramatically at some times than it does at others.

Musical transmission, or the means whereby each generation passes on musical beliefs and practices to succeeding generations, is also a dynamic process that promotes musical change. Formally and informally, whether by such means as instruction or osmosis, practice or participation, example or observation, reflection or sensibility, musical transmission forges new understandings and practices as it also preserves past wisdom and ways of participating in music. And this suggests a broad array of ways in which musical learning, as learning in other subjects, can be fostered.

Several practical applications of this analysis have also been suggested for music instruction. I have suggested the importance of musical institutions such as MENC as a means of forging coalitions of a broad array of organizations that are representative of cultural and artistic life. Within this context, teachers can help to transform music through studying deeply the various musics of which they claim to be exponents, acquiring the skills to "think in" those musics, having a deep and broad knowledge of the particular music they teach, developing their own and their students' musical imaginations, and broadening the means of instruction they employ to include imaginative thinking as an essential part of the work of music, culture, and life in general. To this end, play, problem-centered approaches, and opportunities to deepen and broaden musical knowledge systematically are essential to the educational process. Teachers also need to be more skillful as politicians, willing to work with their colleagues to demand and secure appropriate support, recognition, and remuneration for their work. Building support for music or any sort of education comes at a price. It cannot be left to others to defend. Rather, it requires teachers who are apt, skillful, and courageous enough to insist that the requisite support be given to their work so that it can be done with integrity.

5

Creating Alternatives

What should music education be like? What should be its effects on the people it comprises, the communities in which it takes place, and the general education and wider society of which it is a part? A prescriptive plan is out of the question because it does not take into account the human passion for transcending past practice and the inherent situatedness and particularity of music education, or the many different ways in which it is carried on from time to time and place to place. At some point, however, ideas need to be put into practice. How is this possible in the absence of a unilateral and final solution? These questions take on an urgency because of the need to commit to principles and practices that address and redress the pervasive and systemic problems in music education and society at large that I sketched earlier.

One way of approaching these questions is to propose principles that can be interpreted and practiced in different ways, and are symptomatic of what transforming music education might look like and what its effects might be. I offer them with the important caveats that the formulation is incomplete, their practical effects cannot be fully anticipated, other perspectives may be valuable, and better solutions may be found in the future. In taking this approach, I use the word *transformation* in the special, quite technical sense already outlined; intuitive and commonsense interpretations cannot do justice to the richness of the idea, given its ambiguous and problematical nature. Also, consistent with notions of education and music, the descriptor "transforming" applied to music education is intentionally ambiguous, including both the quality of becoming, whereby music education is in the process of being transformed, and the sense of agency, whereby music education has a transformative effect on those involved in it, on music, on education, and on society at large. Nor is there ever a time when one has arrived at the end of transformation; it is an ongoing process. This inherent ambiguity, or what Goodman might term "promiscuity,"[1] enriches the conception and practice of music education and invokes imagination, intuition, and feeling along with reason as ways of designing plans and implementing programs; it is also problematical in that it necessitates special care in clarifying meanings, elucidating practices, and ensuring that some do not presume to act on behalf of others without regard to their wishes. As I have shown, transformation has both a light and dark side, and the musician-teacher needs to be constantly watchful that potential good is not turned into evil and the best of intentions become the worst of realities.

Ways of Thinking

Among the symptoms of transforming music education, music educators and those interested in their work need to break out of the little boxes of restrictive thought and practice and reach across the real and imagined borders of narrow and rigid concepts, classifications, theories, and paradigms to embrace a broad and inclusive view of diverse music educational perspectives and practices. A global and historical view of music and education exemplifies "soft boundaries"; that is, inherent fuzziness at the edges of its theoretical concepts and their practical expressions.[2] This softness, fuzziness, murkiness, or untidiness results from the complex and dialectical nature of the music education enterprise and causes theoretical and practical difficulties in articulating ideas and implementing them, or in formulating strategies and rationalizing them. I have suggested that music educators are often interested in the territory "in between" theoretical types—that is, at their intersection or in their vanishing points. Of particular interest are those cases where teacher meets student, musical form meets function, theory meets practice, one idea meets another, one instructional method meets another, one music meets another, and so on. This quality of living in the "eye of paradox," as Deanne Bogdan puts it,[3] is enormously challenging to all involved in musical education, be they musicians, researchers, teachers, students, or the public.

There has been too much cataloguing of schools and "isms," reducing ideas and approaches simplistically into categories, and dehumanizing them further by referring to them by acronyms.[4] Rather than forging genuinely open spaces for dialogue and inquiry, cliques of scholars and practitioners cluster around certain ideas, methods, or "regulative ideals" that guide their work, in which agnostics or dissenters are excluded, feel marginalized, or believe themselves compromised. Such groups serve mainly sectarian or political purposes as means by which particular approaches and points of view are polarized, popularized, and foisted upon the profession at large.

The little boxes of restrictive labels, slogans, and either/or dichotomies that have plagued music education in the past have introduced an almost doctrinaire or ideological note into discussions among scholars and practitioners in the field. Such thinking is misguided because it suggests that things are simpler than they actually are, and wrongheaded because it fails to deal fairly with the nuances in and complexities of philosophical and other writings. For

example, Alperson's tripartite classification of philosophies of music education as formalist aesthetic, aesthetic cognitivist, and praxial, while useful in
pointing to certain broad differences among philosophers, overstates them
and omits other philosophical views such as instrumentalism.[5] Moreover, his
historical sketch is cast from a particular philosophical perspective that biases
his account. He cannot escape from the limitations of his own point of view
any more than can the rest of us, and the situation is much more complex
than these categorical distinctions might suggest.

Still, breaking out of the little boxes of restrictive and rigid thinking does
not suffice.[6] This metaphor captures the process of deconstruction, of analyzing and challenging conventional wisdom and daring to reject it in favor
of a different point of view. This is an important step in transformation; however, it does not go far enough toward the object of reconstruction and recon-
ceptualization, nor does it establish and commit to alternative perspectives of
what music education could or should become and what its impact could be
on education and society generally. In addressing this question, the notion of
transformation that I have sketched in these pages requires thoroughly re-
envisioning and re-constituting musical education individually and institutionally. It involves clarifying the aims of musical education in our time and
working out the ways in which they may be reached. It suggests nothing less
than pervasive and systemic educational and musical change. And, in the
process, it necessitates directly addressing the profoundly dehumanizing
institutional problems that afflict music, education, and society today.

The ongoing search for wisdom may be admirable; however, the claims
of musical and educational practice require commitment to certain ends.
What are these ends? In unraveling a philosophical knot, one invariably
creates another. Tracking down the nature of transformation opens the
question-set: "Transformation for what?" "Toward what goods should
music education be directed?" These questions go to the heart of the aims
of education, to what it should be about and for. The ethical ideals with
which I began this study and to which I now return—justice, civility, goodness, fidelity, and mutuality—may appeal intuitively, yet their meaning and
the implicit interrelationship of ethical and musical ends among other
issues are problematical, cannot be taken simply at face value, and require
further explanation and defense. Nor is my list of values complete. Each
institution brings its own particular perspectives to bear, be they familial,
religious, political, musical, or economic. And it is clear that fleshing out
these assumptions remains an important task for the future.

One argument might run as follows. Assuming that such ideals as justice,
civility, goodness, fidelity, and mutuality are necessary for a democratic society
to prosper, music education serves to nurture and transform society as well as
the individuals it comprises. It is effective in this task when it embodies the
qualities of a civilized society yet to come. Oppressive structures are endemic
to music education as to society, and these oppose civility and humanity. By
privileging some and marginalizing others, the establishment ensures that

some voices are heard while others are silenced in the public spaces, some cultural expressions and visions of civility are advocated while others are repudiated. This exclusivity, under whatever guise, no matter how well meaning, is to the detriment of all. However, where these oppressive structures are undermined, society is enriched in terms of the discourse, conduct, and cultural expressions of its members. By tackling the dehumanizing forces in music education, music educators and those interested in their work can create a miniature society that presages a more civil society; in this way, music education can model not only general education but also society yet to come.[7]

In the multicultural societies of our time, teachers and students need to be willing to live and let live; to resist the temptation, no matter how strong, to coopt traditions within their own particular worldviews. Big countries have always sought to impose their culture on small countries, and cultural imperialism is alive and well today.[8] Likewise, in the world of the arts, Langer describes the tendency of one art form to overpower another when they are combined. As she puts it: "There are no happy marriages in art—only successful rape."[9] Does the same principle also holds true with musics and musical genres? I suspect so. To my ears, in a recording of Queen songs by the London Symphony Orchestra, popular music assimilates classical symphonic orchestral sound. Likewise, the classical sound of an Ives symphony co-opts and assimilates the New England folk tunes and hymns of Ives's time. Either way, one music seems to overpower the other, even as both may be changed in the process. Some intermingling of musical traditions is inevitable in our world; however, instead of seeking to assimilate other musical traditions within Western classical or popular musics, music educators need to also allow and encourage the many different ways of making and taking music on their own terms.

It is also important to respect secrets and to allow cultures predicated on certain initiation rites and secretive about their rituals to choose not to share their cultures and musics. This principle was brought home to me when I visited Uluṟu, formerly known as Ayers Rock, in central Australia. Even as an Australian citizen, I felt that I was an outsider looking in; I might watch, listen, and learn about native culture, but certain knowledge would be withheld from me because I am not initiated into the tribe's secrets. Respecting another's secrets requires one to be willing to accept gracefully and gratefully what different others are willing to share without pressing them further than they are willing to go. My experience at Uluṟu taught me that not every society is open, willing to share its culture and music. I might hope that the aboriginal people of Australia would be more open to those outside their culture, but if they are not, I may need to be content with a partial if also incorrect view of that culture. I should approach all musics in an attitude of humility, receptive to what the other is willing to teach me and share with me, hopeful that the other might become less exclusive in regard to his or her culture as I am of mine and that in the process of sharing what we can, we will both be enriched.[10]

One of the most important attributes of the student or teacher in a multicultural world is the necessity to de-center self—to become, as it were, the "other" to one's own culture, able to look critically at it as if one were an outsider. In so doing, I learn to approach the music with which I have identified in the past as if it were not my own, as if from the outside looking in. I also learn to look at another's music empathetically, putting myself, as it were, in the other's place, trying imaginatively to grasp how it might feel to be the other in his or her musical tradition, or how it might feel to be the other looking at the tradition with which I have been identified. In so doing, I become more sympathetic to the other's view of her or his tradition and less commonsensical and arrogant about my own. I come to see the ways in which the tradition(s) in which I have grown up share commonalities and differences with others, how we have constructed similar and different realities, and why these similarities and differences exist. What I take to be my "own" tradition is thereby de-centered. My sense of self changes with my changing perceptions of the traditions with which I have grown up and those of others. I am now more critical and understanding of, and sympathetic and open to, my own and these other disparate musical beliefs and practices because I see them more critically and sympathetically, less egocentrically and ethnocentrically. And the lines between my traditions and those of others become more blurred as I accept and learn from the other's point of view, and the other learns from mine.

The fact that music and education are culturally embedded suggests that the human elements of music should be celebrated. Rather than rejecting music because it is a Western construct or education because it is culturally entrenched, I may move from music alone to think of music together with the other arts, such that its boundaries are deliberately blurred.[11] Thus seen, music becomes a human expression within the larger context of life. It is approached more as a humanity than a science, holistically rather than atomistically.[12] And its functional as well as formal aspects constitute the basis for understanding what it is and what it contributes to individual and communal experience.

In this view, education is predicated on sharing what one knows and values. Students come with already formed musical perspectives, and these need to be taken seriously, listened to, challenged, and validated because musical beliefs and practices constitute a part of self. The teacher is anxious to enlarge learners' horizons, to show them what is not readily accessible to them and how to approach disparate musics beyond those with which they have already identified. On the other hand, the student has much to contribute to the teacher's understanding. Both are conversation partners, fellow travelers on the path to wisdom. The teacher may have the advantage of experience and maturity, the student of naïveté and youth. Within the bounds and limits of what is possible or permissible to be shared, each has an opportunity to learn from the other.

Transforming practice is an educational and musical value. Just as the artist seeks to transcend past practice, to go beyond it in compelling ways, so the teacher challenges and reinvents traditional paradigms; corrects past limitations and flaws; and enlarges and reframes ideas to include musical function as well as form, improvisation as well as composition, performance as well as listening, contextual as well as sonic phenomena, practice as well as theory. Such transformations take into account the many ways in which music is influenced by such social factors such as gender, class, ethnicity, age, sexuality, and economic status, and its role as an agent of propaganda and oppression on the one hand or education and liberation on the other. As the status quo is challenged and displaced, so new futures and means to reach them are envisaged and created. And as I have shown earlier, this human and imaginative drive toward transformation constitutes the wellspring of a vital and dynamic musical experience.

Ways of Being

One of the compelling aims of musical education is captured in the metaphor of the living organism, in the sense of vitality that pervades its every aspect.[13] The notion of art as a living and vital entity possessing qualities of livingness, liveliness, lifelikeness, vitality, and dynamism is old and pervasive in musical and aesthetic literature. Seeing music education as a vital and living entity is a natural extension of such ideas as Whitehead's argument that the educator's aim is to bring knowledge alive in the quest for wisdom, the metaphor of living form in Langer's conception of art, the resonance between teaching and artistry in the work of Howard, among others, and the many references to curriculum as aesthetic discourse.[14]

Seeing music education as a living thing also resonates with the symptoms of transformation outlined earlier, including its dynamic, evolutionary, metamorphic, systemic, dialectical, political, spiritual, active-reflective, inspirational, and imaginative qualities. All sentient beings are dynamic in the sense that they are in a constant state of becoming. They evolve through time and from place to place and undergo a metamorphosis in that their very forms and shapes change over time. People confront the many dialectics in their everyday lives as they decide how to put "this with that," and they are political creatures, bound by the necessities of social life to interact with others in political as well as social ways. As spiritual beings, they invent narratives, myths, rituals, and systems of belief that create meaning in the phenomenal world as they also engage whatever lies beyond it. Thinking imaginatively prompts them to grasp intellectually and passionately the alternative possibilities that might improve their lot and act to realize them practically. As living exemplars, they, in turn, inspire others to reflect on and then act to transform their situations. As such, transforming music educators are passionate about what they do because for them, passing on the living traditions of the past as they also reshape them in the present is the vital work of directly engaging the hearts and minds of their students, of bringing living knowledge and living beings together in the celebration of music making and taking. Transforming music education is alive; its institutions are vital and relevant to individual members and public alike;[15] its teachers are imbued with energy, passionate about their art, and eager to communicate it to others; and its students embrace knowledge as a living entity that is central to their lives. Its influence is directly felt on society as it ennobles humanity, enriches culture, and promotes civility. As a living thing, it transforms the hearts, minds, and lives of its teachers, students, and all affected by its work.

At the heart of transforming musical education are the people involved in it, particularly students and teachers. Teaching and learning are human endeavors, holistic experiences that are construed intellectually, emotionally, physically, and spiritually. A dialectical view of the relationship between the curriculum and the student suggests that the human dimensions of music education are just as important as the material to be learned and taught and cannot be separated from it. Building curriculum solely around subject matter, programs of study, and abstract objectives derived from expert knowledge of the field of music is short-sighted because it fails to take sufficient account of the ways in which knowledge is socially and individually constructed and of the centrality of teacher-student interaction in the learner's and teacher's experience. The word *experience* is understood here in the deep sense of a profound impact on the person, one that is practical and relevant to the needs and interests of student, teacher, and public alike; perceived as significant by the individual undergoing it; and vividly remembered by him or her. The vitality of transforming music education results from its integration with, and its necessity and relevance to, the rest of the lives of its participants. As such, it constitutes, for them, an imperative. It cannot subsist on the fringes of education or the margins of personal awareness as arid theory, disconnected knowledge, or meaningless practice. Rather, it is regarded by those involved in it as essential—even rare and precious—and it expects, even demands, to be taken seriously in the hearts and minds of teachers, students, and the public, something to be aspired to and to inspire toward better practice and something to be celebrated joyfully.

Its inspirational and practical qualities are clearly in dialectic. It motivates people to gain wisdom, wider understanding, and greater tolerance and respect for and cooperation with different others. It hopes for the best of its teachers, students, and public, and it celebrates the present moment as it also takes fullest advantage of it. Yet it also recognizes human frailty and limitation, and it takes into account the specific circumstances of peoples, times, and places as it also seeks to broaden and deepen musical and educational experience. As such, it is optimistic, manifestly farsighted, and hopeful yet realistic, present-centered, and practical—an attitude that prevents it from being utterly utopian and impractical on the one hand and bogged down in pessimism and despair on the other.

Its educational present-centeredness derives from a sense of duty, reverence, and integrity on the part of all of its participants. In a sense, one cannot do anything about the past because it is already history, while the future has yet to unfold in unexpected ways. However, the present offers a unique opportunity in which to transform music, education, and society. Duty arises from the obligation to seek wisdom and exemplify best practice, to reshape past traditions in ways that improve and otherwise transcend them. Reverence connotes the spiritual sense of wonder and awe at the importance of the present moment and the value of the subject matter—a sense that one is on holy ground at this moment in time. And integrity highlights the carefulness and fidelity with which students and teachers approach their subject matter. Interestingly, this educational present-centeredness parallels musical present-centeredness as, for example, the listener's attention shifts moment by moment to a piece unfolding over time.[16] The musician likewise demonstrates duty, reverence, and integrity—duty with respect to the claims of musical practice; reverence regarding the spiritual quality of music, its immateriality, and the wonder felt by participants in the rituals of which music is the raison d'être or forms a part; and integrity in the carefulness and fidelity with which the process of musical transformation transpires.

Music education comes alive when it is experienced holistically. It comes alive when its educational aims are spiritual as well as material; when its participants celebrate the present, transcend past practice, and come to love wisdom; and when duty, reverence, and integrity are central to the educational and musical enterprise. It comes alive when learners view knowledge as relevant to their lives; within their powers to grasp; challenging, inspiring, and encouraging them to move beyond past attitudes, abilities, and attainments. And it comes alive as it impacts the lived experience of its public in ways that are humanizing and civilizing. Full of hope, courage, joy, and faith, such music educators dare to put people at the center of the music educational process. They challenge the unquestioned assumptions, stultified attitudes, and irrelevant practices of the passé and the status quo. And they seek to meet directly the needs, interests, and aspirations of people where they are rather than the abstract claims and expectations of experts far removed from their particular situations.

A living thing cannot be standardized. It cannot be reduced to formulaic approaches, procedures, or instructional methods. Langer's observation that throughout history, generative ideas have typically been reduced to narrow and restrictive interpretations that gradually lose their power[17] is borne out in the field of music education. As disciples propagate their prophet's ideas, they also participate in those ideas' destruction by proceeding to codify them. Their interpretations are inevitably partial and stultifying; they lack the liveliness and imperative of the original idea, especially seeing that it is embodied in the person of its creator; and their doctrines and practices eventually squeeze the life out of the ideas at their origin. National standards, state curriculum guidelines, codified instructional methods, and the like, no matter how well intentioned, cannot bring music education alive.[18] They attend to the symptoms of the problem rather than fixing it at its roots, thereby neglecting fundamental and pervasive problems. Insisting or recommending that teachers follow particular approaches or meet certain mandated objectives overlooks the many different ways and particular situations in which teachers and students come together; their differing needs, interests, and abilities; and the varying constraints on their work. More profoundly, such an approach neglects the diversity of musical beliefs and practices, the multifaceted nature of music itself, the richness and possibilities inherent in this diversity, and the transformative quality of musical experience. It takes people—living according to their particular perspectives, abilities, interests, and needs, and interacting with others in the instructional setting—to bring education alive. The people are at its heart not the procedures.

I am struck by the role that individual personality plays in developing approaches to music instruction. Each of the music curricular methods that has wide currency internationally was inspired by a person with an idea. How different they were and are. Instead of focusing teacher training efforts on preparing disciples or technicians of these methods, it is much more important that teachers discover and articulate their own perspectives and voices and develop the skills and confidence to forge their own particular approaches. One need not constantly reinvent the wheel, and traditional methods may be helpful in providing examples for teachers to consider, but a transformation in music teaching will occur only if teachers are encouraged to find their own imperatives. There are many roads to musical understanding and wisdom. There are many ways of teaching and learning. The power to set one's own expectations, to design and implement one's own curriculum, and to inspire others to follow one's example results in diversity, not standardization. Only when individual teachers and students are inspired by the examples of others and choose to raise their expectations of themselves, when musical instruction directly addresses their specific interests and needs, does music education comes alive in the hearts and minds of all involved.

The living beings at the heart of music education deserve to be valued, respected, and heard in the private and public spaces; they have the right to freedom, compassion, justice, equality, and integrity. All have the right to a humane education, to learn the culture of their personal heritage as well as that of different others and, in the process, to become better and more informed people, prepared to take their places fully in a diverse society. If all are to have this opportunity, it is necessary to concentrate resources in those places and situations in which poverty, disease, and neglect have been especially evident, or those areas of the curriculum that have been ill served in the past—notably, elementary and preschool education, especially in rural and urban areas in which there is widespread poverty, or in such specialties as music composition, performance, or listening, when they have been ignored. With these objectives in mind, if music education is to take its place in the public arena, it will be political, directly involved in civil rights issues. In the United States, for example, music educators will be outraged at the lack of educational resources devoted to some inner-city or rural schools, at the widespread tolerance of musical ignorance beyond popular culture, at the sterility of the classical tradition and its failure to engage sufficiently the popular culture of our time or the interests and needs of the common people, and at the lack of a deep knowledge and appreciation of the wellsprings of American culture. They will act decisively and determinedly to remedy this situation.

Likewise, music educators will resist religious, commercial, and other pressures that seek to impose certain values on teachers and muffle or silence their voices. These pressures are enormous in the United States.[19] Conservative religious groups, among other interest groups, wield enormous political power in textbook and repertoire selection and regularly challenge the teaching of religion and religious music in publicly supported schools. Commercial influences are felt in the textbook production and adoption process, commercial advertising in schools, and the efforts to construe education as vocational training and ensure accountability by applying fiscal criteria as the principal yardsticks for educational institutions and standardized tests as measures of teachers' effectiveness. The specific problems raised by these religious and economic pressures, among others, are particular to the places in which music education is carried on, and the situation in the United States is doubtless exacerbated by the cultural milieu, narrow readings of the constitutional prohibition of establishing religion in publicly supported schools, the local control of education, and its resulting fragmentation. Whatever the nature of the specific problems, however, external pressures subvert music education wherever it is found, and music educators and others interested in their work, wherever they are, must resist these pressures.

It is also less threatening to go abroad to other nations and collect their musics, to focus on the exotic and the different, than to confront the many diverse musical experiences at home, especially in a culture that is "monochromatic" despite its claims of diversity.[20] In the United States, for example, one comes face-to-face with the lack of freedom; unfinished racial business; a profound neglect of native peoples and other invisible minorities; and injustice and discrimination on the basis of gender, age, language, religion, color, ethnicity, class, or lifestyle, among the host of barriers that separate people. Too often, there is widespread apathy toward pervasive problems of poverty, anxiety, and fear; a lack of appreciation for the fine arts; and a lack of care for the natural environment. Each place and situation has its own particular set of challenges, and these cannot be met in standardized ways. Looking abroad for exotic musical cultures can mask a widespread lack of interest in or indifference to the makers and takers of the many diverse yet marginalized musics of our own place.

Notwithstanding these differences, finding and cultivating common threads, shared musical understandings and practices, is entirely consistent with celebrating musical diversity. This is so because of the crucial distinction between standardizing instructional methods or ends and identifying common or shared purposes. Each musical practice has specific rules that undergird it and a corresponding sense of "rightness" on the part of its exponents and public. Construed globally, however, the commonalities that emerge across musics tend to be general rather than specific, construed phenomenally as well as theoretically. Although there may be consensus within a particular practice, or similarities from one musical practice to another, such themes and common expectations, even though widely shared, are general and partial and cannot be relied upon as the sole or principal driver for instructional decision-making. Specific personal and musical factors are of equal if not greater importance, and these defy standardization.

Transcending past practice impels music educators to promote a rich array of musical and educational experiences, to resist and even defy political efforts to standardize methods and objectives in ways that often exemplify the world of commerce by showing that standardization is ultimately irrelevant to transforming music education as it is to all the arts and education generally. Standardization deflects attention from the needs and interests of the people who are the central concern of educators, does not go to the heart of education, and can be subverted easily by teachers and students alike. For example, where statewide or nationally standardized music examinations are in place, teachers regularly teach to the examination, thereby narrowing the curriculum and undermining the intended purpose of the specified standards. Many music teachers are also cynical of and resist new curricular innovations, and they regularly interpret well-known music instructional approaches such as those of Kodály or Suzuki in different ways, thereby changing those approaches' original intent. Teaching and learning are ultimately human endeavors; there is much to teach and learn, and many valid ways in which to teach and learn. Cultural, societal, institutional, and group differences affect the beliefs and values that undergird teaching and learning music and the practices that express them. Rather than being funneled toward predetermined ends and prosaic methods, diversity can be encouraged and celebrated. Instead of teaching every young person to know and do certain musical things, music education can ensure that every young person experiences music in ways that are relevant to, and meaningful in, her or his particular reality. Through exploring the many musical expressions that musical culture comprises, from the differing perspectives of peoples, times, and places, music can come alive for individual students and teachers, and its effects can spread throughout the community, enriching the musical and cultural fabric of society.

One might worry that unless detailed curricular standards are in place, music education will neither improve nor be shown to be accountable to its public. There is the case of the high school music teacher, for example, whose curriculum consists entirely of teaching her students popular songs from lyric sheets and entirely by rote; unless standards are in place and she is forced to ensure that her students attain them, one might say, she will not improve her music curriculum. True, some teachers are motivated, at least in the short term, by the stick rather than the carrot, and the political reality is that certain standards are more or less mandated from place to place. However, it does not require codified standards to conclude that a curriculum consisting entirely of the rote teaching of a limited repertoire of pop songs at the secondary school level is philosophically problematical on at least two grounds. First, although it highlights oral/aural learning, it fails to develop musical skills such as sight-singing or sight-reading that might enable students to go on to learn other musics. And second, although it engages students' interest in popular culture, it fails to introduce them to other less accessible musics such as classical traditions, jazz, or vernacular musics from other cultures that would broaden their understanding. Learning skills that will enable one to apply knowledge gained to a new area and moving outward from the known to the unknown are well-established pedagogical principles.[21] If this teacher is going to make a genuine, lasting change in her program, she needs new ways of thinking and being as a musician and teacher. Standards may make her feel inadequate or tell her what she must accomplish, but they don't provide her the inward impetus or help to reach the stated ends. Rather, she needs to raise her expectations of herself and her students and imagine what she and they might be able to accomplish together. And she needs the time; musical and pedagogical skills; instructional resources; and community, administrative, and collegial support and encouragement to raise her expectations of her students and realize her new aspirations for them.

As a living thing, transforming music education necessitates improving on the status quo, doing things differently or better than they have been done in the past. It may also mean actively subverting standards because they codify and institutionalize established or past practice. Realizing human potential relies on the exercise of personal choice, on an individual's decision to improve her or his practice, and music teaching and learning cannot be transformed in the absence of the teacher's and learner's decision to make this happen.[22] As I have suggested earlier, over the long term, the desire to transcend past practice is nurtured not so much by external directive as by a change of mind and heart, as one commits to certain ideals and works along with others over the long haul to carry them into practice.

Ways of Acting

Ways of thinking and being within a community of music educators committed to transforming music education play out in ways of action. Thinking divergently and critically; living as spiritual beings in harmony with the earth and the things in it, as part of a community of others growing and adapting to change; committing to unmasking and resisting the many oppressive and dehumanizing systemic forces in society; creating a more just, inclusive, and civil society; and transforming music, education, and society, as I have suggested earlier, imply significant changes in the practices of teaching, leading, music making and taking,[23] and learning. My purpose here is to flesh out in a few respects some particular ways of acting consistent with notions of transformation that I have advanced in preceding chapters, or some specific symptoms, if you will, of what transforming music education might look like.

Teaching

Music teachers are typically preoccupied with a wide array of tasks, including developing musical imagination; interpretative capacity; the ability to listen; skills in composing, improvising, and performing; and critical judgment. Their specific tasks differ depending on a host of factors, including the musical traditions in which they work; their performing instruments; the backgrounds and personalities of students they teach; their own teaching personae, training, and preferences; and the times and places in which they work. Notwithstanding these differences, all teachers have certain aims for their students, arrange a program of study for them, communicate what they wish their students to do (through explaining, questioning, and/or showing), and evaluate their students' progress toward particular ends.

The liveliness of transforming teaching arises from the fact that it is genuinely open-ended. A teacher opens dialogues or conversations with a student; cares for the student and the subject matter; reflects before, in the midst of, and after instruction; and forges an instructional process that delights in questions, resists foreclosing options, engages the many, sometimes conflicting tensions that abound in education and music, and relates knowledge to the lived experience of teacher and student. Such approaches resist the prosaic ways and pat answers of the past and demand the best of teacher and student in transcending the status quo and forging better theory and practice in the future. A profound optimism tempered with realism, search for wisdom tempered with practicality, and respect for tradition tempered with ambition for change demands more, not less, of teachers and students in imaginative and critical thinking, musical teaching and learning skills.[24]

Dialogical or conversational teaching relies on improvised responses of showing and telling. There are many ways of conversing through such means as rehearsals, discussions, teacher presentations, or demonstrations. Whatever the specific approach, the teacher is reflecting in the midst of action, devising strategies on the spot, and attempting to take advantage of the present moment, no matter how unexpected the particular circumstances.[25] This improvisational or rhapsodic quality of transforming teaching extends to how music is taught, and the explicit connection between music and teaching as improvisation represents a fresh and forward-looking approach pointing the way to models of teaching that reflect the subject matter more closely than traditional, pre-scriptive, corseted, and teacher-directed methods can do.[26] In this way, teach-ing more closely approximates the nature of music making and taking itself, and the medium more clearly reflects the message.

Transforming teaching is first and foremost personal business. It necessi-tates the sorts of teachers who are dedicated and knowledgeable musicians; understand their personal strengths and weaknesses; and have a clear vision of what they seek to accomplish, high expectations of themselves and oth-ers tempered with compassion and realism, a love of the musics of which they are exponents and the particular people, young or old, whom they instruct, and a desire to communicate their knowledge to their students and to improve the musical traditions of which they are heirs. To accomplish this requires people of integrity who are bright, articulate, tactful, compassion-ate, and astute, the best musicians and communicators, the very cream of society. Their preparation requires a broad education, academic challenge, extensive opportunities to practice the art of teaching guided by experienced mentors who exemplify the highest professionalism in their lives and work, high academic and musical expectations, and time to reflect on that practice. Such high expectations reflect the fact that music education is central to music because it is vital to the survival of any musical practice.

Seeing that teaching, like the art of music, involves learning ways of acting or doing, all the learning about theoretical principles of music and education, no matter how vital, cannot substitute for extended teaching practice or apprenticeship under the guidance of expert teachers. Just as it is more time-consuming to learn the practical skills and procedural knowl-edge of being a musician than to learn the theoretical or propositional knowledge about music, so it takes much longer to become an expert teacher of music than to learn the theory about it—a reality that needs to be reflected in teacher preparation and professional development pro-grams. This being said, however, theory is important, and bridging the divide between theory and practice is a tall order that requires revaluing practice, forging strong links between theory and practice, and providing extensive opportunities for teachers at all levels to improve their grasp of theory as well as practice and to see the connection between the two. To ensure this, theoretically oriented music education courses at every level need to be permeated with applications to practice, just as practical experi-ences need to be imbued with opportunities for research and reflection. And the more closely that teaching experiences mirror real-life situations, the more seriously students can be expected to take their theoretical study, and the greater its inspirational value in prompting them to find their own teaching styles as they also hone the practical craft of teaching.

Outstanding music teachers have been with us since antiquity. Their expectations of themselves and their students are typically high, and they inspire their students to do things that the latter never dreamed possible. Too often, the work of these teachers continues in relative obscurity. Many are women whose efforts are transforming the cultural lives of the communities in which they live and work. These teachers seek constantly to improve their practice, search for greater understanding, and influence the lives of generations of children and youth by dint of their humility, passion, diligence, and integrity. Irrespective of the particular educational fads of the time, they continue to broaden and deepen the musical understanding of their students while also inspiring them to be better people. Telling and listening to their stories can bring alive the many and varied ways in which music educators think, are, and act; it can highlight the many ways in which music instruction can be carried on effectively, the impact that it can have on the hearts and minds of students, and the importance of being true to oneself and to one's beliefs, passions, strengths, and weaknesses as a teacher and learner. The systematic study of these stories can provide opportunities to sharpen critical thinking skills, apply theory to practice, and highlight the need for careful analysis and well-devised strategies that address the challenges and realize the possibilities of each instructional situation.[27] Reflection and discussion of the questions raised can also focus teacher and student attention on the questions themselves, foster a love of the questions and respect for divergent solutions, cultivate imaginative thinking, and prompt teachers to try out alternative strategies and work to improve their practice.

To transform music teaching systemically requires the collective efforts of teachers, administrators, and others interested in the work of music education. When teachers are active partners in dialogue about the issues they face and have opportunities to practice skills themselves rather than simply watching others or hearing about how to do them, organizations and meetings of music teachers can be especially helpful in improving teaching practice. As teachers genuinely engage ideas and are heard in the public spaces, they can think new thoughts and be inspired to transform their own practice. They require extended opportunities in professional meetings for dialogue in seminar or discussion formats with other teachers, where leaders and fellow teachers pose questions that prompt participants to think through issues and alternative strategies for themselves. They need to be able to try out practical skills in master class formats where they can receive feedback from others and hone skills in the company of others. In these among other ways, meetings, symposia, and other gatherings of music teachers and administrators can be powerful agents for transforming music education.

Importantly, transforming music teaching needs to include the various societal institutions that are engaged in music education, be they family, religion, commerce, politics, or music profession. Reinventing music teaching with this reality in mind suggests preparing people who may later earn their livelihoods while doing the work of music education in such diverse worlds as business, engineering, entertainment, arts administration, music therapy, church music, studio instruction, music performance, government, social work, architecture, instrument design and manufacture, mass media, community schools and colleges, clinical psychology, and geriatric services. To prepare students for this new world, fostering such projects as joint programs that combine music education with other fields of study or multitrack programs that allow students to specialize in the particular specialties in music education in which they expect to work or teach can provide opportunities for dialogue among people from fields that are now isolated from one another, and can open up opportunities for young and old alike to transform musical culture.

Leading

It would be wishful thinking to suppose that all music teachers are willing and eager to improve their practice and transform their teaching. Human nature being what it is, many prefer the safety of the status quo; they are afraid of change and look to leaders for direction, guidance, support, assistance, and even protection. Leaders are vital to transforming music education because they provide the context in which music teachers work that affects their lives, happiness, and willingness to transcend past practice and forge something better for the future. If leaders are to act toward transforming music education, they need to understand how to achieve this. Seeing that educational transformation operates best through persuading rather than dictating to others, a humane approach to leadership suggests that leaders exemplify in their own work with teachers the same attitudes and values that they wish teachers, in turn, to model with their students, and that they act with, rather than on behalf of, other teachers to improve music instruction. A leader requires not only knowledge of the subject matter but also administrative knowledge and practical skill. These leadership skills are best acquired, like other arts, through practice combined with theoretical study, requiring opportunities for music administrators and teachers to hone their leadership skills, reflect on their practice, and share their insights with each other. Inspectors, supervisors, and administrators are, in some ways, relics of the old industrial second-wave worldview, and it is not surprising that they often think of their positions hierarchically, and themselves primarily as means of quality control, to ensure certain standardized products. However, if leaders are to influence teachers toward transforming their teaching, or if teachers are to assume a genuinely collegial rather than subordinate relationship with their administrators, leaders need to practice leadership differently than in the past. They may need to reinvent their positions, work alongside teachers rather than issue directives to them, and do everything within their power to create humane environments that foster transforming music teaching and learning. This is not an easy task. The conflict between consultative and inspecting roles is sometimes difficult to resolve, for administrator and teacher alike, and shifting the balance toward a collaborative and consultative role may be difficult to achieve. It may also be difficult if not impossible to acquire the power to effect change, and there are limits to the ability of administrators, no matter how skilled or well-meaning, to improve a situation; they also work within an organizational context and are subject to external pressures from those to whom they are accountable. Still, leaders can do all in their power to work for change and to subvert oppressive and dehumanizing management systems.

It is difficult to imagine transforming music education without also transforming the perspectives and practices of the administrators and colleagues of the institutions in which music teachers work or the public to whom they are responsible. For this reason, a comprehensive plan for transforming music education needs to address music education in centers of advanced learning such as universities, colleges, conservatories, and institutes. Changing the present reality of musically and culturally uninformed educational and community leaders and policy makers requires working toward a more central role for the arts in the academy and in the general education of tertiary students. In our time, the demands of the information age for a sophisticated workforce emphasize advanced education and necessitate artistic among other education that fosters imaginative, intuitive, and logical thinking. Just as nineteenth-century music educators developed a plan for musical instruction in the general education of all students in elementary and secondary schools, so twenty-first-century music educators need also to develop a plan for the musical and artistic education of students at centers of advanced learning. Taking the arts seriously in tertiary education can eventually affect elementary, secondary, and tertiary education by changing the nature of the administrative, collegial, and public context in which music teachers work.

Because transformation plays out over long periods of time, over decades or even centuries, music education leaders and policy makers must stay the course of their decisions over the long haul. Without the long-term commitment to particular plans of action, transformation founders on the shoals of fashion and faddishness. It takes time, sometimes multiple generations, to work out ideas in practice. Just as the development of a rich musical culture in Germany and Austria during the eighteenth and nineteenth centuries was the outgrowth of centuries of musical education and political patronage, so the singing schools in Britain and the United States during the same period eventually flowered in the choral and orchestral societies in the nineteenth and twentieth centuries, and the nineteenth-century military and town bands in the United States eventually expanded in instrumental music education in twentieth- and twenty-first-century public schools. These long-term developments would not have been possible in the absence of the persistence and commitment of their protagonists over generations. Taking the long view avoids the distractions and fads that lurk along the way and helps to make possible transforming music education.

Music Making and Taking

In a mass-mediated, information-driven, multicultural world, the pressures toward change—toward depreciating, neglecting, and even excluding traditional ways of thinking and acting—are pervasive and powerful. If the young abandon or forget their musical heritage, they can become disconnected from the past that shaped their forbears with a resulting loss of a sense of personal identity, security, and even community, and along with increasing isolation, a less secure basis from which to connect with different others. Lewis Rowell's example of the Greek mythical figures, Clotho and Atropos, the spinner of thread and the one who prepares to sever it, shows that musical change brings some measure of discontinuity, and I cannot see how this can be avoided.[28] Still, transformation is a matter of both selecting what to keep and deciding what new to embrace; tradition and change, Clotho and Atropos, are both implicated. Transforming music education necessarily engages popular music if for no other reason than that it is the folk music of our time; it forms the inescapable backdrop of contemporary life. Beyond this reality, however, lies the task of deepening a learner's understanding of how this music is made and its function in daily life. Popular music constitutes a bridge to other great and little traditions that are also this student's particular heritage, seeing as these traditions are often invoked in the popular culture of a place and time. Beyond them are other traditions even further removed from the student in time and place. If the practices of great and little traditions are to be kept alive and flourish, music educators also need to take particular care of those traditions that are out of the limelight, less accessible to the majority of people, yet valuable as a part of the rich mosaic of cultural heritage and musical expression. Given music's living, vital quality, its exponents seek to transcend past practice. Practitioners have a dual responsibility—to the past as well as to the future. This conserving quality of transformation suggests that teachers underscore the musical traditions that have led to present practice and, where possible or appropriate, keep them alive. One might propose, for example, that shawms, sackbuts, and viols, as historic artifacts, no longer play a vital role in contemporary music making. Why take time for their study and keep their practice alive, when their immediate usefulness has passed? Surely a school would be better served by having synthesizers, electric guitars, and saxophones. My reply is that the matter is not this simple. It is in the nature of the educational enterprise that teachers push the borders of ignorance backward toward antiquity, just as they also push outward toward other places or traditions, or forward toward the future. Understanding early music is key to grasping the roots of Western civilization and classical music; it is vulnerable now because it is out of the limelight and, as such, can easily be ignored, and if not practiced, lost. The very fact that early music is so strange and inaccessible to many ears makes it especially interesting and vital as a part of musical education; shawms, sackbuts, and viols may have an important place in music education even though, and possibly because, they are rarely heard in today's popular music.

With the benefit of a musical education, music makers of whatever practice are in a better position to decide what of past practice to keep and what to discard. As such, they can preserve and enrich the particular popular and traditional musics of which they are the exponents or to which they adhere. For example, Western musicians can build a rejuvenated and transformed classical tradition that juxtaposes musics as it also melds others and draws from the vernacular musics of our time. Popular musicians can tap into the resources of the Western classical tradition and thereby enrich popular music making. Musicians steeped in particular vernacular traditions can acquire skills and understandings that broaden their perspectives on the diversity of cultural expressions and open their hearts and minds to other different musics. As such, transforming music education enables music makers of all sorts to cross over between or collaborate with music makers from other traditions, just as it also promotes the transformation of those traditions themselves; it removes barriers and creates bridges of understanding between and among musics and those who make and take music, so that people can travel more easily between them.

The musical world I envisage does not valorize one music as better than another but exemplifies a plethora of rich traditions, many less popular than others, yet nevertheless supported and enriched by the transformative efforts of musicians. Commonalities as well as differences provide a leitmotif for the study of these disparate traditions. Musics are engaged critically with a view to making them more humane, better understood by those outside as well as inside the particular tradition. And the study of each tradition takes into account the different perspectives and practices of people in time and place.

I worry about the fragility of a remarkable classical tradition that grew up in the West and, while representative of European perspectives, has been contributed to by musicians from every continent. Despite its relative unpopularity in our time, this tradition represents a phenomenal achievement by men and women who mined the potential of its sounds and scales. Likewise, jazz constitutes one of the uniquely North American contributions to the world of music, yet, like its classical cousins, it has become the province of a relatively few practitioners, its contributions largely ignored by most people. These traditions are precious accomplishments. The young, especially in the West, need to become acquainted with them, as they also come to understand how these traditions relate to their own worlds of music. Only as this occurs will their understanding broaden as it also deepens. And in passing on these traditions, teachers can help ensure that these musics continue to live and doubtless change.

The embarrassment of musical riches in our time poses a tremendous challenge for the music teacher in that it is often more difficult to decide what musical repertoire or activities to exclude rather than what to include within the program of study. On the other hand, the reality that music is practiced and requires knowing how to go on in as well as knowing about it constitutes a limitation to the musics that can reasonably be studied.[29] The deeper one digs, the more likely a musical practice turns out to be constituted of several or even many practices, each with its own specific rules. To return to our example of early music, all depends on which particular early music one is talking about, of which time, which place, or which composer or practitioner. Even within a musical practice, there are differences as well as commonalities. For practical reasons, teachers need to be very selective regarding the particular music(s) studied and examples chosen. Not only does this approach obviate curricular diversity, but it also reinforces the importance of the present instructional moment and of the teacher's choice of exemplary music of whatever sort or tradition. As such, it demands higher rather than lower expectations of teachers and their students. With so much to learn, time cannot be frittered away in entertaining students but becomes precious amid the opportunity to push back the borders of ignorance and deepen understanding not only of music but also of self, others, and whatever lies beyond.

That music is so diverse suggests a polyglot of instructional programs, each filling a somewhat specialized niche. One might expect to find programs fostering early musics, contemporary musics, popular musics, classical musics, and traditional musics of all sorts, each focusing on the array of musical experiences such as composing, improvising, performing, listening, producing, and distributing, in which the teacher is skilled. This diversity of programs across the various agencies of music education reflects the diversity of music itself. One imagines the esoteric and especially fragile traditions being nurtured and transformed along with those that lie within the musical mainstream. All of these musics are valued, while also criticized. Even as new musics emerge from the coalescence of others, so teachers ensure that less accessible but historically valued musics are not silenced by the hegemony of those that are currently fashionable or politically or economically viable. Instead of capitulating to popular culture, programs foster the more esoteric, classical traditions. As such, the dialectic between musical elitism and universalism plays out in music education, and both ideals coexist, sometimes tenuously. This reality fosters a multiform rather than uniform curriculum in which the needs of the few and those of the many are met in a host of different ways and the needs and interests of minorities are protected.

There is also the musical imperative of making music, whether it be through composing, improvising, performing, and listening to music as a practical activity, something not only thought about but done in the context of a musical community, tradition, practice, or ritual. Hence the importance of communities of musicians, structures of rules, and sets of practices that constitute the frameworks in which people make music. And in the information age, at a time when much learning is individual, and the young have more limited opportunities in general education to develop life and social skills than in the past, group music making provides a welcome opportunity for communal or social learning that balances an increasing reliance on individual and technologically driven learning in society at large.

Learning

In learning there is a sense in which one engages in the process of rediscovery, in finding that which has been lost. One goes over the ground again, inquires once more, rethinks theoretical problems, and reinvestigates phenomenal events. Certainly, some of the same philosophical, musical, and educational problems that confront us today have been grappled with in the past, and there is a sense of returning to well-worn themes. Likewise in science, the basic foundations of proceeding slowly with great care, regarding results with skepticism, and if possible refuting them, evidences a similar mind-set in which the student returns again and again to the questions and evidence to review, refine, and, if possible, improve upon past understandings.

Still, whether it be philosophy, science, or any other field of inquiry, there is also the sense that one has not gone over this territory before, that changes in place and time have changed both the frame in which questions are asked and addressed and the significance or meaning attached to the findings. True, astronomers in the past attempted to map the heavens and understand the place of planet Earth in the universe. However, the tools and information at their disposal could not come close to contemporary understandings made possible by recent technological inventions and the cumulative efforts and persistence on the part of astronomers and other scientists over the millennia of recorded history. The universe of the present is a radical and new departure from the limited understandings of the past. This is new territory not visited before in the annals of recorded human history. Likewise it is in music education. Though possibly less dramatic than astronomical developments, researchers continue to uncover new and different insights on music teaching and learning, just as teachers and their students continue to advance their understandings.[30]

The very ambiguity of music—its texts, scores, practices, and meanings—necessitates the constant discovery and rediscovery of ways of making and taking music. Many new musical ideas and interpretations arise during the compositional or improvisatory process, or during the re-study, re-performance, or re-hearing of a particular piece of work. The many different possible compositions that may be derived from the same scale, the many different score readings of a particular musical work, and the many different nuances of musical meaning grasped by the listener come as fresh discoveries, as if one has not heard this particular feature before. Discovering the many facets of a musical belief or practice helps bring the music alive. And bringing and keeping music alive and growing, and discovering and rediscovering its many aspects, necessitates imaginative and divergent thinking.

Curiosity—an inquisitiveness concerning peculiar phenomena, wondering about why things are as they are—is one of the drivers of imaginative thinking and creative action. In the territory between fancy, abstract thought, and perception, one imaginatively explores the terrain of the might-have-been or might-be and wonders what if such-and-such were the case. The music maker spins out musical and other ideas in a variety of ways and, in the process, discovers new insights and creates new music that also threatens to break with the past. In oral traditions, the music is remembered and reconstituted as the performers together enact and reenact the rituals of which music is a part. Yes, there is the old, but importantly, the music is rediscovered in new and differing ways. As such, musical knowledge comes with the force of insight. Music thus reenacted is not only rediscovered in some respects but discovered anew in others. Such curiosity, a love of wisdom and a desire to know better and more fully, is the lifeblood of transforming music education. No matter how expressed, whether through such diverse means as scientific research, reflection on practice, music composition, performance, listening, or technical production, curiosity and a desire to make sense or meaning of the phenomenal world and whatever lies beyond drive the search for better ideas and practices on the part of music teachers, students, and all those interested in their work. And they point to the might-yet-be, to the possibility, even probability, of new forms of music and musical instruction in the future.

Given the importance of learning as a key element of transforming music education, it is imperative to create the sorts of conditions in which it can flourish. What are these conditions? I submit that they are the selfsame ideals of mutuality, respect, freedom, and fidelity, among others that ground this study. The creative edge is easily dulled, and it is up to music education policy makers to devise the kinds of conditions that foster divergent thinking, individual expression, and carefulness, among the host of qualities that allow and encourage risk taking and discovery on the part of teachers and their students. Fostering such values as well-articulated and fair policies, professional conduct, intellectual prowess, inclusiveness of and respect for differing points of view, broad perspectives, and dispassionate attitudes establishes the conditions in which learning can flourish. Breaking out of the restrictive ideas and practices of the past is not done to disparage the status quo just for the sake of doing so. Rather, the commitment to learning provides clear reasons for transforming music education by finding better ways of musical instruction; creating a richer musical culture; and fostering greater happiness, nobility, sensitivity, and understanding in those who are involved in or affected by its work.

Toward a Better World

How would the ways of thinking, being, and acting in transforming music education affect the participants, communities of musicians and educators, and society at large? How would the world be better for transforming music education? In unpacking these questions, I want to address specifically the pervasive and systemic problems of gender, worldview, music, education, tradition, and mind-set in music education with which I began this book, to show how they can be re-visioned and practiced differently. Showing how music education might be different also portends how its effects might ripple outward to change the wider education, society, and culture of which it is a part. My sketch is of a transforming music education already in place, or as if it were already in place. Couching it in the present tense is an act of faith, a clear-eyed vision of what could be.

Transforming music education affirms the contributions of women and men, boys and girls, in all areas of musical and music educational life, regardless of gender. It is devoted to breaking down barriers of gender that prevent some from reaching the potential they might otherwise attain, thereby enriching and celebrating the musical gifts and experiences of all members of society. It repudiates exclusive masculine prerogatives and perspectives; insists on the inclusion of feminine and masculine viewpoints in all facets of music and music educational life; protects the more fragile minority perspectives; and embraces work and play, pleasure and understanding, intellection and sensibility as elements of musical and educational experience. It criticizes extant musical traditions insofar as they are mainly the work of men or embody sexist thought and practice. And it reconstructs notions of gender in music and society, affirms both femininity and masculinity, avoids restrictive stereotypes of males and females, and recognizes androgynous qualities within the well-developed personality. It welcomes and affirms people of whatever sexuality within the worlds of music making, thereby validating them as persons of worth. And it transforms relationships between males and females and makes an inclusive and egalitarian learning community, and its effects ripple outward into the wider world as it changes the hearts and minds of teachers and their students.

Artistic, information-based, and symbolic-centered ways of meaning making are included alongside scientifically oriented, factory-based, and technocratic worldviews. Transforming music education recognizes the importance of intuition, reason, and feeling as valid means of intellection. It affirms the multiplicities and pluralities in contemporary society and respects and sustains minority belief and practice while also seeking societal unity and mutual understanding. As such, it has a profound impact on every aspect of music education. It prepares people who can work in the arts and sciences, among other symbol systems, critical thinkers who bring imagination and intuition together with reason and who can thrive in a world in which information and technology must be balanced with wisdom and humanity. It engenders individuality while fostering community, and open-mindedness toward different others while developing a sense of personal tradition. It prepares people to live in an uncertain and changing world by helping them forge a basis for personal faith and conviction and cope successfully with the changes and uncertainties they confront in their lives. It stresses spiritual values in a materialistic age while preparing people to succeed in their chosen ways of life. And it celebrates the diversity and richness of musics around the world and provides students with tools by which to negotiate these musics while also keeping sight of the value and richness of the traditions to which they are heirs.

The plethora of classical and vernacular traditions that make up the musics of the world—their respective theories and practices, similarities and differences, ways of making and taking music—form the subject matter of transforming music education. It approaches these musical beliefs and practices comparatively, respecting their differences yet looking beneath the surface to see the commonalities in ways people make musical meaning. It rejects simplistic or Eurocentric definitions of music and music education, understanding that while the Western classical concept of music focuses predominantly on human constructions of sounds, this is a minority perspective, and what Westerners understand as music represents a small part of larger, artistically unified constructs in which the arts combine within rituals to express human meaning making. It recognizes that while people in other cultures may not have words that equate to Western notions of music, they nevertheless do what Westerners think of as music; they act musically and borrow aspects of Western music, just as Westerners borrow from theirs. This conceptually fuzzy notion of music, in which rules for making and taking music are determined within the context of particular practices, necessitates forging an alternative paradigm by which music and musical instruction can be studied contextually, ethnologically, and comparatively as well as formally, curatorially, and normatively.[31] It also involves reshaping musical beliefs and practices when they militate against the values that frame the transformative process and undergird the civil society—values such as justice, civility, equality, goodness, and mutuality. This view of music pervades every aspect of music education. It prepares people to care for and about musical experience, respect and care for the musical traditions of others, and treasure their own musical heritages and reshape them where necessary. It provides them with the skills to express themselves musically in a variety of ways, as composers, performers, producers, distributors, or listeners, and to integrate music as a vital part of daily living. And it constitutes opportunities to experience human creative and musical genius at work, to aspire to excellence not only musically but also in the rest of life, to become not only better musicians but also better people.

Here is a broad view of education that is both directive and liberative, didactic and dialogical, subject-centered and student-centered. Not only does it construe teaching variously,[32] but it constitutes an agent of transmission as well as transformation in society. As such, this educative view impacts every aspect of transforming music education. It engages teacher and student actively in the instructional process and, through exposition and dialogue, constitutes a liberative as well as conservative agent. It assumes a prophetic role within society by embodying, exemplifying, or expressing the shape of things to come; it constitutes a living example at a micro level of how society might work at the macro level. As with prophets of our past and present, it may also be an irritant to society because it subverts the status quo, undermines cherished privilege, and challenges established tradition. Inspiration arises from the power of example. Where some may doubt the possibility of transformation or lack the imagination or ability to construct transforming education, demonstration offers hope for, and practical knowledge in, realizing its ideals. As such, it is necessarily a grassroots movement. Where directed institutionally, as it may be on occasion, its leaders rely upon the practical instances and demonstrations throughout the field, and these instances are persuasive to music educators and those interested in their work. Far from constituting a superficial restructuring of educational institutions, such transforming education becomes a life-changing process for all engaged in it. It seeps throughout the system, affecting all.

Musical and educational traditions are respected yet criticized and re-visioned. Transforming music education anchors in particular places and times and yet embraces wider national, regional, and global perspectives. In the West it is cognizant of the popular musics with which teacher and student identify, takes a curatorial approach to the Western classical tradition and other Western vernacular traditions, yet enlarges learners' understandings of musics beyond the West. It treats tradition not as something set in stone but as a dynamic, living thing that adapts to changing circumstances, in which it is being forged by those who practice and identify with it. As a process as well as a product, it is in a state of becoming as well as being. It is both idealistic and realistic, straddling the worlds of the possible and the actual, and negotiating the tensions between values and their expression musically and educationally. As such, it affords learners the opportunity to participate in making, preserving, and transforming past beliefs and practices in the context of present realities. It also affirms and celebrates the participants in the process of socially constructing traditions and building bridges of understanding between them.[33] Its dialectical approach to tradition enriches civility and culture and benefits all humankind.

Transforming music education resists the pitfalls of dystopian or utopian mind-sets, settling, instead, in the region of optimistic realism. It takes seriously Schiller's caution to "think of [people] as they ought to be when called upon to influence them; think of them as they are, when tempted to act on their behalf."[34] It is hopeful while practical, drawing from past experience yet not bound by it, imaginative yet reasonable, daring yet cautious. The dialectical nature of mind-set affects every area of music education. It takes an optimistic view of instruction while recognizing the discontinuity between possibility and actuality, views teaching as helpful to learning while also recognizing the importance of the learner's decision in realizing her or his potential, and sets tasks for the learner just out of the learner's grasp yet within her or his ability to accomplish. Rather than jumping on current fads or bandwagons without careful and critical reflection, music education policy makers weigh the advantages and disadvantages of each option and exercise discretion regarding the alternatives they select. Each commitment is provisional in the sense that it is revisited and reexamined from time to time, abandoned only when the weight of philosophical argument or empirical evidence suggests that it is reasonable to do so.

Within the context of commitment to such ideals as justice, equality, mutuality, and fidelity, transforming music education addresses each of the systemic and dehumanizing flaws in music and education. All of its facets are infused by a broad and dialectical vision that calls for reshaping the institution of music education as well as the individual experience of its members. A paradigmatic shift toward transforming music education can be realized, practically, in many different ways. Its dialectical nature is not an invitation to some bland meld of alternatives or to a uniform approach mandated for all. Rather, as I have pointed out, each of these dialectics may be difficult to reconcile, and a variety of possibilities emerge. How, for example, does one find a way between the claims of generally shared expectations concerning musical belief and practice that suggest the possibility of certain musical standards with those of protecting differences, minority perspectives, and alternative ways of making and taking music? How does one combine objectives of uniformity on the one hand and multiformity on the other, transmission on the one hand and transformation on the other, atomistic approaches on the one hand and holistic approaches on the other? In response to these questions, my earlier metaphor of drama suggests that one or another possibility may be in the foreground at a particular time or that aspects may be reconciled at different levels of generality. What is important is that options are not prematurely foreclosed and that one may constitute a foil for another.

At first glance, these dialectics might seem to be mutually contradictory or exclusive. On further examination, they can be worked through, although the particular solutions reached are likely to differ from time to time and place to place, and they necessitate living with tension and paradox. Solutions, where found, turn out to be inherently shortsighted, problematical, and fallible. Each generation of music educators grapples with solving these dialectics and revisits its aims and methods from the perspectives of its particular time and place. For example, the idea of comprehensive musicianship, construed as a broad preparation in music history, theory, composition, performance, and listening, is among the historically resilient aims of music education to resurface in various modern music education philosophies.[35] This notion, originally formulated in terms of Western classical music, has been rethought and broadened to include diverse musics and comparative and contextual approaches to music as part of culture. Generally speaking, musicians may agree with the appropriate shape of comprehensive musicianship, and their professional common sense may constitute the basis for some practical commonality in terms of certain broad objectives of music education. However, as music teachers apply these general principles to their studios, classrooms, and all the other places in which they teach, they may also embrace multiformity as a guiding principle. This is not surprising in view of the fact that teachers have long realized that there ought to be room for a variety of ways to reach common goals and that there may and should be dissent about the aims of musical education. So it is possible that the dialectics of uniformity and multiformity can be resolved, to some extent, in terms of different levels of generality or specificity, aspects of music education, or differences between theory and practice.

Genuine, ongoing, and widespread dialogue constitutes a key to transforming music education. A dialogue, as I conceive it, is a conversation in which each person listens to, genuinely hears, and respects all of the other participants. It is truly open-ended in that it may result in divergent opinions and convictions among the participants, who may criticize professional common sense and offer alternatives to it. In transforming music education, instead of having leaders decide what is best for music educators, dictate to or persuade others of their plans under the guise of building consensus, and achieve compliance by dint of influence, authority, pressure, or force, dialogue occurs widely throughout the profession, and ideas and plans seep up through the system, later to be facilitated and implemented by leaders. Nor is dialogue constrained by external dicta that define the parameters in which it takes place or spell out the conclusions it must reach. Instead, participants delight in the questions. Their conversations invite active engagement, prompt individual commitment, and inspire to transformative action.

There is always the danger that virtues will be turned into vices, that oppressive forces will prove too resistant to change or transformative elements too fragile to survive in the long term. This necessitates constant vigilance on the part of music education policy makers. A dialogical approach goes a long way toward liberating learners and equipping them with the critical skills they need to resist the pitches and pressures of authority figures. Instead of being told what to do, learners discover what they must do. Not only does its open-endedness allow learners to grapple with dialectical issues in their own terms, but as they participate in this conversation, the process of personal and institutional transformation in music education is set in motion, even if its ends remain forever out of reach.

For transformative music education to be life-changing, it needs to translate into practical plans and policies. Collective action is essential for an institution to survive, and leaders are charged with forging such plans and policies. How can music education policy makers break free from the strictures of top-down, paternalistic, and managerial thinking? Among the possibilities, they can re-vision their roles and responsibilities and draw on alternative leadership models that foster such values as consensus, equality, inclusiveness, and cooperation among participants. They can rethink notions of consensus and consensus building and seek to ascertain if there is consensus before formulating their plans rather than waiting until after plans are laid to build support for them. They can take a longer view, moving slowly and carefully, recognizing that education is a long-term enterprise and that no administrative action may be better than ill-considered action. And they can take a broader view of music education, realizing the limitations of their perspectives and the fallibility of their plans.

It is just as important to journey toward transformation as to arrive at one's destination. In a sense, one never arrives, because the ends sought seem to keep moving away as one travels toward them, and the conception of these ends changes along the way. In the search for wisdom, the questions the philosopher asks are central to the transformative process. Philosophy assists music educators and those interested in their work in formulating questions about the aims and methods of music education. It helps learners frame the questions and critically think through possible answers, formulate concepts and carefully engage them, and prepare practical solutions and evaluate their respective merits. Participating in this questioning process in shared and genuinely open dialogue is personally and communally transformative. It provides an opportunity for individual learners to critically examine their perspectives, plans, and programs, and it enables the community of learners to benefit from the differing insights of others. In so doing, they may imagine what might and should be done, and they gain the courage to transform their particular situations.

If some are reluctant to embrace a transforming vision of music education, there is always the hope that practical examples of such music education may persuade them to change their minds. Notwithstanding that philosophers throughout recorded history may have wished that their ideas would take hold systemically, this rarely seems to have been the case. Instead, their visions captured the imaginations of some administrators, teachers, or students, who, in many, varied ways and to differing degrees, sought to cultivate music and transform the lives of young and old alike in their particular spheres of influence, be it studio or classroom, vocal or instrumental ensemble, opera house or concert hall. Sometimes, transforming music education begins in an obscure classroom and ripples out into the lives of students and colleagues, eventually catching the attention of music educators more widely. At other times, it is fostered by leaders in the musical or educational world who are in the position to implement a national system of music education or even to build international support for it. Whatever the particular ways in which it occurs, transforming music education begins with individuals, wherever they may be, and their responsibilities toward transforming music education are important, irrespective of their specific roles in musical and educational life, whether elementary classroom teacher, college professor, studio teacher, orchestra board member, university trustee, church musician, software designer, fine arts consultant, or superintendent of schools.

Coda

The picture of transforming music education that I have sketched challenges music educators to raise their expectations of themselves, their colleagues, their students, and their publics; to look beyond the ordinary; and to aspire to distinction in every aspect of their work. Transforming music education seeks excellence in every facet of its enterprise. It embraces and fosters the best in music of whatever genre. Its policy makers and teachers exemplify and epitomize the highest standards of professionalism as musicians and educators. Far from being a retreat from high expectations, transforming music education challenges music educators to significantly raise their sights in every area and at every level. Schoolchildren can acquire sophisticated musical knowledge and demonstrate superb musicianship. Undergraduates can read widely, demonstrate professionalism in and devotion to their work, and cherish intellectual prowess, musical passion, and practical skill. Graduate students can aspire to scholarly excellence, creativity, and a rich professional life as mentors, musicians, and educators. Professors can exemplify in their work and creative output the best in scholarship, performance, composition, or whatever their particular gifts and interests predispose them to create. There is no room in transforming music education for laziness and lack of carefulness, anti-intellectualism and lack of learning, narrowness and rigidity of thinking, opportunism and lack of professionalism. Rather, transforming music education appeals to the highest aspirations of musicians, educators, and their publics. The richness of its conception meets the challenges of our time and offers hope toward enriching human experience. And it calls for a revolution in the institution of music education; a pervasive, systemic, ongoing, and radical intervention in the status quo; and a conversion of the hearts and minds of all those involved in its work.

I have often reflected on the fate of Plato's cave dweller who, having been dragged out into the sunlight, caught a vision of another possibility for existence.[36] When he went back into the cave to tell his fellows what he had seen and persuade them to leave the cave, they were so angry with him that they considered killing him. Imagine Plato telling this story and thinking about his teacher, Socrates, who had been forced to drink the hemlock because he incurred the ire of his contemporaries. I return to this story again and again because it underscores the discomfort the philosopher brings to people satisfied with the status quo, the pervasive human tendency to resist the transformative action for which he or she calls, and the courage the philosopher must have in the face of concerted opposition.[37] As I have shown in these pages, the ideal of transforming music education challenges and benefits not only individuals but the societies of which they are a part, and I must follow the idea wherever it leads and whatever the consequences. Was the mission of Plato's caveman hopeless? I think not. Excellent teacher that he was, Plato probably would have thought it worthwhile that one person had seen the sunlight even if the rest of the cave people wouldn't follow their prophet. Still, I wonder, maybe with Plato, how much better it might have been for all had others been willing to take a risk and walk out into the sunshine.

NOTES

1. Setting the Stage

1. One account of these changes for music composition and the possibilities for music education is provided by Edward Williams, "'Obsolescence and Renewal' (Musical Heritage, Electronic Technology, Education and the Future)," *International Journal of Music Education* no. 37 (2001): 13–31.

2. Jacques Attali, *Noise: The Political Economy of Music,* trans. Brian Massumi (Minneapolis: University of Minnesota, 1985), 19, makes the point that repetition silences others "by mass-producing a deafening, syncretic kind of music, and censoring all other human noises."

3. Kurt Blaukopf, *Musical Life in a Changing Society,* trans. David Marinelli (Portland, Oreg.: Amadeus Press, 1992), chap. 3.

4. For a discussion of notions of what educators ought to bring to these "multiplicities and pluralities," see Maxine Greene, *The Dialectic of Freedom* (New York: Teachers College Press, 1988), chap. 4. On educational issues arising out of this conservatism, see Michael Apple, *Official Knowledge: Democratic Education in a Conservative Age,* 2d ed. (New York: Routledge, 2000).

5. The homogeneity of core beliefs, values, expectations, and aspirations in American society evoked by Amitai Etzioni's "monochrome" metaphor, in his *The Monochrome Society* (Princeton, N.J.: Princeton University Press, 2001), suggests that while Americans may evidence an array of beliefs and values, they are all shades of one color rather than various colors of the rainbow.

6. This resistance against liberal ideologies of all stripes is evident in responses to feminism; see Susan Faludi, *Backlash: The Undeclared War against American Women* (New York: Crown Publishers, 1991).

7. The rationale for music education has changed relatively little since music entered the publicly supported schools of Boston in the first part of the nineteenth century; see Estelle R. Jorgensen, "Justifying Music Instruction in American Public Schools: An Historical Perspective," *Bulletin of the Council for Research in Music Education* no. 120 (Spring 1994): 17–31.

8. This is seen, for example, in contemporary music education and in its history in the United States. Michael L. Mark and Charles L. Gary, *A History of American Music Education* (New York: Schirmer Books, 1992); and Michael L. Mark, *Contemporary Music Education,* 3d ed. (New York: Schirmer Books, 1996).

9. The Music Educators National Conference, now known as the MENC—The National Association for Music Education, led a consortium of arts organizations in formulating and publishing *The National Standards for Arts Education: What Every Young American Should Know and Be Able to Do in the Arts,* ed. Michael Blakeslee (Reston, Va.: Music Educators National Conference, 1994).

10. On philosophical fallacies, see Anthony Weston, *A Rulebook for Arguments,* 2d ed. (Indianapolis: Hackett, 1992), chap. 10. Also, see Estelle R. Jorgensen, "What Are the Roles of Philosophy in Music Education?" *Research Studies in Music Education* no. 17 (December 2001): 19–31.

11. This point is made in Estelle R. Jorgensen, *In Search of Music Education* (Urbana: University of Illinois Press, 1997).

12. Estelle R. Jorgensen, "Philosophical Issues in Music Curriculum," in *New Handbook of Research in Music Teaching and Learning*, ed. Richard C. Colwell and Carol Richardson (New York: Oxford University Press, March 2002), 48–62.

13. Samuel Lipman, *The House of Music: Art in an Era of Institutions* (Boston: David R. Godine, 1984), 263, 265.

14. *Growing Up Complete: The Imperative for Music Education*, The Report of the National Commission on Music Education (Reston, Va.: Music Educators National Conference, 1991), 3.

15. Lucy Green, *Music on Deaf Ears: Musical Meaning, Ideology, and Education* (Manchester: Manchester University Press, 1988), chap. 6. For an account of the story of British Secondary School Music in the twentieth century, see Stephanie Pitts, *A Century of Change in Music Education: Historical Perspectives on Contemporary Practice in British Secondary School Music* (Aldershot, Hampshire: Ashgate, 2000).

16. For example, Robert Walker, "Music Education Freed from Colonialism: A New Praxis," *International Journal for Music Education* 27 (1996): 2–15, suggests that *music* is a Western term for a particular Western cultural activity and that the Ghanaian words *dwom* or *agror* might do just as well as *music* (pp. 8–10). Also, see Robert Walker, *Musical Beliefs: Psychoacoustic, Mythical, and Educational Perspectives* (New York: Teachers College Press, 1990).

17. Estelle R. Jorgensen, "Engineering Change in Music Education: A Model of the Political Process Underlying the Boston School Music Movement," *Journal of Research in Music Education* 31 (1983): 67–75; Bernarr Rainbow, *Land without Music: Musical Education in England 1800–1860 and Its Continental Antecedents* (London: Novello, 1967); and Bernarr Rainbow, *Music in Educational Thought and Practice: A Survey from 800 B.C.* (Aberystwyth, Wales: Boethius Press, 1989).

18. Warren Bennis and Patricia Ward Biederman, *Organizing Genius: The Secrets of Creative Collaboration* (Reading, Mass.: Addison-Wesley, 1997), make the point that in today's world, most creative projects are accomplished within the context of groups rather than individually, as in the past. Likewise, Donald Arnstine, *Democracy and the Arts of Schooling* (Albany: State University of New York, 1995), chap. 8, points to the important role of school systems on educational practice.

19. John Dewey, *The Public and Its Problems* (Denver: Alan Swallow, c. 1927).

20. Henry Zentner, *Prelude to Administrative Theory: Essays in Social Structure and Social Process* (Calgary: Strayer Publications, 1973), chap. 7.

21. Blaukopf, *Musical Life in a Changing Society*, chaps. 2 and 11.

22. *National Association of Schools of Music 2001–2002 Handbook* (Reston, Va.: National Association of Schools of Music, 2001).

23. Blaukopf, *Musical Life in a Changing Society*, chap. 22, points to the influence of the metropolis on contemporary life and the fact that it is difficult for individuals and groups to be noticed in the noise and competition for attention. One sees only a small portion of what is to be seen and heard. Sound becomes comparatively lost in the pervasively visual emphasis in contemporary society. Among the writers to study culture—in particular, the influence of the mass media as an educational agency—one thinks of Henry A. Giroux's writing; for example, his *Fugitive Cultures: Race, Violence, and Youth* (New York and London: Routledge, 1996), and his *Impure Acts: The Practical Politics of Cultural Studies* (New York and London: Routledge, 2000). For a compilation of some of his important essays, see Henry A. Giroux, *Pedagogy*

and the Politics of Hope: Theory, Culture, and Schooling: A Critical Reader (Boulder, Colo.: Westview Press, 1997).

24. Elisabeth Schüssler Fiorenza, *But She Said: Feminist Practices of Biblical Interpretation* (Boston: Beacon Press, 1992), has stated publicly that she coined the term *kyriarchy* to connote these systemic forces of oppression because she came to believe that the term *patriarchy* was both passé and limited; it had become hackneyed, and it didn't do justice to the systemic oppression that transcends patriarchal beliefs and practices. Its connotation to the *Kyrie* should not be missed, in its plea for divine help—for mercy, justice, and grace.

25. Jorgensen, *In Search of Music Education.*

26. Estelle R. Jorgensen, "On Teaching Music with Care," *Quarterly Journal of Music Teaching and Learning* 7, no. 2 (1997): 65–76; Nel Noddings, *Caring: A Feminine Approach to Ethics and Moral Education* (Berkeley: University of California Press, 1984); Nel Noddings, "On Community," *Educational Theory* 46, no. 3 (Summer 1996): 245–267; and Aaron Schutz, "Caring in Schools Is Not Enough: Community, Narrative, and the Limits of Alterity," *Educational Theory* 48, no. 3 (Summer 1998): 373–393.

27. Greene, *The Dialectic of Freedom*, chap. 2, agrees that the American perception of freedom is illusory and that despite ideals of freedom and democracy, many are silenced, marginalized, and oppressed. Jane Roland Martin, *Coming of Age in Academe: Rekindling Women's Hopes and Reforming the Academy* (New York and London: Routledge, 2000) writes of her personal journeys of realization within the academy. And Martha Nussbaum, *Cultivating Humanity: A Classical Defense of Reform in Liberal Education* (Cambridge, Mass.: Harvard University Press, 1997) argues for academic reform toward humane educational ideals.

28. On needs and drives, see a classic statement in Abraham H. Maslow, *The Farther Reaches of Human Nature* (1971; reprint, Harmondsworth, Middlesex: Penguin, 1976), and his *Religions, Values, and Peak Experiences* (1964; reprint, Harmondsworth, Middlesex: Penguin, 1976). On the collective consciousness, see C. G. Jung, *The Archetype and the Collective Unconscious*, trans. R. F. C. Hull, 2nd ed. (Princeton, N.J.: Princeton University Press, 1969); C. G. Jung, *The Development of Personality*, trans. R. F. C. Hull, 3rd ed. (Princeton, N.J.: Princeton University Press, 1970); C. G. Jung, *The Structure and Dynamics of the Psyche*, trans. R. F. C. Hull, 2nd ed. (Princeton, N.J.: Princeton University Press, 1969); and C. G. Jung, *The Undiscovered Self*, trans. R. F. C. Hull (Boston: Little, Brown, 1958). Blaukopf, *Musical Life in a Changing Society*, 43, notes that Émile Durkheim sees collective consciousness as the "subject matter" of sociology. See Émile Durkheim, *The Rules of Sociological Method*, ed. Steven Lukes; transl., W. D. Halls (New York: Free Press, 1982). For another view of the relationship of collective consciousness and music, see Max Weber, *The Rational and Social Foundations of Music*, ed. and trans. Don Martindale, Johannes Reidel, and Gertrude Neuwirth (Carbondale: Southern Illinois University Press, 1958).

29. Paulo Freire, *Pedagogy of the Oppressed*, trans. Myra Bergman Ramos (New York: Continuum, 1990).

30. As I have pointed out elsewhere, in Jorgensen, *In Search of Music Education*, 80, and in Estelle R. Jorgensen, "The Artist and the Pedagogy of Hope," *International Journal of Music Education* 27 (1996): 36–50, this notion of *conscientization* is a complicated, dialectical concept. Freire largely abandoned using the word *conscientização* because he believed it to be widely misinterpreted.

31. Greene, *The Dialectic of Freedom*, 17; bell hooks, *Teaching to Transgress: Education as the Practice of Freedom* (New York and London: Routledge, 1994), chap. 7; and

Parker J. Palmer, *The Courage to Teach: Exploring the Inner Landscape of a Teacher's Life* (San Francisco: Jossey-Bass, 1998), are among those to address the importance of solidarity with others in the search for freedom.

32. Among those to raise this question were John Shepherd and his colleagues in their book, *Whose Music? A Sociology of Musical Languages* (London: Latimer, 1977).

33. This issue became a central theme in the Tanglewood Symposium, whose members weighed in on the side of including popular and other world musics beyond the Western classical tradition; see Robert A. Choate, ed., *Documentary Report of the Tanglewood Symposium* (Washington: MENC, 1968), 139.

34. hooks, *Teaching to Transgress*, passim.

35. Arnstine, *Democracy and the Arts of Schooling*, 196–198, 202, writes of the anesthetic effect of schooling.

36. Michael Chanan, *Musica Practica: The Social Practice of Western Music from Gregorian Chant to Postmodernism* (London: Verso, 1994), chap. 10, coins the term "electronified" music.

37. This is not a new idea. Christopher Small, *Music–Society–Education: A Radical Examination of the Prophetic Function of Music in Western, Eastern, and African Cultures with Its Impact on Society and Its Use in Education* (London: John Calder, 1977), is among those to make similar claims.

38. Werner Jaeger, *Paideia: The Ideals of Greek Culture*, trans. Gilbert Highet, 2d ed., 3 vols. (New York: Oxford University Press, 1945), notes that the word *paideia* resists easy translation. It has been rendered variously as philosophy, education, and culture, but none of these words when taken alone does justice to the original Greek conception. As an ideal and practice, it straddles the theoretical and phenomenal worlds.

39. This is the case, for example, in Plato's *Republic*, trans. Robin Waterfield (New York: Oxford University Press, 1993).

40. On the arts as central elements of general education, see Friedrich Schiller, *On the Aesthetic Education of Man in a Series of Letters*, ed. and trans. Elizabeth M. Wilkinson and L. A. Willoughby (Oxford: Clarendon Press, 1967); John Dewey, *Art as Experience* (New York: G.P. Putnam's Sons, 1934); Herbert Read, *Education through Art* (London: Faber and Faber, 1958); Harry Broudy, *Enlightened Cherishing: An Essay on Aesthetic Education*. The 1972 Kappa Delta Pi Lecture. (Urbana, IL: University of Illinois Press for Kappa Delta Pi, 1972); Mortimer Adler, *Reforming Education: The Opening of the American Mind* (New York: Macmillan, 1977); Mortimer Adler et al., *The Paideia Program: An Educational Syllabus* (New York: Macmillan, 1984); Elliot W. Eisner, *Cognition and Curriculum Reconsidered*, 2d ed. (New York: Teachers College Press, 1994); Maxine Greene, *Releasing the Imagination: Essays on Education, the Arts, and Social Change* (San Francisco: Jossey-Bass, 1995); and Charles Fowler, *Strong Arts, Strong Schools: The Promising Potential and Shortsighted Disregard of the Arts in American Schooling* (New York: Oxford University Press, 1996).

41. For a discussion of education as enculturation, see Jorgensen, *In Search of Music Education*, 23–29.

42. The names of some prominent teachers from Canada, Great Britain, continental Europe, and the United States are recorded in Kenneth Simpson, ed., *Some Great Music Educators: A Collection of Essays* (Borough Green, Kent: Novello, 1981); Rainbow, *Music in Educational Thought and Practice*; F. Paul Green and Nancy F. Vogan, *Education in Canada: A Historical Account* (Toronto: University of Toronto Press, 1991); Mark and Gary, *A History of American Music Education*; Gordon Cox, *A History of Music Education in England, 1872–1928)* (Aldershot, Hampshire: Scolar Press, 1993); George

N. Heller, *Historical Research in Music Education: A Bibliography*, 3d ed. (Lawrence, Kans.: Division of Music Education and Music Therapy, University of Kansas, 1995); and Pitts, *A Century of Change in Music Education.* Participants in Vision 2020: The Housewright Symposium on the Future of Music Education, issued a declaration to guide the future of school music teaching and learning in the United States. See Clifford K. Madsen, ed., *Vision 2020: The Housewright Symposium on the Future of Music Education* (Reston, Va.: MENC, 2000), 219–220.

43. Charlene Morton, "Feminist Theory and the Displaced Music Curriculum: Beyond the 'Add and Stir' Projects," *Philosophy of Music Education Review* 2, no. 2 (Fall 1994): 106–121.

44. In the Northern Indian classical tradition, for example, that which is old is often valued because it is old. See Daniel M. Neuman, *The Life of Music in North India: The Organization of an Artistic Tradition* (Detroit: Wayne State University Press, 1980).

45. Estelle R. Jorgensen, "Musical Multiculturalism Revisited," *Journal of Aesthetic Education* 32, no. 2 (Summer 1998): 77–88; Estelle R. Jorgensen, "Justifying Music in General Education: Belief in Search of Reason," in *Philosophy of Education 1996*, ed. Frank Margonis (Urbana, Ill.: Philosophy of Education Society, 1996), 228–236; and Jorgensen, *In Search of Music Education.*

46. Freire, *Pedagogy of the Oppressed*, 19–21.

47. Israel Scheffler, *In Praise of the Cognitive Emotions and Other Essays in the Philosophy of Education* (New York and London: Routledge, 1991), 13, 130–131, also cautions against "radical skepticism," "the *rejection* of all expectation—in effect, the denial of all belief."

48. Henry Zentner, "The Construction of Types and Standards in Sociology: A Critical Reassessment," *International Journal of Critical Sociology* 3 (1979): 49–59.

49. This notion of the "ground between" is evocative of Martin Buber's notion of the "between" in human relationships; see, for example, his *Between Man and Man*, trans. Ronald Gregor Smith (1947; reprint, London and Glasgow: Collins, Fontana Library, 1961).

50. The discontinuity between theory and women's experience, as Jean Grimshaw, *Philosophy and Feminist Thinking* (Minneapolis: University of Minnesota Press, 1986), 75, observes, is one of the "central themes of feminism." Theories that are articulated in such strictly logical and rational terms as were my "ideal types" seem remote from the lived experience of teachers and students—a factor that doubtless contributes to the lack of interest by many teachers in academic research and philosophical inquiry.

51. There is little emphasis on choice theory in music education or on how music educators make decisions. See Estelle R. Jorgensen, "An Analysis of Aspects of Type IV Music Instruction in a Teacher-Student Dyad," *Quarterly Journal of Music Teaching and Learning* 6, no. 1 (Spring 1995): 16–31; Estelle R. Jorgensen, "Aspects of Private Piano Teacher Decision-making in London, England," *Psychology of Music* 14, no. 2 (1986): 111–129; Estelle R. Jorgensen, "On the Decision-making Process in Music Education," *Journal of Educational Thought* 19, no. 3 (1985): 218–237; and Estelle R. Jorgensen, "On a Choice-based Instructional Typology in Music," *Journal of Research in Music Education* 29 (1981): 97–102. Hypothesis generation tends to look backward by estimating the likelihood of what might happen based on past evidence, while choice theory, drawing on past experience, looks forward by forecasting how people will behave in the future.

52. Émile Jaques-Dalcroze, *Rhythm, Music, and Education*, trans. Harold F. Rubinstein (New York: Arno Press, 1921); Percy A. Scholes, *Music, the Child, and the*

Masterpiece: A Comprehensive Handbook of Aims and Methods in All That Is Usually Called "Musical Appreciation" (London: Oxford University Press, 1935); *The Selected Writings of Zoltán Kodály*, trans. Lili Halápy and Fred Macnicol (London: Boosey and Hawkes, 1974); Carl Orff and Gunild Keetman, *Orff-Schulwerk: Musik für Kinder*, 5 vols. (Mainz: B. Schott's Sohne; New York: Schott Music Corporation, 1950–1954); Shinichi Suzuki, *Nurtured by Love: A New Approach to Education*, trans. Waltraud Suzuki (New York: Exposition Press, 1969); R. Murray Schafer, *The Thinking Ear: Complete Writings on Music Education* (Toronto: Arcana Editions, 1986); Patricia Shehan Campbell, *Lessons from the World: A Cross-Cultural Guide to Music Teaching and Learning* (New York: Schirmer Books, 1991); and Doreen Rao, *Choral Music Experience—Education through Artistry* (New York: Boosey and Hawkes, 1987–1991).

53. Polly Carder, ed., *The Eclectic Curriculum in American Music Education: Contributions of Dalcroze, Kodály, and Orff*, 2d ed. (Reston, Va.: MENC, 1990); and Estelle R. Jorgensen, "Curriculum Design in Music," *College Music Symposium* 28 (1988): 94–105.

54. Carol Gilligan, *In a Different Voice: Psychological Theory and Women's Development* (Cambridge, Mass.: Harvard University Press, 1982); Lyn Mikel Brown and Carol Gilligan, *Meeting at the Crossroads: Women's Psychology and Girls' Development* (New York: Ballantine Books, 1992); and Jill McLean Taylor, Carol Gilligan, and Amy M. Sullivan, *Between Voice and Silence: Women and Girls, Race and Relationship* (Cambridge, Mass.: Harvard University Press, 1995).

55. In music, for example, one thinks of two prominent American basal series: Judy Bond et al., coordinating authors, *Share the Music*, 7 vols. (New York: Macmillan, 2000); and Jane Beethoven et al., program authors, *The Music Connection*, 8 vols. (Morristown, N.J.: Silver Burdett Ginn, 2000).

56. This cyclicality is evidenced throughout curriculum history. See William F. Pinar et al., *Understanding Curriculum: An Introduction to the Study of Historical and Contemporary Curriculum Discourses* (New York: Peter Lang, 1994), chap. 4, for evidence of the ahistoricity and cyclicality of curricular ideas during the twentieth century. For a discussion of the cyclicality of multicultural music education, see Therese M. Volk, *Music, Education, and Multiculturalism: Foundations and Principles* (New York: Oxford University Press, 1998).

57. Pinar et al., *Understanding Curriculum*, points to the interest of teachers and educational institutions in the economic and political success of their innovations.

58. Iris M. Yob, "Can the Justification of Music Education Be Justified?" in *Philosophy of Education 1996*, ed. Margonis, 237–240.

59. Morton, "Feminist Theory and the Displaced Music Curriculum," describes some of the difficulties in such an approach.

60. Vernon A. Howard, *Artistry: The Work of Artists* (Indianapolis, Ind.: Hackett, 1982), chap. 6.

61. Keith Swanwick, *Music, Mind, and Education* (London and New York: Routledge, 1988); Keith Swanwick, *Musical Knowledge: Intuition, Analysis and Music Education* (London and New York: Routledge, 1994); Keith Swanwick, *Teaching Music Musically* (New York: Routledge, 1999); and June Boyce-Tillman, "Conceptual Frameworks for World Musics in Education," *Philosophy of Music Education Review* 5, no. 1 (Spring 1997): 3–13.

62. Nicholas C. Burbules and Thomas A. Callister Jr., "Knowledge at the Crossroads: Some Alternative Futures of Hypertext Learning Environments," *Educational Theory* 46, no. 1 (Winter 1996): 23–50.

63. Ibid., 35, 36.

64. The potentially rich relationship between dialectic and dialogic is noted by Deanne Bogdan, "Book Review," *Philosophy of Music Education Review* 6, no. 1 (Spring 1998): 71–73.

65. Freire, *Pedagogy of the Oppressed*, chap. 4, contrasts dialogical and anti-dialogical education; Greene, *The Dialectic of Freedom*, chaps. 4 and 5, and Greene, *Releasing the Imagination*, part 3, point to the importance of dialogue as a means toward discovering freedom within community.

66. Walker, "Music Education Freed from Colonialism"; and Henry Kingsbury, "Situations, Representations, and Musicalities: An Anthropological Perspective," *Philosophy of Music Education Review* 5, no. 2 (Fall 1997): 86–91.

67. Jorgensen, "Musical Multiculturalism Revisited." My approach is consistent with dialectical and dialogical approaches to music by such writers as Charles Keil and Steven Feld, *Music Grooves: Essays and Dialogues* (Chicago: University of Chicago Press, 1994), 20, who believe that "music is our last-best source of participatory consciousness and it has this capacity not just to model but maybe to enact some ideal communities." However, Keil and Feld's musical metaphor of "grooving" in which "the phallic needle drops into the vaginal groove" (p. 23) should be challenged for its mechanistic quality, exclusivity, and the passive role accorded the feminine role in sexuality and, implicitly, in music. That two men conduct the conversation omits the perspectives of different others that would doubtless change substantially the nature and tenor of the dialogue. Nor do they trust their dialogues, preferring, rather, to insert extended academic discourses in their book by way of propping their dialogues up with the very "rationalism and empiricism" that they decry because of its tendency to "squeeze the participatory out from everybody's lives" (p. 24).

68. For Maxine Greene, "Metaphors and Multiples: Representation, the Arts, and History," *Phi Delta Kappan* (January 1997): 387–394, these forces become so strong as to more or less mandate a pluralistic approach to education.

69. Estelle R. Jorgensen, "Music Education as Community," *Journal of Aesthetic Education* 29, no. 3 (Fall 1995): 71–78; and Noddings, "On Community." On the limitations of a dialogical approach to education, see Alison Jones, "The Limits of Cross-Cultural Dialogue: Pedagogy, Desire, and Absolution in the Classroom," *Educational Theory* 49, no. 3 (Summer 1999): 299–316.

70. Noddings, "On Community," 258.

71. Yob, "Can the Justification of Music Education Be Justified?"

72. Noddings, "On Community," 266–267. To this end, Noddings cautions against "pushing for collective goals and demanding a collective identity" (p. 267).

73. Scheffler, *In Praise of the Cognitive Emotions*, 126–139.

74. Estelle R. Jorgensen and Iris M. Yob, "Theory into Practice and Practice into Theory in Music Education: A Philosophical Conversation," Presentation to the Research in Music Education Symposium II, University of Exeter, U.K., April 2001.

75. Estelle R. Jorgensen, "A Dialectical View of Theory and Practice," *Journal of Research in Music Education* 49, no. 4 (Winter 2001): 343–359.

76. At first glance, it may appear that the author's text is not privileged; that is to say, the author does not decide which route(s) the learner will travel, and in what order. Rather, the learner decides which texts to pursue and how to pursue them. In fact, however, the learner manipulates material that is privileged in that it has been assembled and written by the author.

77. This is true, for example, in the formulation of national standards in music, which are arranged conceptually rather than in terms of psychological characteristics. Also, see John Dewey's essay, *The Child and the Curriculum*, in John Dewey, *The Child and the Curriculum* and *The School and Society*, combined edition (Chicago and London: University of Chicago Press, 1956), 3–31. Even when theorists construed music more broadly, the search for a universal theory was evident in the latter part of the twentieth century. See, for example, Jay Rahn, *A Theory for All Music: Problems and Solutions in the Analysis of Non-Western Forms* (Toronto: University of Toronto Press, 1983).

78. On this point, Jerome Bruner has been misunderstood to say that the structure of the subject matter is inherent in the subject itself. His later writings suggest, however, that the learner's psychological makeup and cultural background also factor into the structure of the subject. See, for example, Jerome Bruner, *Acts of Meaning* (Cambridge, Mass.: Harvard University Press, 1990).

79. The notion of the search for the one high road of education was debunked by writers during the mid-nineteenth century, when various competitive methods were in vogue. See "On Simplifying Instruction in Vocal Music," *English Journal of Education* 4 (1846): 360.

80. Joseph J. Schwab, "The Practical: Arts of Eclectic," *School Review* 79 (1971): 493–542; Joseph J. Schwab, *The Practical: A Language for Curriculum* (Washington: National Education Association, 1970); and Israel Scheffler, *Reason and Teaching* (Indianapolis and New York: Bobbs-Merrill Co., 1973), 181–197.

81. Deanne Bogdan sees this indeterminacy in my notion of praxis and the subject matter of music as underscoring "the element of the experiential" in a theory of music education and as virtually recuperating the "disadvantages" of my dialectical approach. Personal communication, 30 October 1996.

82. On the applicability of philosophical analysis to curricular decision making, see Scheffler, *Reason and Teaching*; Paul S. Hirst, *Knowledge and the Curriculum: A Collection of Philosophical Papers* (London: Routledge and Kegan Paul, 1974); P. H. Hirst and R. S. Peters, *The Logic of Education* (London: Routledge and Kegan Paul, 1970); and Robin Barrow, *Giving Teaching Back to Teachers: A Critical Introduction to Curriculum Theory* (Sussex: Wheatsheaf Books; Totawa, N.J.: Barnes and Noble, 1984). Rather than turning to philosophy, recent reconceptualist thinking about curriculum has drawn principally from the social sciences, theology, and feminist thought. See, for example, William F. Pinar, ed., *Curriculum: Toward New Identities* (New York: Garland, 1998); and Pinar et al., *Understanding Curriculum*.

83. For a discussion of this point and the distinction between philosophical and scientific refutation, see Jorgensen, "Justifying Music in General Education," in *Philosophy of Education 1996*, ed. Margonis.

2. Justifying Transformation

1. There is an embarrassment of riches on these themes; among the host of writers that might be named, one thinks, for example, of John Dewey, *Democracy and Education: An Introduction to the Philosophy of Education* (New York: Macmillan, 1916); Noddings, *Caring*; Greene, *The Dialectic of Freedom*; Freire, *Pedagogy of the Oppressed*; Jane Roland Martin, *The Schoolhome: Rethinking Schools for Changing Families* (Cambridge, Mass.: Harvard University Press, 1992); hooks, *Teaching to Transgress*; Arnstine, *Democracy and the Arts of Schooling*; and Nussbaum, *Cultivating Humanity*.

2. The case for this view in music education is made in Jorgensen, *In Search of Music Education.*

3. The need for such a moral and spiritual emphasis in education is underscored by David E. Purpel, *The Moral and Spiritual Crises in Education: A Curriculum for Justice and Compassion in Education* (New York: Bergin and Garvey, 1989).

4. In his notion of *praxis*, Freire, *Pedagogy of the Oppressed*, 76, notes that it is not enough to become conscious of the need for change; one must also "work to transform the world." Ira Shor, *Empowering Education: Critical Teaching for Social Change* (Chicago and London: University of Chicago Press, 1992), is among those to apply Freire's ideas to the American college classroom.

5. This radical and critical pedagogy is evident in the work of Giroux, who notes the role of the arts and culture as a vital part of educational transformation. See, for example, Henry A. Giroux, *Theory and Resistance in Education: A Pedagogy for the Opposition* (New York: Bergin and Harvey, 1983); Giroux, *Fugitive Cultures*; Giroux, *Pedagogy and the Politics of Hope*; and Giroux, *Impure Acts*.

6. Among those to challenge male aesthetic perspectives are Sophie Drinker, *Music and Women: The Story of Women in Their Relation to Music* (New York: Coward-McCann, 1948); Catherine Clément, *Opera, or, the Undoing of Women*, trans. Betsy Wing (Minneapolis: University of Minnesota Press, 1988); Heide Göttner-Abendroth, *The Dancing Goddess: Principles of a Matriarchal Aesthetic*, trans. Maureen T. Krause (Boston: Beacon Press, 1991); Susan McClary, *Feminine Endings: Music, Gender, and Sexuality* (Minneapolis: University of Minnesota Press, 1991); John Shepherd, *Music as Social Text* (Cambridge: Polity Press, 1991), chap. 8; Lydia Goehr, *The Imaginary Museum of Musical Works: An Essay in the Philosophy of Music* (Oxford: Clarendon Press, 1992); Christine Battersby, *Gender and Genius: Towards a Feminist Aesthetic* (Bloomington: Indiana University Press, 1993); Marcia J. Citron, *Gender and the Musical Canon* (New York: Cambridge University Press, 1993); Hilda Hein and Carolyn Korsmeyer, eds., *Aesthetics in Feminist Perspective* (Bloomington: Indiana University Press, 1993); and Susan Crook and Judy Tsou, eds., *Cecilia Reclaimed: Feminist Perspectives on Gender and Music* (Urbana: University of Illinois Press, 1994). Writers such as Madeline Grumet, *Bitter Milk: Women and Teaching* (Amherst: University of Massachusetts Press, 1988); Deanne Bogdan, *Re-educating the Imagination: Towards a Poetics, Politics, and Pedagogy of Literary Engagement* (Portsmouth, N.H.: Boynton/Cook; Toronto: Irwin, 1992); Greene, *Releasing the Imagination*; Julia Koza, "Aesthetic Education Revisited: Discourses of Exclusion and Oppression," *Philosophy of Music Education Review* 2, no. 2 (Fall 1994): 75–91; Roberta Lamb, "Feminism as Critique in the Philosophy of Music Education," *Philosophy of Music Education Review* 2, no. 2 (Fall 1994): 59–74; and Lucy Green, *Music, Gender, Education* (Cambridge: Cambridge University Press, 1997), direct their attention to male views of the arts (notably music) in education, and cite historical, literary, and empirical evidence of patriarchy and sexism. And Marianne Kielian-Gilbert, "The Woman in the Music (On Feminism as Theory and Practice)," *College Music Symposium* 40 (2000): 62–78, takes a dialectical perspective that situates feminist musical contribution at the intersection of theory and practice.

7. There is also a growing body of gender research in music education. See, for example, Roberta Lamb, "Women Composers in School Music Curricula, Grades 5–8: A Feminist Perspective," in *The Musical Woman: An International Perspective*, vol. 3 (1986–1990), ed. J. Zaimont (New York: Greenwood Press, 1991), 682–713; Julia Koza, "Picture This: Sex Equity in Textbook Illustrations," *Music Educators Journal* 78 (1992): 28–33; Julia Eklund Koza, "The 'Missing Males' and Other Gender Issues in

Music Education: Evidence from the Music Supervisors' Journal, 1914–1924," *Journal of Research in Music Education* 41, no. 3 (Fall 1993): 212–232; Julia Eklund Koza, "Females in 1988 Middle School Music Textbooks: An Analysis of Illustrations," *Journal of Research in Music Education* 42, no. 2 (Summer 1994): 145–171; Jason Zervoudakes and Judith Tanur, "Gender and Musical Instruments: Winds of Change?" *Journal of Research in Music Education* 42, no. 1 (Spring 1994): 58–67; Elizabeth S. Gould, "Getting the Whole Picture: The View from Here," *Philosophy of Music Education Review* 2, no. 2 (Fall 1994): 92–98; Barbara Payne, "The Gender Gap: Women on Music Faculties in American Colleges and Universities, 1993–94," *College Music Symposium* 36 (1996): 91–102; Carolyn Livingston, "Women in Music Education in the United States: Names Mentioned in History Books," *Journal of Research in Music Education* 45, no. 1 (Spring 1997): 130–144; and Sondra Wieland Howe, "Reconstructing the History of Music Education from a Feminist Perspective," *Philosophy of Music Education Review* 6, no. 2 (Fall 1998): 96–106. Special issues of the *British Journal of Music Education* (November 1993), *Quarterly Journal of Music Teaching and Learning* (Winter 1993 and Spring 1994), and *Philosophy of Music Education Review* (Fall 1994) have been devoted to feminist perspectives on music education.

8. This is consistent with the findings of Ellen Koskoff and her colleagues in Ellen Koskoff, ed., *Women and Music in Cross-Cultural Perspective* (Urbana: University of Illinois Press, 1989).

9. Maxine Greene, *Landscapes of Learning* (New York: Teachers College Press, 1978), chap. 11, borrowed Alfred Schutz's notion of "wide-awakeness."

10. Scholes, *Music, the Child, and the Masterpiece,* 81.

11. Paulo Freire, *Pedagogy of Hope: Reliving Pedagogy of the Oppressed,* trans. Robert R. Barr (New York: Continuum, 1994), 65–68.

12. Gould, "Getting the Whole Picture." On queer theory and musicology, see, for example, Philip Brett, Elizabeth Wood, and Gary C. Thomas, eds., *Queering the Pitch: The New Gay and Lesbian Musicology* (New York: Routledge, 1994).

13. Anthony E. Kemp, *The Musical Temperament: Psychology and Personality of Musicians* (Oxford: Oxford University Press, 1996), 108–120. This androgynous quality and the feminization of the field of music—that is, its association with women and gay men—seems to counter the view that formal music making is grounded in masculine perspectives and practices.

14. Claire Detels, *Soft Boundaries: Re-Visioning the Arts and Aesthetics in American Education* (Westport, Conn.: Bergin and Garvey, 1999) chap. 1, distinguishes between "hard boundaries" and "soft boundaries."

15. On ideal-typical matriarchal and patriarchal aesthetics, see Heide Göttner-Abendroth, "Nine Principles of a Matriarchal Aesthetic," in *Feminist Aesthetics,* ed. Gisela Ecker, trans. Harriet Anderson (Boston: Beacon Press, 1985), 81–94.

16. One thinks, for example, of Baldassarre Castiglione, *The Book of the Courtier,* trans. George Bull (Harmondsworth and Baltimore: Penguin Books, 1976).

17. Green, *Music, Gender, Education.*

18. Leonard Meyer, *Emotion and Meaning in Music* (Chicago: University of Chicago Press, 1956).

19. Shepherd, *Music as Social Text.*

20. Zentner, "The Construction of Types and Standards in Sociology," would define these instances as empirical types.

21. Albert Lord, *The Singer of Tales* (Cambridge, Mass.: Harvard University Press, 1960); Catherine Ellis, *Aboriginal Music: Education for Living* (St. Lucia, Queensland:

University of Queensland Press, 1985); and Steven Feld, *Sound and Sentiment: Birds, Weeping, Poetics, and Song in Kaluli Expression*, 2d ed. (Philadelphia: University of Pennsylvania Press, 1990).

22. Göttner-Abendroth, "Nine Principles of a Matriarchal Aesthetic," in *Feminist Aesthetics*, ed. Ecker.

23. Green, *Music, Gender, Education.*

24. Small, *Music–Society–Education*, chaps. 3 and 4.

25. The impact of scientific thinking in music education is described in Estelle R. Jorgensen, "Some Observations on the Methodology of Research in Music Education," *Canadian Music Educator* 20, no. 2 (1979): 45–50.

26. This is the clear impression conveyed in National Commission on Excellence in Education, *A Nation at Risk: The Imperative for Educational Reform* (Washington: U.S. Government Printing Office, 1983).

27. Small, *Music–Society–Education*, chap. 9.

28. Small's stretch toward musical artistry is reminiscent of the forward-looking views of Jacques Attali or Walter Wiora, who suggested that a new musical and cultural worldview was emerging. See Attali, *Noise*; and Walter Wiora, *The Four Ages of Music*, trans. M. D. Herter Norton (New York: W. W. Norton, 1965).

29. Alvin and Heidi Toffler, *Creating a New Civilization: The Politics of the Third Wave* (Atlanta: Turner Publishing Co., 1994).

30. Susanne K. Langer, *Philosophy in a New Key: A Study in the Symbolism of Reason, Rite, and Art*, 3d ed. (Cambridge, Mass.: Harvard University Press, 1957); Howard Gardner, *Frames of Mind: The Theory of Multiple Intelligences* (New York: Basic Books, 1983); Jerome Bruner, *On Knowing: Essays for the Left Hand*, exp. ed. (Cambridge, Mass.: Harvard University Press, 1979); and Bruner, *Acts of Meaning*. For a recent account and extension of Langerian ideas and their relevance to explaining the relationship between music and emotion, see Laird Addis, *Of Mind and Music* (Ithaca, N.Y.: Cornell University Press, 1999).

31. These principles are exemplified in curricular writing. See Philip Phenix, *Realms of Meaning: A Philosophy of the Curriculum for General Education* (1964; reprint, Ventura, Calif.: Ventura County Superintendent of Schools Office, 1986); Eisner, *Cognition and Curriculum Reconsidered*; Greene, *The Dialectic of Freedom*; Greene, *Releasing the Imagination*; Pinar et al., *Understanding Curriculum*, 20; and William E. Doll Jr., *A Post-Modern Perspective on Curriculum* (New York: Teachers College Press, 1993).

32. For example, Flo Conway and Jim Siegelman, *Snapping: America's Epidemic of Sudden Personality Change* (Philadelphia: Lippincott, 1998), point to a significant rise in the incidence of people unable to cope psychologically.

33. This tendency is lamented, for example, in Jonathan Rosenbaum, "The Danger of Putting Our Cultural Destiny in the Hands of Business," *Chronicle of Higher Education*, 17 April 1998, A64. Also, Christopher Small, *Musicking: The Meaning of Performing and Listening* (Hanover and London: Wesleyan University Press, 1998), notes the pervasive impact of business thought and practice on the symphony orchestra concert.

34. This view is sketched in Jorgensen, *In Search of Music Education*, 3. The Gaia hypothesis is sometimes construed within the context of postpositivism in contrast to the earlier positivistic paradigm undergirding the scientific worldview. See Egon G. Guba, ed., *The Paradigm Dialog* (Newbury Park, Calif.: Sage Publications, 1990).

35. Douglas John Hall, *The Steward: A Biblical Symbol Come of Age*, rev. ed. (Grand Rapids, Mich.: William B. Eerdmans Publishing Co.; New York: Friendship Press, 1990).

36. Howard, *Artistry*; and Vernon A. Howard, *Learning by All Means: Lessons from the Arts* (New York: Peter Lang, 1992).

37. For a discussion of the implications of Howard's ideas for music teacher preparation, see N. Carlotta Parr, "Towards a Philosophy of Music Teacher Education," *Philosophy of Music Education Review* 7, no. 1 (Spring 1999): 55–64. Among those who follow Howard in significant respects, see David J. Elliott, *Music Matters: A New Philosophy of Music Education* (New York: Oxford University Press, 1995).

38. For example, see Ruth M. Stone, *Dried Millet Breaking: Time, Words, and Song in the Woi Epic of the Kpelle* (Bloomington: Indiana University Press, 1988); and Christopher Small, *Music in a Common Tongue: Survival and Celebration in African-American Music* (New York: Riverrun Press, 1994).

39. Nelson Goodman, *Of Mind and Other Matters* (Cambridge, Mass.: Harvard University Press, 1952), 168–172, turns the current scientific bias in the academy on its head in "Message from Mars."

40. In this respect it is prophetic of society; see Attali, *Noise*.

41. Henry Raynor, in *A Social History of Music: From the Middle Ages to Beethoven*, and *Music and Society Since 1815*, two volumes in one, unabridged (1972, 1976; reprint, New York: Taplinger, 1978), chaps. 4–6; and Abram Loft, "Musicians' Guild and Union: A Consideration of the Evolution of Protective Organization Among Musicians" (Ph.D. diss., Columbia University, 1950; Ann Arbor: University Microfilms, 1950).

42. On anthropological and ethnomusicological accounts of American conservatories and music schools, see Henry Kingsbury, *Music, Talent, and Performance: A Conservatory Cultural System* (Philadelphia: Temple University Press, 1988); and Bruno Nettl, *Heartland Excursions: Ethnomusicological Reflections on Schools of Music* (Urbana: University of Illinois Press, 1995).

43. Arnold Perris, *Music as Propaganda: Art to Persuade, Art to Control* (Westport, Conn.: Greenwood, 1985); and Estelle R. Jorgensen, "Music and International Relations," in *Culture and International Relations*, ed. Jongsuk Chay (New York: Praeger, 1990), 56–71.

44. Alan Yorke-Long, *Music at Court: Four Eighteenth Century Studies* (London: Weidenfeld and Nicolson, 1954); and Lipman, *The House of Music*. Battersby, *Gender and Genius*, 2, 4, shows how males coopted such "feminine" qualities of genius as intuition, imagination, and emotion while denying attributions of genius to female artistic expression.

45. One would not then be surprised by the finding in Green, *Music on Deaf Ears*, that Western classical music more or less remains the mainstay of English school music programs.

46. John Blacking, *How Musical Is Man?* (London: Faber and Faber, 1976). Although Kingsbury, "Situations, Representations, and Musicalities," warns against putting too much stock in evidence from pre-Independence South Africa, Blacking's point seems well taken and resonates with the experience of other countries that have been colonized by European powers.

47. Jorgensen, *In Search of Music Education*, chap. 2.

48. Neil Postman, *Teaching as a Conserving Activity* (New York: Dell Publishing Co., 1979).

49. A reader may take issue, for example, with the particular social and political interpretation of the development of tonality in European classical music in Shepherd, *Music as Social Text*, chap. 6.

50. The interconnectedness of classical and vernacular music is underscored by Sidney Finkelstein, *Composer and Nation: The Folk Heritage in Music*, 2d ed. (New York: International Publishers, 1989).

51. Rose Rosengard Subotnik, "The Challenge of Contemporary Music," in *What Is Music? An Introduction to the Philosophy of Music*, ed. Philip Alperson (1987; reprint, University Park: Pennsylvania State University, 1994), 359–396.

52. Yahlin Chang, "Cross Over Beethoven," *Newsweek*, 20 April 1998, 60–62, comments on these sorts of crossovers between classical and popular music as possibly "the only future classical music has" (p. 62).

53. Henry A. Giroux, *Border Crossings: Cultural Workers and the Politics of Education* (New York and London: Routledge, 1992), uses the metaphor of crossing and recrossing borders that mark differences of culture, race, and gender.

54. Jorgensen, "On Teaching Music with Care." On musical obligation, see Morris Grossman, "Performance and Obligation," in *What Is Music?* ed. Alperson, 255–281.

55. Freire, *Pedagogy of the Oppressed*, chaps. 3 and 4.

56. Scheffler, *Reason and Teaching*, chap. 6.

57. Dewey, *The Child and the Curriculum*.

58. As Peter Kivy, *Authenticities: Philosophical Reflections on Musical Performance* (Ithaca, N.Y.: Cornell University Press, 1995), shows, the concept of musical authenticity is ambiguous and culturally interpreted, which leads him to refer to it in the plural. Also, see the critique of the ideal of authenticity, or *Werktreue*, in Goehr, *The Imaginary Museum of Musical Works*, especially, chaps. 4 and 9. Goehr points out that this ideal has its roots in nineteenth-century thought and that analytical approaches such as those by Nelson Goodman, *Languages of Art: An Approach to the Theory of Symbols* (Indianapolis: Hackett, 1976); and Jerrold Levinson, *Music, Art, and Metaphysics: Essays in Philosophical Aesthetics* (Ithaca, N.Y.: Cornell University Press, 1990), are flawed because they do not take a historical perspective on musical practice.

59. Jerome S. Bruner, *The Process of Education* (Cambridge, Mass.: Harvard University Press, 1960).

60. Jerome S. Bruner, *The Relevance of Education* (1971; reprint, New York: W. W. Norton, 1973); Bruner, *On Knowing*; Jerome S. Bruner, *Actual Minds, Possible Worlds* (Cambridge, Mass.: Harvard University Press, 1986); Bruner, *Acts of Meaning*; and Bruner, *The Culture of Education*.

61. Arguments contra state-mandated standards are suggested in Thomas F. Kelly, "Why State Mandates Don't Work," *Phi Delta Kappan* 80, no. 7 (March 1999): 543–546.

62. Freire, *Pedagogy of the Oppressed*, 68.

63. Scheffler, *Reason and Teaching*, chap. 6.

64. Aaron Copland, *Music and Imagination* (Cambridge, Mass.: Harvard University Press, 1952); Nicholas Cook, *Music, Imagination, and Culture* (Oxford: Clarendon Press, 1990); and Mary J. Reichling, "Images of Imagination," *Journal of Research in Music Education* 38, no. 4 (Winter 1990): 282–293.

65. Scheffler, *Reason and Teaching*, chap. 6.

66. Martin Buber, *I and Thou*, trans. Walter Kaufmann (New York: Charles Scribner's Sons, 1970).

67. Critics may view Freire's accounts of working with the Brazilian peasants or in the schools of São Paulo in this light; however, Freire recognizes this pitfall and

cautions his readers to avoid it. See Paulo Freire, *Pedagogy of the City*, trans. Donaldo Macedo (New York: Continuum, 1993); and Freire, *Pedagogy of Hope*.

68. Greene, *Dialectic of Freedom*, passim.

69. Martin, *Coming of Age in Academe*, describes the difficulties that women face in attempting to change traditional academic education.

70. Edward D. Myers, *Education in the Perspective of History*, with a concluding chapter by Arnold J. Toynbee (New York: Harper and Brothers, 1968).

71. Pitirim Sorokin, *Social and Cultural Dynamics*, vol. 1 (New York: Bedminster, 1937).

72. Schiller, *On the Aesthetic Education of Man*, passim, especially letters 24–27.

73. Harold O. J. Brown, *The Sensate Culture: Western Civilization between Chaos and Transformation* (Dallas: Word Publishing Co., 1996).

74. Giroux is one of the strongest critics of mediated culture during recent decades. In a succession of books and essays, he criticizes Western culture for its sexism, racism, classism, and portrayal of violence and challenges educators to critically engage the purveyors of culture, contest the "taken-for-granted" cultural assumptions of the establishment, and open students to the possibilities of a humane and inclusive education. Among his essay collections, one thinks especially of Giroux, *Pedagogy and the Politics of Hope*.

75. Attali, *Noise*, chap. 4, discusses the impact of musical repetition.

76. Robert H. Frank and Philip J. Cook, *The Winner-Take-All Society: How More and More Americans Compete for Ever Fewer and Bigger Prizes, Encouraging Economic Waste, Income Inequality, and an Impoverished Society* (New York: Free Press, 1995). Thus, a few musical "stars" command exorbitant salaries, fees, and royalties, while most others who are not stars, even those whose musical talents might be comparable or surpass those of the stars, have far lower salaries, fees, and royalties.

77. On the problems of technology and society, see Charles Taylor, *The Ethics of Authenticity* (Cambridge, Mass.: Harvard University Press, 1992).

78. Among the criticisms of multiculturalism, see Yehudi O. Webster, *Against the Multicultural Agenda: A Critical Thinking Alternative* (Westport, Conn.: Praeger, 1997).

79. Schiller, *On the Aesthetic Education of Man*, 61.

80. Maya Angelou, *I Know Why the Caged Bird Sings* (New York: Random House, 1969); and Jonathan Kozol, *Savage Inequalities: Children in America's Schools* (New York: Crown Publishers, 1991).

81. Gilbert Highet, *The Art of Teaching* (New York: Vintage Books, 1950), 176–188; and A. S. Neill, *Summerhill: A Radical Approach to Education* (London: Victor Gollancz, 1973).

3. Transforming Education

1. David Tyack and Larry Cuban, *Tinkering toward Utopia: A Century of Public School Reform* (Cambridge, Mass.: Harvard University Press, 1995); and Martin Bickman, "Thinking toward Utopia: Reconstructing the Tradition of the Active Mind," *Phi Delta Kappan* 80, no. 1 (September 1998): 75–78.

2. Langer, *Philosophy in a New Key*; Howard, *Artistry*; Goodman, *Languages of Art*; and Estelle R. Jorgensen, "On Philosophical Method," in *Handbook of Research on Music Teaching and Learning: A Project of the Music Educators National Conference*, ed. Richard Colwell (New York: Schirmer Books, 1992), 91–101.

3. An earlier draft of material in portions of this chapter is to be found in Estelle R. Jorgensen, "What Does It Mean to Transform Education?" in *Philosophy of*

Education, 2000, ed. Lynda Stone (Urbana, Ill.: Philosophy of Education Society, 2001), 242–252.

4. Adler, *Reforming Education*; Adler et al., *The Paideia Program*; Roland S. Barth, *Run School Run* (Cambridge, Mass.: Harvard University Press, 1980); Bruner, *The Culture of Education*; Eisner, *Cognition and Curriculum Reconsidered*; John I. Goodlad, *A Place Called School: Prospects for the Future* (New York: McGraw-Hill, 1984); and Theodore R. Sizer, *Horace's Compromise: The Dilemma of the American High School* (Boston: Houghton Mifflin, 1984).

5. *America 2000: An Educational Strategy: Sourcebook* (Washington: U.S. Department of Education, 1991); and *National Standards for Arts Education*, ed. Blakeslee.

6. Myers, *Education in the Perspective of History*.

7. For Jean Piaget, *The Origins of Intelligence in Children*, trans. Margaret Cook (New York: International Universities Press, 1952), 416, *accommodation* denotes the organism's active and differentiated responses to the environment and constitutes an adaptive, biological, psychological, and evolutionary mechanism. See Jean Piaget, *Behavior and Evolution*, trans. Donald Nicholson-Smith (New York: Pantheon Books, 1978), passim; and Jean Piaget, *Adaptation and Intelligence: Organic Selection and Phenocopy*, trans. Stewart Eames (Chicago: University of Chicago Press, 1980), passim. This process of accommodating to the environment is governed by accommodation norms. See Jean Piaget, *The Grasp of Consciousness: Action and Concept*, trans. Susan Wedgwood (London: Routledge and Kegan Paul, 1977), 351.

8. Morton, "Feminist Theory and the Displaced Music Curriculum."

9. Green, *Music on Deaf Ears*, chap. 6.

10. Piaget's notion of assimilation is "correlative" with that of accommodation; see Piaget, *Origins of Intelligence in Children*, 416. *Assimilation* denotes the process whereby organizing structures are intellectually constructed—for example, during the sensorimotor developmental phase of intelligence the young child learns to classify and manipulate materials in her or his environment. Indeed, for Piaget, intelligence is "an organizing activity" in which some things are subsumed in others. See Jean Piaget, *The Child and Reality*, trans. Arnold Rosin (New York: Grossman Publishers, 1973), 82, 407–419.

11. Freire, *Pedagogy of the Oppressed*, chap. 4.

12. Göttner-Abendroth, "Nine Principles of a Matriarchal Aesthetic," in *Feminist Aesthetics*, ed. Ecker.

13. Detels, *Soft Boundaries*.

14. Susanne K. Langer, *Feeling and Form: A Theory of Art Developed from Philosophy in a New Key* (London: Routledge and Kegan Paul, 1953), chap. 2. Support for the concept of "soft boundaries" can be found in Susanne K. Langer, *The Practice of Philosophy* (New York: Henry Holt and Co., 1930), 50, 59–60, 62, 65, 67, 89, 165. See Mary J. Reichling, "A Woman Ahead of Her Time: The Langer Legacy," *Philosophy of Music Education Review* 6, no. 1 (Spring 1998): 17, 18.

15. Langer, *Feeling and Form*, chap. 3; Scheffler, *In Praise of the Cognitive Emotions*, 3–17; and Iris M. Yob, "The Cognitive Emotions and Emotional Cognitions," in *Reason and Education: Essays in Honor of Israel Scheffler*, ed. Harvey Siegel (Dordrecht: Kluwer Academic Publishers, 1997), 43–57.

16. James E. Loder, *The Transforming Moment: Understanding Convictional Experiences* (San Francisco: Harper and Row, 1981), chap. 3.

17. Estelle R. Jorgensen, "On the Recruitment Process in Amateur Ensembles," *Canadian University Music Review* no. 6 (1985): 293–318.

18. For a discussion and criticism of this dialectical approach, see Jorgensen, "Justifying Music in General Education," in *Philosophy of Education 1996*, ed. Margonis; Yob, "Can the Justification of Music Education Be Justified?"; and Jorgensen, "What Does It Mean To Transform Education?" in *Philosophy of Education, 2000*, ed. Stone. I.A. Richards, *How to Read a Page: A Course in Efficient Reading with an Introduction to a Hundred Great Words* (New York: W. W. Norton, 1942): 221, notes Socrates' enjoyment of dialectical thought and sees it as the "highest form of REASON."

19. Donald A. Schön, *Educating the Reflective Practitioner: Toward a New Design for Teaching and Learning in the Professions* (San Francisco: Jossey-Bass, 1987), chap. 2.

20. Compare Howard, *Learning By All Means*, chap. 1.

21. Freire, *Pedagogy of the Oppressed*, 75 n.

22. Greene, *The Dialectic of Freedom*, chap. 4.

23. Martin, *The Schoolhome*.

24. Greene, *The Dialectic of Freedom*, chap. 1.

25. Scott Russell Sanders, *Staying Put: Making a Home in a Restless World* (Boston: Beacon Press, 1993).

26. Palmer, *Courage to Teach*, chap. 7, offers an approach to developing these sorts of communities as a basis for educational change.

27. For a description of social processes in music in terms of developmental phases, see Jorgensen, "On the Recruitment Process in Amateur Ensembles."

28. For a criticism of this view of transformation, see Sophie Haroutanian-Gordon, "Estelle Jorgensen's Vision of 'Transformation,'" in *Philosophy of Education, 2000*, ed. Stone, 253–257. Haroutanian-Gordon faults the ambiguity of my view of transformation, a quality that I envisage as a strength because of its appeal to imaginative thinking and the variety of perspectives that it offers. I cannot agree with her endorsement of Hans-Georg Gadamer's view of transformation, because his notion of transformation as grounded in artistic perception in the eye of the beholder is not sufficiently broad.

29. Dewey, *Art as Experience*, 267.

30. Bogdan, *Re-educating the Imagination*; Cook, *Music, Imagination, and Culture*; Greene, *Releasing the Imagination*; Karen Hanson, *The Self Imagined: Philosophical Reflections on the Social Character of Psyche* (New York: Routledge and Kegan Paul, 1986); Howard, *Artistry*, chap. 5; Howard, *Learning By All Means*, chap. 1; Reichling, "Images of Imagination"; and Mary Warnock, *Imagination* (Berkeley: University of California Press, 1978).

31. Reichling, "Images of Imagination."

32. Dewey, *Art as Experience*, 267.

33. Freire, *Pedagogy of Hope*. In his *Pedagogy of the Heart*, 101–107, Freire links faith and hope in the context of a religious persuasion.

34. Estelle R. Jorgensen, "Religious Music in Education," *Philosophy of Music Education Review* 1, no. 2 (Fall 1993): 103–114; Diana Apostolos-Cappadona, "On the Music of the Spheres: Unifying Religion and the Arts," *Philosophy of Music Education Review* 3, no. 2 (Fall 1995): 63–68; Iris M. Yob, "Religious Music and Multicultural Education," *Philosophy of Music Education Review* 3, no. 2 (Fall 1995): 69–82; Austin Caswell, "Sacred Music in the Classroom: A Pluralistic View," *Philosophy of Music Education Review* 3, no. 2 (Fall 1995): 83–90; and Anthony J. Palmer, "Music Education and Spirituality: A Philosophical Exploration," *Philosophy of Music Education Review* 3, no. 2 (Fall 1995): 91–106.

35. This spiritual quality is captured in Freire, *Pedagogy of the Heart*, passim.

36. The focus on imminence and transcendence of the present moment in Parker J. Palmer, *Let Your Life Speak: Listening for the Voice of Vocation* (San Francisco: Jossey-Bass, 2000), echoes a persistent concern among educational philosophers. See, for example, Alfred North Whitehead, *The Aims of Education and Other Essays* (New York: Macmillan, 1929), 14.

37. Whitehead, *The Aims of Education*, chap. 1.

38. Joe L. Kincheloe and William F. Pinar, eds., *Curriculum as Social Psychoanalysis: The Significance of Place* (Albany: State University of New York, 1991); and Marjorie O'Loughlin, "Listening, Heeding, and Respecting the Ground at One's Feet," *Philosophy of Music Education Review* 5, no. 1 (Spring 1997): 14–24.

39. Neil Postman and Charles Weingartner, *Teaching as a Subversive Activity* (New York: Dell Publishing Co., 1969); Estelle R. Jorgensen, "Modelling Aspects of Type IV Music Instructional Triads," *Bulletin of the Council for Research in Music Education* no.137 (Summer 1998): 43–56; Jorgensen, "An Analysis of Aspects of Type IV Music Instruction in a Teacher-Student Dyad"; and Jorgensen, "On a Choice-based Instructional Typology in Music."

40. This is seen, for example, in external examinations by British and other conservatory systems in the British tradition. Rather than going beyond the repertoire listed for examination, many teachers, driven by the desire to have their students do well in their examinations, teach only the specific examination pieces. The same goes for English high school music examinations at the ordinary and advanced levels. In developing their curricula, teachers are often guided by the kinds of questions typically asked in these examinations; they sometimes teach to those questions. Thus, national examinations can have the effect of limiting or restricting education, rather than ensuring high standards of broad education as they are intended to do.

41. *America 2000*; and *National Standards for Arts Education*, ed. Blakeslee.

42. MENC Task Force for National Standards in the Arts, *The School Music Program: A New Vision, The K-12 National Standards, Prek Standards, and What They Mean to Music Educators.* (Reston, VA.: Music Educators National Conference, 1994), pp. 1, 2.

43. Mark and Gary, *A History of American Music Education*. Present standards in music education are rooted in earlier publications; see, for example, *The Contemporary Music Project for Creativity in Music Education* (Washington: MENC, 1968); *The School Music Program: Description and Standards* (Vienna, Va.: MENC, 1974); and *The School Music Program: Description and Standards*, 2d ed. (Reston, Va.: MENC, 1986).

44. David Campbell, "The Coriolanus Syndrome," *Phi Delta Kappan* 78, no. 8 (April 1997): 640–643.

45. In music, this idea comes across in sources as diverse as Aboriginal songmen facing their pupils and breathing a song into them (see A. P. Elkin, "Arnhem Land Music," *Oceania* 24, no. 2 [1953]: 81–109), and Hildegard of Bingen, who in her letters refers to song as the breath of God (see *Hildegard of Bingen's Book of Divine Works with Letters and Songs*, ed. Matthew Fox [Santa Fe, N.M.: Bear and Co., 1987], 354–359, Letter 41).

46. Jorgensen, "Engineering Change in Music Education."

47. Ibid.

48. For example, the Jaques-Dalcroze, Kodály, Orff, and Suzuki instructional approaches are among those introduced into the United States through demonstrations. See Mark and Gary, *A History of American Music Education*, 357–361.

49. Howard, *Learning by All Means*, chap. 7.

50. Ibid., 116–121.

51. Estelle R. Jorgensen, "William Channing Woodbridge's Lecture, 'On Vocal Music as a Branch of Common Education' Revisited," *Studies in Music* (University of Western Australia) no. 18 (1984): 1–32.

52. Haman A. Alexander, "Editorial: Inclusiveness and Humility in Religious Education," *Religious Education* 91, no. 2 (Spring 1996): 142–145.

53. On artistic foresight, see Howard, *Artistry*, chap. 5.

54. Schwab, "The Practical: Arts of Eclectic."

55. Scheffler, *Reason and Teaching*, 181–197.

56. For a description of the dialectical character of theory and practice, see Estelle R. Jorgensen, "A Dialectical View of Theory and Practice," *Journal of Research in Music Education* 49, no. 4 (Winter 2001): 343–359.

57. Lawrence Baines, "Future Schlock: Using Fabricated Data and Politically Correct Platitudes in the Name of Education Reform," *Phi Delta Kappan* 78, no. 7 (March 1997): 493–498.

58. John Dewey, *Experience and Education*. The Kappa Delta Pi Lecture series (New York: Collier Books, 1938), 29.

59. One of the important insights in Patricia Shehan Campbell, *Songs in Their Heads: Music and Its Meaning in Children's Lives* (New York: Oxford University Press, 1998), is the focus on what can be learned by listening to the young. Too often, music education policy is derived in the absence of such listening, and I suggest that it would be helped by applying Campbell's insight to include listening to other students, teachers, administrators, and the public at large.

60. Gareth Morgan, *Images of Organizations* (Beverly Hills, Calif.: Sage Publications, 1986).

61. Douglas M. McGregor, "Theory X and Y," in *Organizational Theory: Selected Readings*, 2d ed., ed. D. S. Pugh (Harmondsworth, Middlesex: Penguin, 1984), 317–333.

62. Paul S. George, *The Theory Z School: Beyond Effectiveness* (Columbus, Ohio: National Middle School Association, 1983); James Lewis Jr., *Excellent Organizations: How to Develop and Manage Them Using Theory Z* (New York: J. L. Wilkerson Publishing Co., 1985); and William G. Ouchi, *Theory Z: How American Business Can Meet the Japanese Challenge* (Reading, Mass.: Addison Wesley, 1981).

63. Warren Bennis and Burt Nanus, *Leaders: The Strategies for Taking Charge* (New York: Harper and Row, 1985).

64. Freire, *Pedagogy of the Oppressed*. For example, Jimmy Carter found that developing simple agricultural reforms in African countries required the cooperation of individual farmers and collectives as well as powerful government officials. Working with farmer cells was not enough; one also needed to work with government leaders, departments, and agencies in a multiprong strategy.

65. Educational writers have come down on both sides of the issue of choice in schooling, curriculum, instructional methods, and the like. Among the foremost to frame the debate in economic terms and advocate educational choice are Milton and Rose Friedman, *Free to Choose: A Personal Statement* (New York: Harcourt Brace Jovanovich, 1980).

66. Exercising choice is not only a personal matter. It often involves collective action. Palmer, *Courage to Teach*, chap. 7, emphasizes the importance of moving from individual conviction of the need for certain choices to finding other like-minded

people with whom to discuss and forge the sorts of political action that will impact education generally.

67. Pinar et al., *Understanding Curriculum*.

68. Greene, *The Dialectic of Freedom*, chap. 5; and Greene, *Releasing the Imagination*, chap. 10.

69. Bogdan, *Re-educating the Imagination*.

70. Arnstine, *Democracy and the Arts of Schooling*.

71. Martin, *The Schoolhome*; and Maria Montessori, *The Absorbent Mind*, trans. Claude A. Claremont (1967; reprint, New York: Dell, 1980).

72. Grumet, *Bitter Milk*; and Noddings, *Caring*.

73. Howard, *Learning by All Means*, 10, 11. Metaphorical teaching also needs to be rooted in an understanding of the physical and psychological processes involved in music making and taking.

74. J. P. Guilford, "Creativity," *American Psychologist* 5 (1950): 444–454; Milton C. Nahm, *Genius and Creativity: An Essay in the History of Ideas* (1956; reprint, New York: Harper and Row, 1956); Morton A. Bloomberg, ed., *Creativity: Theory and Research* (New Haven: College and University Press, 1973); Goodman, *Languages of Art*; Howard, *Artistry*; Mihaly Csikszentmihalyi, *Creativity: Flow and the Psychology of Discovery and Invention* (New York: Harper Collins Publishers, 1996); Linda Melrose, *Creative Personality and the Creative Process: A Phenomenological Perspective* (Lanham Md.: University Press of America, 1988); Doris B. Wallace and Howard E. Gruber, eds., *Creative People at Work: Twelve Cognitive Case Studies* (New York: Oxford University Press, 1989); John Brockman, ed., *Creativity* (New York: Simon and Schuster, 1993); and Howard Gardner, *Creating Minds: An Anatomy of Creativity Seen through the Lives of Freud, Einstein, Picasso, Stravinsky, Eliot, Graham, and Gandhi* (New York: Basic Books, 1993). The research literature on unusual musical talent indicates that some musicians have prodigious intellectual ability. See Rosamund Shuter-Dyson and Clive Gabriel, *The Psychology of Musical Ability*, 2d ed. (London: Methuen, 1981), chap. 11.

75. In writing about the spiritual dimension of education, Yob, "Images of Spirituality," sketches the history of Western philosophical and theological notions of body, mind, and spirit or soul, and the Cartesian body/mind bifurcation that dominated enlightenment and subsequent modern educational thought and practice, all of which tended to de-valorize body, soul, and spirit as foci of instruction.

76. Arnstine, *Democracy and the Arts of Schooling*, shows the importance of things of value in school curriculum and instruction; however, he skirts the issue of exactly how these values are determined. In listing dispositions, one privileges certain attributes that are societally grounded. However, I cannot see how education can avoid such privileging, because it is not a value-neutral undertaking. This question of value is one that merits further study in music education.

77. Notwithstanding that the effect of teacher expectations on student learning has been studied in general education; see, for example, Roy Nash, *Teacher Expectations and Pupil Learning* (London: Routledge and Kegan Paul, 1976); and Barbara Smey-Richman, *Teacher Expectations and Low-achieving Students* (Philadelphia: Research for Better Schools, 1989). A review of the subject index in Colwell, ed., *Handbook of Research in Music Teaching and Learning*, turned up limited evidence of the study of expectations in music instruction (p. 720).

78. Israel Scheffler, *Of Human Potential: An Essay in the Philosophy of Education* (Boston: Routledge and Kegan Paul, 1985); and Scheffler, *In Praise of the Cognitive Emotions*, 24–29.

79. Blacking, *How Musical is Man?*

80. Shuter-Dyson and Gabriel, *Psychology of Musical Ability*, part 3.

4. Transforming Music

1. Jorgensen, *In Search of Music Education*, chap. 2.

2. My provisional list of musical images may be read in counterpoint with that in Wayne D. Bowman, *Philosophical Perspectives on Music* (New York: Oxford University Press, 1998), and serves a different purpose than his. Whereas Bowman's interest is in describing various philosophies of music, mine draws from literatures in philosophy, sociology, psychology, musicology, and music theory, to distinguish various sorts of music curricula.

3. The word *curriculum* is also an ambiguous term. For a philosophical discussion of some of these issues in music curriculum, see Jorgensen, "Philosophical Issues in Curriculum," in *New Handbook of Research in Music Teaching and Learning*, ed. Colwell and Richardson.

4. Blaukopf, *Musical Life in a Changing Society*; and Zentner, *Prelude to Administrative Theory*, chap. 7. Traditionally, sociological research in music fell through the cracks of various research specialties, and musicologists, especially in the North American tradition, were more interested in studying musical beliefs and practices than their social and contextual ramifications, which they typically left to sociologists and anthropologists of music, social historians, and music educators. More recently, there has been a reawakening of interest in social and ethnological approaches to music within musicology, following in the footsteps of some scholars in the past who took a broad view of musical life in society. Among those to emphasize the relationship of music and society, see Curt Sachs, *The Rise of Music in the Ancient World, East and West* (London: J. M. Dent and Sons, 1944); John H. Mueller, *The American Symphony Orchestra: A Social History of Musical Taste* (Bloomington: Indiana University Press, 1951); Wilfrid Dunwell, *Music and the European Mind* (London: Herbert Jenkins, 1962); Raynor, *A Social History of Music*; Jane Bowers and Judith Tick, eds., *Women Making Music: The Western Art Tradition, 1150–1950* (Urbana: University of Illinois Press, 1986); McClary, *Feminine Endings*; Shepherd, *Music as Social Text*; Blaukopf, *Musical Life in a Changing Society*; Citron, *Gender and the Musical Canon*; John Shepherd and Peter Wicke, *Music and Cultural Theory* (Cambridge: Polity Press, 1997) and Derek B. Scott, ed., *Music, Culture, and Society: A Reader* (New York: Oxford University Press, 2000). For their part, music teachers tended to see their field quite narrowly as focused on school music in the West rather than encompassing broader issues of musical socialization and enculturation. Contra this narrow conception of music education, see Jorgensen, *In Search of Music Education*, passim. And in the social sciences, sociologists often focused on popular musics and anthropologists on vernacular musics. Sociological studies of popular culture include Simon Frith, *Sociology of Rock* (London: Constable, 1978); Simon Frith, *Art into Pop* (London: Methuen, 1987); Simon Frith, *Music for Pleasure: Essays on the Sociology of Pop* (New York: Routledge, 1988); Simon Frith, *Performing Rites: On the Value of Popular Music* (Cambridge, Mass.: Harvard University Press, 1996); and Peter Wicke, *Rock Music: Culture, Aesthetics, and Sociology*, trans. Rachel Fogg (Cambridge: Cambridge University

Press, 1990). Anthropological and ethnomusicological studies of vernacular musics include those by Alan P. Merriam, *The Anthropology of Music* (Evanston: Northwestern University Press, 1964); and Bruno Nettl, *The Western Impact on World Music: Change, Adaptation, and Survival* (New York: Schirmer Books, 1985). Sociological investigations of classical music include those by Pete Martin, *Sounds and Society: Themes in the Sociology of Music* (Manchester: Manchester University Press, 1995); Shepherd et al., *Whose Music?*; and Shepherd, *Music as Social Text*.

5. Jorgensen, *In Search of Music Education*, chap. 2.

6. Jane Roland Martin, "The Wealth of Cultures and the Problem of Generations," in *Philosophy of Education, 1998*, ed. Steven Tozer (Urbana: University of Illinois Press, 1999), 23–38. For a case study of musical transmission, see Marie McCarthy, *Passing It On: The Transmission of Music in Irish Culture* (Cork: Cork University Press, 1999).

7. Examples of critiques of contemporary classical music include those by Copland, *Music and Imagination*; Subotnik, "The Challenge of Contemporary Music," in *What Is Music?* ed. Alperson; Rose Rosengard Subotnik, *Deconstructive Variations: Music and Reason in Western Society* (Minneapolis: University of Minnesota Press, 1996); McClary, *Feminine Endings*; Goehr, *The Imaginary Museum of Musical Works*; Austin B. Caswell, "Canonicity in Academia: A Music Historian's View," in *Philosopher, Teacher, Musician: Perspectives on Music Education*, ed. Estelle R. Jorgensen (Urbana: University of Illinois Press, 1993), 129–145; Citron, *Gender and the Musical Canon*; F. Joseph Smith, "Toward a Phenomenology of Music: A Musician's Composition Journal," *Philosophy of Music Education Review* 3, no. 1 (Spring 1995): 21–33; Small, *Music–Society–Education*; and Small, *Musicking*. For a popularist criticism regarding how music is taught in the academy, see Sammie Ann Wicks, "The Monocultural Perspective of Music Education," *Chronicle of Higher Education*, 9 January 1998, A72.

8. Choate, ed., *Documentary Report of the Tanglewood Symposium*.

9. Contrast, for example, the compositional, improvisatory, and cross-cultural approaches by John Paynter, *Music in the Secondary School Curriculum: Trends and Developments in Class Music Teaching* (Cambridge: Cambridge University Press, 1982); Schafer, *The Thinking Ear*; Campbell, *Lessons from the World*; and Campbell, *Songs in Their Heads*, with the traditional approaches to Western classical music advocated by the followers of Kodály (Lois Choksy, *The Kodály Context: Creating an Environment for Musical Learning* [Englewood Cliffs, N.J.: Prentice-Hall, 1981]); Lois Choksy, *The Kodály Method: Comprehensive Music Education from Infant to Adult* [Englewood Cliffs, N.J.: Prentice-Hall, 1988]); Dalcroze (Marie-Laure Bachmann, *Dalcroze Today: An Education Through and Into Music*, trans. David Parlett [Oxford: Clarendon Press, 1991]); and Suzuki (John D. Kendall, *Listen and Play by John Kendall* [Evanston, Ill.: Summy Birchard, 1961]; John D. Kendall, *The Suzuki Violin Method in American Music Education* [Reston, Va.: MENC, 1978]; Elizabeth Mills, *In the Suzuki Style: A Manual for Raising Musical Consciousness in Children* [Berkeley, Calif.: Diablo Press, 1974]; and Susan Grilli, *Preschool in the Suzuki Spirit* [Tokyo: Harcourt Brace Jovanovich Japan, 1987]).

10. For example, the *National Standards for Arts Education* are arranged conceptually in terms of Western art forms despite the inclusion of vernacular and/or classical traditions outside the West.

11. Green, *Music on Deaf Ears*; and Green, *Music, Gender, Education*.

12. On Venda musical life, see Blacking, *How Musical Is Man?* In a visit to the Collins Living Learning Center, Indiana University, Bloomington, Emily Terhune, a South African journalist, remarked that Venda women are the victims of sexist

practice. For example, they are often forced to carry water long distances to their homes because the men, who are in charge of political affairs, arrange for water to be delivered closest to their fields, not their homes.

13. For example, in 2000 the Musashino Academia Musicae, a private music school in Tokyo, had a larger piano faculty and piano student enrollment than the entire enrollment in the music school at Indiana University, according to the *Herald Times* (Bloomington, Indiana), 5 January 2001, A1, A7.

14. Kivy, *Authenticities*, chap. 4, notes a "great divide" in musical history between the time when music was a mixed or multimedia event and that when it became a pervasively sonic or concert hall event.

15. Immanuel Kant, *The Critique of Judgement*, trans. James Creed Meredith (Oxford: Clarendon Press, 1952); and Eduard Hanslick, *On the Musically Beautiful: A Contribution towards the Revision of the Aesthetics of Music*, ed. and trans. Geoffrey Payzant (Indianapolis: Hackett, 1986).

16. The inclusion of performance as an aesthetic aspect is defended in Hilde Hein, "Performance as an Aesthetic Category," *Journal of Aesthetics and Art Criticism* 28, no. 3 (Spring 1970): 381–386.

17. While Kivy, *Authenticities*, examines questions related to the performance of music in the Western classical tradition, Francis Sparshott, "Aesthetics of Music: Limits and Grounds," in *What Is Music?* ed. Alperson, 53, 74–76, refers, more broadly, to various musics and to the concept of "rightness" whereby a specific musical performance is judged with reference to the expectations of the particular tradition or "praxis (what musicians do)" of which this performance is an instance.

18. On the notion of articulated or significant form, see Langer, *Philosophy in a New Key*, chap. 8.

19. The nature of aesthetic judgments predicated on distancing oneself from the art work are spelled out in Kant, *Critique of Judgement*. For Kant, judgment applies to things felt and, as such, complements pure and practical reason.

20. For example, see Julius Herford, "The Choral Conductor's Preparation of the Musical Score," in *Choral Conducting: A Symposium*, ed. Harold A. Decker and Julius Herford (Englewood Cliffs, N.J.: Prentice-Hall, 1973), 177–230. Cook, *Music, Imagination, and Culture*, 68, notes a difference between many listeners' perception of musical form and that of the "arbiters of musical taste." And the relatively few experimental studies of subjects' listening to extended musical examples reported by Rita Aiello, "Can Listening to Music Be Experimentally Studied?" in *Musical Perceptions*, ed. Rita Aiello with John Sloboda (New York: Oxford University Press, 1994), 273–282, suggests how problematic this research is and how varied are the listener responses, even among musicians.

21. For a defense of musical formalism, see Wayne D. Bowman, "The Values of Musical 'Formalism,'" in *Philosopher, Teacher, Musician*, ed. Jorgensen, 41–59.

22. Copland, *Music and Imagination*, chap. 2, coins the term "sonorous image."

23. Walker, "Music Education Freed from Colonialism." Walker further argues for the cultural embeddedness of music education in his essay, "Multiculturalism and Music Re-attached to Music Education," *Philosophy of Music Education Review* 8, no. 1 (Spring 2000): 31–39.

24. Scheffler, *In Praise of the Cognitive Emotions*, 30–41.

25. Among the psychologists studying aspects of musical ability, perception, cognition, and development, one thinks of Shuter-Dyson and Gabriel, *The Psychology of Musical Ability*; Diana Deutsch, ed., *The Psychology of Music* 2nd ed. San Diego:

Academic Press, 1999); David Hargreaves, *The Developmental Psychology of Music* (New York: Cambridge University Press, 1986); Mary Louise Serafine, *Music as Cognition: The Development of Thought in Sound* (New York: Columbia University Press, 1988); John A. Sloboda, ed., *Generative Processes in Music: The Psychology of Performance, Improvisation, and Composition* (Oxford: Clarendon Press, 1988); Carol L. Krumhansl, *Cognitive Foundations of Musical Pitch* (New York: Oxford University Press, 1990); Jeanne Shapiro Bamberger, *The Mind behind the Musical Ear: How Children Develop Musical Intelligence* (Cambridge, Mass.: MIT Press, 1991); Mari Reiss Jones and Susan Holleran, eds., *Cognitive Bases of Musical Communication* (Washington: American Psychological Association, 1992); Aiello and Sloboda, *Musical Perceptions*; Harold E. Fiske, *Selected Theories of Music Perception* (Lewiston, N.Y.: Edwin Mellen Press, 1996); Kemp, *The Musical Temperament*; Irene Deliege and John Sloboda, *Perception and Cognition of Music* (Hove, East Sussex: Psychology Press, 1997). Following Langer's emphasis on symbolism in her *Philosophy in a New Key*, other philosophers in the latter part of the twentieth century to take up specifically the symbolic properties of music and the arts include Meyer, *Emotion and Meaning in Music*; Gordon Epperson, *The Musical Symbol: A Study of the Philosophic Theory of Music* (Ames: Iowa State University, 1967); Goodman, *Languages of Art*; Peter Kivy, *Music Alone: Philosophical Reflections on the Purely Musical Experience* (Ithaca, N.Y.: Cornell University Press, 1990); Jean-Jacques Nattiez, *Music and Discourse: Toward a Semiology of Music*, trans. Carolyn Abbate (Princeton, N.J.: Princeton University Press, 1990); V. Kofi Agawu, *Playing with Signs: A Semiotic Interpretation of Classical Music* (Princeton, N.J.: Princeton University Press, 1991); Raymond Monelle, *Linguistics and Semiotics in Music* (Chur, Switzerland: Harwood Academic Publishers, 1992); Stephen Davies, *Musical Meaning and Expression* (Ithaca, N.Y.: Cornell University Press, 1994); Roger Scruton, *The Aesthetics of Music* (Oxford: Clarendon Press, 1997); and Joseph P. Swain, *Musical Languages?* (New York and London: W.W. Norton and Co., 1997).

26. In an inherently ambiguous symbol system, such as music, the imagination plays a prominent role. See Reichling, "Images of Imagination"; Mary J. Reichling, "Images of Imagination: A Philosophical Study of Imagination in Music with Application to Music Education" (D.M.E. diss., Indiana University, 1991); and Mary J. Reichling, "Imagination and Musical Understanding," *Quarterly Journal of Music Teaching and Learning* 3, no. 4 (Winter 1992): 20–31. For a discussion of the impact of culture on musical imagination, see Cook, *Music, Imagination, and Culture*. And for composers' reflections on musical imagination, see Copland, *Music and Imagination*; and Roger Sessions, *The Musical Experience of Composer, Performer, Listener* (New York: Atheneum, 1962).

27. This more conservative view of musical narrative is taken, for example, by Carolyn Abbate, *Unsung Voices: Opera and Musical Narrative in the Nineteenth Century* (Princeton, N.J.: Princeton University Press, 1991), especially xii–xv; Jean-Jacques Nattiez, "Can One Speak of Narrativity in Music?" *Journal of the Royal Musical Association* 115, no. 2 (1990): 240–257; Jean-Jacques Nattiez, "The Concepts of Plot and Seriation Process in Music Analysis," trans. Catherine Dale, *Music Analysis* 4 (1985): 107–118; Jean-Jacques Nattiez, "Reflections on the Development of Semiology in Music," *Musical Analysis* 8, no. 1 and 2 (March/July 1989): 21–76; and Fred Everett Maus, "Music as Narrative," *Indiana Theory Review* 12 (Spring and Fall 1991): 1–34. For Maus, "The comparisons are not between individual compositions and individual plays or novels; rather, individual compositions or genres of compositions are thought to be dramatic or narrative in some more general way," and he explores the musical bases

for why these comparisons are made with reference to musical examples drawn from the late classical and romantic periods. Maus, "Music as Narrative," 1.

28. According to Anthony Newcomb, "Schumann and Late Eighteenth-Century Narrative Strategies," *Nineteenth-Century Music* 11, no. 2 (Fall 1987): 164–174, this form of analysis is "a less rigorous, systematic way than semiotics" because it is so intuitive.

29. Langer, *Philosophy in a New Key*, 245.

30. For an introduction to postmodern conceptions of music as narrative, see Lawrence Kramer, *Classical Music and Postmodern Knowledge* (Berkeley: University of California Press, 1995), 98–121. These musical conceptions parallel postmodern thought in curricular theory.

31. Lawrence Kramer, *Music as Cultural Practice, 1800–1900* (Berkeley: University of California Press, 1990), 177.

32. Kramer, *Classical Music and Postmodern Knowledge*, like Maus, "Music as Narrative," and Newcomb, "Schumann and the Late Eighteenth-Century Narrative," draws examples of musical narrativity from late classical and romantic composers such as Beethoven, Schubert, and Schumann, and it is interesting that some of the self-same examples of musical narrativity crop up—for example, the Finale of Beethoven's String Quartet in F Major, op. 135 (explicitly referenced by Beethoven), and Schumann's *Carnaval*. On the close connection between music and narrative in Native American music from the philosophical perspective of a Native American, see the trilogy of essays by Andrea Boyea, "Encountering Complexity: Native Musics in the Curriculum," *Philosophy of Music Education Review* 7, no. 1 (Spring 1999): 31–48; "Native American Music and Curriculum: Controversies and Cultural Issues," *Philosophy of Music Education Review* 7, no. 2 (Fall 1999): 105–117; and "Teaching Native American Music with Story for Multicultural Ends," *Philosophy of Music Education Review* 8, no. 1 (Spring 2000): 14–23.

33. McClary, *Feminine Endings*; Clément, *Opera*; Brett, Wood, and Thomas, eds., *Queering the Pitch*; Jacques Barzun, *The Culture We Deserve* (Hanover, N.H.: Wesleyan University Press, 1989); Ernst Fischer; *The Necessity of Art: A Marxist Approach*, trans. Anna Bostock (Harmondsworth, Middlesex: Penguin, 1963); and James Alfred Martin, *Beauty and Holiness: The Dialogue between Aesthetics and Religion* (Princeton, N.J.: Princeton University Press, 1990).

34. Among women writers to take this view are McClary, *Feminine Endings*; Citron, *Gender and the Musical Canon*; Clément, *Opera*; Green, *Music, Gender, Education*; and Kielian-Gilbert, "The Woman in the Music" (with a rich bibliography of sources on feminist scholarship in music and a view that positions music and feminism at the intersection of theory and practice).

35. Kamer, *Classical Music and Postmodern Knowledge*. Ralph A. Smith makes the point that music ought to be taught as a humanity in his essay, "Teaching Music as One of the Humanities," in *Philosopher, Teacher, Musician*, ed. Jorgensen, 115–128. Also, Dewey, *Democracy and Education*, 258, observes that while music is often defended for its contributions to the humanities, music educators typically take a much more technical and skill-oriented approach, suggesting that music educators ought to teach music as a humanity in a manner consistent with its defense.

36. On great and little musical traditions, see Jorgensen, *In Search of Music Education*, 75–77.

37. Peter Kivy, *Sound and Semblance: Reflections on Musical Representation* (Princeton, N.J.: Princeton University Press, 1984), 196; he notes that "the problem of musical narration lies, clearly, in the propositional poverty of the musical art" (p. 158). He is

inclined, therefore, to treat narration as referring literally to programmatic music, such as Johann Kuhnau's *Biblical Sonatas* or Hector Berlioz's *Symphonie fantastique*. For a representational theory of music, see Addis, *Of Mind and Music*.

38. For example, although Kramer, *Classical Music and Postmodern Knowledge*, chap. 6, acknowledges the disjunction between musical narratives and normal musical processes, he makes the case for musical narrativity by analyzing specific musical scores, as if the narrativity resides primarily within the musical score rather than in conjunction to the ways it is made and taken and its wider cultural purposes—an approach one would not have expected from a postmodern theorist.

39. A starting point for the writings of Glenn Gould (aside from his recordings) is *The Glenn Gould Reader*, ed. Tim Page (Toronto: Lester and Orpen Dennys, 1984). Among scholars to examine Gould's ideas and practices are Gregory Payzant, *Glenn Gould: Music and Mind*, rev. ed. (Toronto: Key Porter Books, 1992) (the first Canadian edition was published in 1978); Elizabeth Angilette, *Philosopher at the Keyboard: Glenn Gould* (Metuchen, N.J.: Scarecrow Press, 1992); Kevin Bazzana, *Glenn Gould: The Performer in the Work: A Study in Performance Practice* (Oxford: Clarendon Press, 1997); and John P. L. Roberts, *The Art of Glenn Gould* (Toronto: Malcolm Lester Books, 1999). Beyond his extensive discography, Alfred Brendel's musical ideas are sampled in his *Musical Thoughts and Afterthoughts* (Princeton, N.J.: Princeton University Press, 1976); and his *Music Sounded Out: Essays, Lectures, Interviews, Afterthoughts* (New York: Farrar Straus Giroux, 1990). Both pianists are very articulate about how and why they approach the performance of particular works by specific composers and their study of musical scores leads them to strongly held convictions. For a collection of essays on musical performance and associated interpretative issues, see Michael Krausz, ed., *The Interpretation of Music: Philosophical Essays* (Oxford: Clarendon Press, 1993).

40. See, for example, Claudia E. Cornett, *Integrating Literature and the Arts throughout the Curriculum* (Upper Saddle River, N.J.: Prentice-Hall, 1999), especially chaps. 11 and 12, on music; and Anne Lowe, "Integration of Music and French: A Success Story," *International Journal of Music Education* 32 (1998): 32–52.

41. On music curricula that seek to accomplish these ends, see, for example, Detels, *Soft Boundaries*, chaps. 7 and 8; Morton, "Feminist Theory and the Displaced Music Curriculum"; and Boyea, "Encountering Complexity," "Native American Music and Curriculum," and "Teaching Native American Music with Story." For ethnological and sociological approaches to music history that have implications for music curriculum, see Caswell, "Canonicity in Academia"; and John Shepherd, "Music and the Last Intellectuals," in *Philosopher, Teacher, Musician*, ed. Jorgensen, 95–114.

42. Theodor Adorno, *Introduction to the Sociology of Music*, trans. E. B. Ashton (New York: Seabury, 1976), 1–20; Sparshott, "Aesthetics of Music"; Alperson, ed., *What Is Music?*; Small, *Musicking*; McCarthy, *Passing It On*; Neuman, *The Life of Music in North India*; and Elliott, *Music Matters*. Whereas Elliott distinguishes between listening and musicing, Small's definition of "musicking" is broader than Elliott's and includes listening as one of its elements. Judging by his remarks at the Philosophy of Music Education International Symposium IV in Birmingham, England, 7–10 June 2000, Elliott's position regarding the centrality of performance in musical praxis seems to have shifted toward greater emphasis on listening than he conveyed in *Music Matters*.

43. See Rainbow, *Music in Educational Thought and Practice*, chap. 12, on the emergence of European conservatories in the nineteenth century.

44. In music and music education, the speculative music tradition has its contemporary revival in projects by Joscelyn Godwin, *Harmonies of Heaven and Earth: The Spiritual Dimensions of Music* (Rochester, Vt.: Inner Traditions International, 1987); and June Boyce-Tillman, "Promoting Well-Being through Music Education," *Philosophy of Music Education Review* 8, no. 2 (Fall 2000): 89–98.

45. On Dewey's notions of experience, see his *Experience and Nature*, 2nd ed. (1929; reprint, New York: Dover Publications, 1958); *Art as Experience*; and *Experience and Education*.

46. Bowman, *Philosophical Perspectives on Music*, chap. 6.

47. Edmund Husserl, *Ideas: General Introduction to Pure Phenomenology*, trans. W. R. Boyce Gibson (1931; reprint, London: Collier Books, 1962); Alfred Schutz, "Fragments on the Phenomenology of Music," *Music and Man* 2, no. 1 and 2 (1976): 5–76; Alfred Pike, *A Phenomenological Analysis of Musical Experience and Other Essays* (New York: St. John's University Press, 1970); Douglas Bartholomew, "Whole/Part Relations in Music: An Exploratory Study," in *Philosopher, Teacher, Musician*, ed. Jorgensen, 175–191; Douglas Bartholomew, "Sounds before Symbols: What Does Phenomenology Have to Say?" *Philosophy of Music Education Review* 3, no. 1 (Spring 1995): 3–9; Smith, "Toward a Phenomenology of Music"; Lawrence Ferrara, *Philosophy and the Analysis of Music: Bridges to Musical Sound, Form, and Reference* (New York: Excelsior Music Publishing, 1991); Judy Lockhead, "Hearing New Music: Pedagogy from a Phenomenological Perspective," *Philosophy of Music Education Review* 3, no. 1 (Spring 1995): 34–42; Arnold Berleant, "Notes for a Phenomenology of Musical Performance," *Philosophy of Music Education Review* 7, no. 2 (Fall 1999): 73–79; and Harris M. Berger, *Metal, Rock, and Jazz: Perception and the Phenomenology of Musical Experience* (Hanover, N.H.: University Press of New England, 1999).

48. Yaroslav Senyshyn, "Kierkegaard's Aesthetic Stage of Existence and Its Relation to Live Musical Performance," *Philosophy of Music Education Review* 4, no. 1 (Spring 1996): 50–63; Yaroslav Senyshyn, "A Kierkegaardian Perspective on Society and the Status of the Individual as a Performing Musician," *Philosophy of Music Education Review* 7, no. 2 (Fall 1999): 80–92; Eleanor Stubley, "Musical Performance, Play, and Constructive Knowledge: Experiences of Self and Culture," *Philosophy of Music Education Review* 1, no. 2 (Fall 1993): 94–102; Mary J. Reichling, "Susanne Langer's Theory of Symbolism: An Analysis and Extension," *Philosophy of Music Education Review* 1, no. 1 (Spring 1993): 3–17; Iris M. Yob, "The Form of Feeling," *Philosophy of Music Education Review* 1, no. 1 (Spring 1993): 18–32; Anthony Palmer, "Consciousness Studies and a Philosophy of Music Education," *Philosophy of Music Education Review* 8, no. 2 (Fall 2000): 99–110; David J. Elliot, "Consciousness, Culture and Curriculum," *International Journal of Music Education* 28 (1996): 1–15; and David J. Elliot, "Music and Affect: The Praxial View," *Philosophy of Music Education Review* 8, no. 2 (Fall 2000): 79–88.

49. See n. 25.

50. Music curricula that seek to foster musicianship include Orff and Keetman, *Orff-Schulwerk: Musik für Kinder*; Carl Orff, *The Schulwerk, 3: Carl Orff/Documentation, His Life and Work*, trans. Margaret Murray (New York: Schott, 1978); Gunild Keetman, *Elementaria: First Acquaintance with Orff-Schulwerk*, trans. Margaret Murray (London: Schott, 1970); Schafer, *The Thinking Ear*; and Paynter, *Music in the Secondary School Curriculum*, Appendix 1. Thomas E. Rudolph, *Teaching Music with Technology* (Chicago: GIA Publications, 1996); and David Brian Williams and Peter Richard Webster, *Experiencing Music Technology: Software, Data, and Hardware* (New York: Schirmer Books, 1996), are geared toward providing teachers with the technical skills

for effectively using technology in learning about, composing, improvising, and performing music. Advances in artificial intelligence offer the prospect of more complex interactions between learner and machines. On artificial intelligence and music education, see Matt Smith, Alan Smaill, and Geraint A. Wiggins, eds., *Music Education: An Artificial Intelligence Approach*, Proceedings of a Workshop held as part of AI-ED 93, World Conference on Artificial Intelligence in Education, Edinburgh, Scotland, 25 August 1993 (London: Springer-Verlag, published in collaboration with the British Computer Society, 1994).

51. Schiller, *On the Aesthetic Education of Man*. Writers on the contributions of play to music education include Stubley, "Musical Performance, Play, and Constructive Knowledge"; Eleanor Stubley, "Field Theory, Play, and Music Education: Performance and the Art of Making Connections," in *On the Sociology of Music Education*, ed. Roger Rideout (Norman: School of Music, University of Oklahoma, 1997), 13–21; and Mary J. Reichling, "Music, Imagination, and Play," *Journal of Aesthetic Education* 31, no. 1 (1997): 41–55.

52. See K. Peter Etzkorn, "The Media as Instruments of Music Education: Some Sociological Reflections," in *On the Sociology of Music Education II*, ed. Roger Rideout and Stephen J. Paul (Amherst, Mass.: Privately published by the editors as a service to music education, 2000), 31–39, on the importance of educating audiences for live musical performance, especially seeing that the media are important agents of music education.

53. See, for example, Plato, *Republic*; Schiller, *On the Aesthetic Education of Man*; and Blaukopf, *Musical Life in a Changing Society*, on music's role in attaining particular political, moral, and social ends; McClary, *Feminine Endings*; Citron, *Gender and the Musical Canon*; Clément, *Opera*; Fischer, *The Necessity of Art*; and Roger L. Taylor, *Arts, an Enemy of the People* (Atlantic Highlands, N.J.: Humanities Press, 1978), on the high arts as means of oppression; Stubley, "Musical Performance, Play, and Constructive Knowledge," on the transformative power of performance; Edward W. Said, *Musical Elaborations* (New York: Columbia University Press, 1991); Chanan, *Musica Practica*; and Allsup, "Music Education as Liberatory Practice," on music education as transformation; and Attali, *Noise*, on music's prophetic role in society.

54. On Church of England choir schools, see Cynthia Hawkins, "Aspects of the Musical Education of Choristers in Church of England Choir Schools" (M.A. thesis, McGill University, 1985). On working-class songs, see Therese M. Volk, "Little Red Songbooks: Songs for the Labor Force of America," *Journal of Research in Music Education* 49, no. 1 (Spring 2001): 33–48.

55. On rationales in the United States, see Jorgensen, "Justifying Music Instruction in American Public Schools." Masafumi Ogawa, "Early Nineteenth Century American Influences on the Beginning of Japanese Public Education: An Analysis and Comparison of Selected Music Textbooks Published in Japan and the United States" (D.M.E. diss., Indiana University, 2000), documents important specific differences between nineteenth-century rationales in the United States and Japan that persist to this day.

56. Regarding the politics of school textbooks, see, for example, Apple, *Official Knowledge*, 2d ed., especially 42–61.

57. Examples include James L. Mursell, *Human Values in Music Education* (New York: Silver Burdett, 1934); James L. Mursell, *Education for Musical Growth* (Boston: Ginn and Co., 1948); and Fowler, *Strong Arts, Strong Schools*.

58. This *"mediated"* rather than *"immediate"* experience in the "assumptive frame of reference" (AFR)—a term borrowed by Edward Tiryakian from Adelbert Ames—is

described in Edward A. Tiryakian, "Sociology and Existential Phenomenology," in *Phenomenology and the Social Sciences*, vol. 1, ed. Maurice Natanson (Evanston, Ill.: Northwestern University Press, 1973), 199.

59. This transformation in the Western classical tradition is documented in Chanan, *Musica Practica*.

60. Freire's *Pedagogy of the Oppressed* and his subsequent *Pedagogy of Hope, Pedagogy of the City*, and *Pedagogy of the Heart* all invoke the necessity for individual transformation to translate into political action. Likewise, Palmer's *Courage to Teach* begins with the teacher's individual self-reflection but transitions to political action in order to transform teaching.

61. Goodman, *Languages of Art*, 252–255.

62. Compare Dewey's metaphor of expressing wine from grapes in his *Art as Experience*, 82.

63. Goodman, *Languages of Art*, 179–192, suggests that musical notation is one of the triumphs of Western classical music.

64. For a discussion of the various "languages" of craft, see Howard, *Artistry*, chaps. 3 and 4.

65. Kivy, *Authenticities*, 133–138, views the performer as an arranger of the composer's score. This overlapping of composing and performing functions contrasts with the earlier characterization of discrete musical roles in Sessions, *The Musical Experience of Composer, Performer, Listener*.

66. The relationship between music, acoustics, and spirituality is explored in Godwin, *Harmonies of Heaven and Earth*; Robin Maconie, *The Concept of Music* (Oxford: Clarendon Press, 1990); and Robin Maconie, *The Science of Music* (Oxford: Clarendon Press, 1997).

67. Cook, *Music, Imagination, and Culture*, passim, especially chap. 1, makes the point that listeners generally listen differently than musicians think they should or do.

68. On women composers in the Western classical tradition, see Diane Peacock Jezic, *Women Composers: The Lost Tradition Found* (New York: Feminist Press, 1988); and Gene Claghorn, *Women Composers and Songwriters: A Concise Biographical Dictionary* (Lanham, Md.: Scarecrow Press, 1996).

69. Sloboda, ed., *Generative Processes in Music*; and Schön, *Educating the Reflective Practitioner*, chap. 8.

70. Grossman, "Performance and Obligation"; and Copland, *Music and Imagination*, 47–57.

71. On "assumptive frames of reference," see Tiryakian, "Sociology and Existential Phenomenology," in *Phenomenology and the Social Sciences*, vol. 1, ed. Natanson, 199–201. For a study of the musician's personality, see Kemp, *The Musical Temperament*.

72. Social histories and theories of the dance include Curt Sachs, *World History of the Dance*, trans. Bessie Schönberg (New York: W. W. Norton, 1937); Philip J. S. Richardson, *The Social Dances of the Nineteenth Century in England* (London: Jenkins, 1960); Frances Rust, *Dance in Society: An Analysis of the Relationship between the Social Dance and Society in England from the Middle Ages to the Present Day* (London: Routledge and Kegan Paul, 1969); Gilbert Rouget, *Music and Trance: A Theory of the Relations between Music and Possession*, trans. Brunhilde Biebuyck (Chicago: University of Chicago Press, 1980); and Judith Lynne Hama, *Dance, Sex, and Gender: Signs of Identity, Dominance, Defiance, and Desire* (Chicago: University of Chicago Press, 1980).

73. Langer, *Problems of Art*, especially chap. 1.

74. Howard, *Artistry*, 173–176.

75. Copland, *Music and Imagination*, chap. 1.

76. Kivy, *Music Alone*. Deanne Bogdan (piano) and Alan Stellings (cello) offered a criticism of Kivy's thesis in their performance workshop, "Toward an Embodied Dialogism: The Amateur and the Atelier in Musical Experience," presented at Holistic Learning: Breaking New Ground, An International Conference, Ontario Institute for Studies in Education, University of Toronto, 24–26 October 1997.

77. Blaukopf, *Musical Life in a Changing Society*, chaps. 20 and 29.

78. Attali, *Noise*, chap. 4.

79. The impact of these processes is sometimes seen in a sinister vein. For example, there are such comments as: "It's the homogenizers who want more musical diversity, more variety in this world beat mix" and "We're living with an *image* of a world of musical diversity and empowerment, but I've come to see that as a world of less and less variety in terms of ownership, control, and who profits," in Keil and Feld, *Music Grooves*, 23. On the other hand, the Internet enables musicians to bypass the large corporation and produce and market recordings independently.

80. Paul R. Farnsworth, *Musical Taste: Its Measurement and Cultural Nature* (Stanford, Calif.: Stanford University Press, 1950); and David J. Hargreaves and Adrian C. North, *The Social Psychology of Music* (Oxford: Oxford University Press, 1997).

81. Mueller, *The American Symphony Orchestra*, passim.

82. Interestingly, Rolling Stones concert attendance did not translate into expected album sales. One commentator speculated that people wanted to see "The World's Greatest Rock n' Roll Band," but its music, while "classic" in that it has not only "endured" but "gained value over the years, turning from Top-40 hits into modern musical monuments," is nevertheless not as relevant as it once was. "Rolling Stones Tour Selling, Album Not," *Herald-Times* (Bloomington, Indiana), 25 October 1997, A7. On Paul Simon's musical, *The Capeman*, see "Simon's Controversial 'The Capeman' Opens," *Herald-Times* (Bloomington, Indiana), 13 December 1997, C5.

83. Rosanne Martorella, *The Sociology of Opera* (South Hadley, Mass.: J. F. Bergin, 1982), chap. 4.

84. Charles Ives, "Essays before a Sonata," in *Three Classics in the Aesthetic of Music* (1920; reprint, New York: Dover, 1962), 103–185.

85. Suzuki, *Nurtured by Love*, 91–94, writes of the deep appeal to him of Mozart's music, a factor that was formative in developing his instructional method.

86. Semiological analyses of musical meaning include Deryck Cooke, *The Language of Music* (Oxford: Oxford University Press, 1959); and Nattiez, *Music and Discourse*.

87. Kivy, *Music Alone*, 101.

88. Small, *Musicking*, on music not being a "thing."

89. Jorgensen, *In Search of Music Education*, chap. 2.

90. For a sketch of the formation of European conservatoires, see Rainbow, *Music in Educational Thought and Practice*, chap. 12. On the development of American educational organizations, see Mark and Gary, *A History of American Music Education*, part IV.

91. Howard, *Learning by All Means*.

92. Gilbert Ryle, *The Concept of Mind* (New York: Harper and Row, 1949).

93. Howard, *Learning by All Means*, 88, 89, 93, 99, 100, 103. In chap. 5 Howard spells out the role of imagination and critical thinking in arriving at artistic mastery; this is not a fixed or permanent point but reflects the artist's conception at a particular moment in time of what an artistic product should be like. He rightly acknowledges that just because a particular practice is thus-and-so does not mean that it constitutes

an ideal for all time. For example, he discusses the various schools of singing impacted by cultural and individual factors, implying that the artist's particular conception of what singing should be may change from time to time.

94. Keil and Feld, *Music Grooves*, believe that such participation is crucial to musical education. When they speak of the fact that music "grooves," they are referring, I think, to this participatory sense of being *in* music, such that it "draw[s] you in and work[s] on you." They believe that "in order to understand what any musician is doing, you have to have done some of it yourself" (p. 29).

95. Howard, *Learning by All Means*, 114–116, 123, 125–127. Howard's example of how he learned from Nicolai Gedda and extrapolated to his own experience is particularly interesting (pp. 125–126). For his discussion of overemphasis, see Howard, *Artistry*, 106–109. An example of the ambiguity and imaginative quality of imitation is shown in Bobby McFerrin's album *Paper Music*, in which he adds vocals to classical instrumental repertoire.

96. Keil and Feld, *Music Grooves*, describe how they acquired much of their musical knowledge and love of the popular music of their time and the music of earlier times by watching and listening to family members and friends. Reading their account, I am struck by the apparent differences between their musical tastes and those typical of their generation and today's young people.

97. Scheffler, *In Praise of the Cognitive Emotions*, 3–17; and Howard, *Learning by All Means*, 144–147.

98. Unfortunately, the word *sensibility* carries a great deal of philosophical baggage, raising the specter of Kant's dichotomy between reason and sensation; see Kant, *The Critique of Judgement*, book 1, para. 3, 44–45. See Howard, *Learning by All Means*, 136–144, for a useful discussion contra Kant's notion of sensibility read as "sensory stimulation or *mere* sensation" (p. 138). I agree with Howard that "sensibility is construed as an active, interpretive *form* of understanding" (p. 139). An alternative term might be the word *feeling*, as construed by Langer in her *Philosophy in a New Key*, although Iris M. Yob, "The Form of Feeling," *Philosophy of Music Education Review* 1, no. 1 (Spring 1993): 18–32, shows that this is also a problematic construct.

99. Yob, "The Cognitive Emotions and Emotional Cognitions."

100. Bowman, *Philosophical Perspectives on Music*, likewise avoids committing to a particular musical image as preeminent. What is yet unclear in Bowman's writing is how his position would play out practically for the music teacher who must choose among a multiplicity of options in designing, implementing, and evaluating curriculum.

101. Pitts, *A Century of Change in Music Education*, chap. 6, traces the history of the present national curriculum in music.

102. Greene, *The Dialectic of Freedom*, chap. 4, coins the terms "multiplicities" and "pluralities" to refer to culture generally, and she speaks of the need to create public spaces in schools where those who have been marginalized, ostracized, and otherwise silenced can be heard.

103. See the "spiral of musical development" developed by Swanwick and Tillman in *Music, Mind, and Education*, 76. As Swanwick, *Musical Knowledge*, explains, even the movement between intuition and analysis requires a back-and-forth emphasis on the part of the music teacher in designing a music curriculum.

104. On zones of tolerance and the impact of teacher and student choice on music instruction, see Jorgensen, "On a Choice-based Instructional Typology in Music"; "An Analysis of Type IV Music Instruction in a Teacher-Student Dyad"; and "Modelling Aspects of Type IV Music Instructional Triads."

105. Detels, *Soft Boundaries.*

106. Caswell, "Canonicity in Academia: A Music Historian's View," in Estelle R. Jorgensen, ed.; *Philosopher, Teacher, Musician: Perspectives on Music Education* (Urbana: University of Illinois Press, 1993), 129–145.

107. On decentering the canon and schools as sites of cultural struggle in a democracy, see Henry A. Giroux, *Border Crossings: Cultural Workers and the Politics of Education* (New York: Routledge, 1992), 149–160.

108. Examples of this criticism can be seen in Roberta Lamb, "Feminism as Critique in Philosophy of Music Education," *Philosophy of Music Education Review,* 2 (2) (Fall 1994):59–74; Thomas A. Regelski, "Scientism in Experimental Music Research," *Philosophy of Music Education Review* 4 (1) (Spring 1996): 3–19; and Paul G. Woodford, "Evaluating Edwin Gordon's Music Learning Theory from a Critical Thinking Perspective," *Philosophy of Music Education Review* 4 (2) (Fall 1996): 83–95.

109. Giroux, *Impure Acts,* 141.

110. Jorgensen, *In Search of Music Education,* chap. 3.

111. For an excellent discussion of the ancient Greek notion of *paideia,* see Jaeger's trilogy of volumes, *Paideia.*

112. For those lovers of jazz, I recommend Paul F. Berliner, *Thinking in Jazz: The Infinite Art of Improvisation* (Chicago: University of Chicago Press, 1994), which is a rich study of how jazz players come to know their art, especially that of improvisation. I am indebted to Lissa May for bringing this study to my attention.

113. Wayne Booth, *For the Love of It: Amateuring and Its Rivals* (Chicago: University of Chicago Press). I am indebted to Anne Sinclair, who found this book for our graduate class. As, at least at the outset, a "bumbling cellist," Booth invites his readers to pursue the life of amateuring into old age, of musicing, even teaching, for the love of it rather than simply as a paid livelihood.

114. See, for example, his comments in Émile Jaques-Dalcroze, "An Essay in the Reform of Music Teaching in Schools (1905)," in *Rhythm, Music, and Education,* trans. Harold F. Rubinstein (New York: Arno Press, 1976), 11–57.

115. Alfred North Whitehead, *The Aims of Education and Other Essays* ([1929]; rpt. New York: Free Press, 1967), chap. 1.

5. Creating Alternatives

1. Goodman, *Languages of Art,* 171, refers to the "promiscuous" use of the word *model.*

2. Claire Detels, "Autonomist/Formalist Aesthetics, Music Theory, and the Feminist Paradigm of 'Soft Boundaries,'" *Journal of Aesthetics and Art Criticism* 52, no. 1 (Winter 1994): 113–126; Detels, *Soft Boundaries*; and Reichling, "A Woman Ahead of Her Time."

3. Bogdan, "Book Review," 73.

4. Use is made of these sorts of abstractions in such texts as Harold F. Abeles, Charles R. Hoffer, and Robert H. Klotman, *Foundations of Music Education* (New York: Schirmer Books, 1984); and Bowman, *Philosophical Perspectives on Music.*

5. Philip Alperson, "What Should One Expect from a Philosophy of Music Education?" in *Philosopher, Teacher, Musician,* ed. Jorgensen, 215–242.

6. Malvina Reynolds invoked the metaphor of the little boxes in another context in her song "Little Boxes": "Little boxes on the hillside/Little boxes made of ticky tacky/Little boxes on the hillside/Little boxes all the same."

7. Greene, *Releasing the Imagination*, passim, refers to the literal and figurative spaces in arts classrooms as a means of bringing about freedom through community.

8. Jeffrey E. Garten, "'Cultural Imperialism' Is No Joke," *Business Week*, 30 November 1998, 26. On the limitations of a dialogical approach to education, see Jones, "The Limits of Cross-Cultural Dialogue."

9. Langer, *Problems of Art*, 86.

10. This idea has been advanced with respect to Native American cultures. See Boyea, "Encountering Complexity."

11. Claire Detels, "Hard Boundaries and the Marginalization of the Arts in American Education," *Philosophy of Music Education Review* 7, no. 1 (Spring 1999): 19–30; and Detels, Soft *Boundaries*.

12. Compare Ralph A. Smith, "Teaching Music as One of the Humanities," in *Philosopher, Teacher, Musician*, ed. Jorgensen, 115–128. This position is probably closer to James Mursell's position than Carl Seashore's (who thought music reduced to a sonic phenomenon); see Estelle R. Jorgensen, "The Seashore-Mursell Debate on the Psychology of Music Revisited," in *The Nature of Musicality: Multi-disciplinary Perspectives*, ed. Don Coffman, Kate Gfeller, David Nelson, and Carlos Rodriguez (Ames: University of Iowa Press), in press.

13. Bogdan, "Book Review," 73, prefers to describe my work as an "anatomy of music education" and refers to the "organicism" of my method.

14. Whitehead, *The Aims of Education*, chap. 1; Langer, *Problems of Art*, passim; Howard, *Artistry*; Eisner, *Cognition and Curriculum Reconsidered*, passim; and Pinar et al., *Understanding Curriculum*, chap. 11.

15. Mark, *Contemporary Music Education*, 302, notes that music education "remains troubled" and that there is a need for "an active, vital profession."

17. Langer, *Philosophy in a New Key*, chap. 1.

16. Jerrold Levinson, *Music in the Moment* (Ithaca, N.Y.: Cornell University Press, 1997).

18. On the failure of state-mandated educational standards, see Kelly, "Why State Mandates Don't Work."

19. Apple, *Official Knowledge*.

20. Etzioni, *The Monochrome Society*.

21. Scheffler, *Reason and Teaching*, chap. 9, makes the twin points that curriculum not only should permit an economical approach to the subject in which the knowledge gained and ways of going about finding it transfer to other areas as well, but it also should broaden as well as deepen the learner's understanding.

22. Scheffler, *In Praise of the Cognitive Emotions*, chap. 2, emphasizes the importance of decision as an element of human potential.

23. Elliott, *Music Matters*, and Small, *Musicking*, use the words "musicing" and "musicking," respectively, to spell out what it means "to music" in the context of what Elliott refers to as a musical practice or Small regards as a social ritual. Similarities and differences in their respective understandings have yet to be articulated.

24. Compare Dewey, *Experience and Education*, chap. 1.

25. Schön, *Educating the Reflective Practitioner*, passim.

26. Christopher J. Smith's model of musical understanding in his dissertation, "I Can Show It to You Better Than I Can Explain It to You: Analyzing Procedural Cues in African-American Musical Improvisations" (Ph.D. diss., Indiana University, 1999), derives from his experience in improvised music making. In such circumstances, the

teacher takes an ethnological approach to music and improvises around a cluster of interrelated cells that take into account musical practice and societal context.

27 Frank Abrahams and Paul Head, *Case Studies in Music Education* (Chicago: G.I.A. Publications, 1998).

28. Rowell, *Thinking about Music*, 210.

29. Jorgensen, "Musical Multiculturalism Revisited."

30. Colwell, ed., *Handbook of Research on Music Teaching and Learning*, passim.

31. This theoretical work is ongoing. See, for example, Rahn, *A Theory for All Music*; and Smith, "I Can Show It to You."

32. On philosophical models of teaching, see Scheffler, *Reason and Teaching*, chap. 6.

33. On musical affirmation and alienation, and the ambiguity of musical meaning, see Green, *Music, Gender, Education*, chap. 5, especially 134, Figure 1.

34. Schiller, *On the Aesthetic Education of Man*, letter 9, p. 61.

35. The notion of comprehensive musicianship as an objective of music education is evident in the writings of Bennett A. Reimer, *A Philosophy of Music Education*, 2d ed. (Englewood Cliffs, N.J.: Prentice-Hall, 1989); Swanwick, *Music, Mind, and Education*; Swanwick, *Musical Knowledge*; Swanwick, *Teaching Music Musically*; and Elliott, *Music Matters*.

36. Plato, *Republic*, VII, 514a–521b.

37. While this was not the point of Plato's allegory, one of the contributions of narrative is the ambiguity of its meaning, and the possibility that it may illustrate quite another principle than the narrator had in mind. This reading of Plato is consistent with Robin Waterfield's view in the Introduction to his translation of Plato's *Republic*.

INDEX

Accommodation, 9, 49–50, 56, 57, 76, 161n7
Acting, 129–139. *See also* Leading; Learning; Music making and taking; Teaching
Actions: consequences of, 11, 67, 68, 70, 85; liberation achieved through, 37; tradition can stifle, 41; individual and collective, 47, 60, 144, 174n60; reflective, 58, 130; expectations are seeds of 75, 76, 129; political, 92, 165n66
Activity, musical image as, 84, 86–88, 92, 101, 117
Adler, Mortimer, 9
Administration, 68, 132, 133–134, 164n59. *See also* Leading
Adorno, Theodor, 86
Aesthetic object, image of music as, 80–82, 84, 87, 92, 101, 114, 117
Aesthetics, 80, 81, 92–93, 156n15
Agency: as symptom of educational transformation, 70–75, 76; music as, 83, 90–92, 101, 117; music education as, 118
Aims: of education, 48, 123; of music education, 120, 125, 143. *See also* Purpose
Alperson, Philip, 86, 120
Ambiguity: of belief and practice, 17, 67, 112; of music 77, 92, 96, 97, 100, 101, 107, 117, 138; of art, 93; fosters experimentation, 113; of knowledge, 115; of transformation, 162n28; of imitation, 176n95; of narrative, 179n37
Angelou, Maya, 44
Apple, Michael, 72
Apprenticeship, 131
Arnstine, Donald, 73, 165n76
Artist: students as, 26; work of, 34, 67, 113, 122, 175n93; teachers as, 44; 111; marketing of, 98, 99
Artistry, 27, 29, 30
Arts: as agency, 3, 9, 26, 32, 39, 73, 74, 155n5; as dynamic process, 13, 123; feminine and masculine views of, 22, 24, 155n6; societal views of, 25, 127; value of, 25, 28; as symbolic system, 27, 29, 48; as work of, 30, 81; and spirituality, 62; interrelatedness of, 77, 84, 85, 86, 110, 141; discourses of, 83; precision in, 93; dance as metaphor of, 96; and education, 111, 115, 122, 128, 134, 140, 178n7; rationality of, 114
Arts of eclectic, 67
Assimilation, 9, 51–52, 56, 57, 76, 161n10
Assumptions: about methods, 12; about education, 38, 46, 68; future tasks and challenges

regarding, 40, 120, 125, 160n74; expectations go beyond, 75; about music, 81, 83, 84; not refuted scientifically, 90; assumptive frames of reference 91, 96, 173n58
Attali, Jacques, 147n2, 157n28
Authenticity, 35, 159n58
Awareness, 13, 97

Bach, J. S.: performance of pieces by, 9, 93–94; family of, 109
Banking education, 35, 40
Barrow, Robin, 18
Bartholomew, Douglas, 88
Barzun, Jacques, 83
Being, 59, 123–129, 139
Berger, Harris, 88
Berleant, Arnold, 88
Berliner, Paul, 177n112
Blacking, John, 32, 75, 158n46
Blaukopf, Kurt, 148n23
Boethius, 86
Bogdan, Deanne, 73, 119, 153n64, 154n81, 175n76, 178n13
Booth, Wayne, 114, 177n113
Boundaries, 15, 24. *See also* Soft boundaries
Bowman, Wayne, 88, 166n2, 176n100
Boyce-Tillman, June, 13, 88, 172n44. *See also* Tillman, June
Boyea, Andrea, 86
Brendel, Alfred, 86, 100, 171n39
Brett, Philip, 83
Broudy, Harry, 9
Brown, Lyn Mikel, 12
Bruner, Jerome, 27, 36, 154n78
Buber, Martin, 38, 151n49
Burbeles Nicholas, 14

Callister, Jr., Thomas, 14
Campbell, Patricia Shehan, 12, 164n59
Canon, musical, 4, 34, 35, 40, 78, 80
Carter, Jimmy, 164n64
Caswell, Austin, 110
Chang, Yahlin, 159n52
Chevé, Émile, 4
Choice: educational, 11, 72, 109; as determinant of potential, 75; of music, 137; theory of, 151n51, 164n66. *See also* Decision-making
Civil rights, and music education, 127
Civilization: world, 41; Western, 135
Classical music: Western, 29, 50, 78–80, 93, 112, 127, 136, 150n33, 159n50, 174n63; common practice of, 80, 93. *See also* Practice

ESTELLE R. JORGENSEN is Professor of Music in the School of Music, Indiana University, where she teaches courses in the foundations of music education. She is the editor of the journal *Philosophy of Music Education Review,* author of *In Search of Music Education,* and a frequent contributor to leading journals in music education.

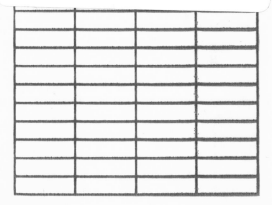